NORTHSTAR 5

READING AND WRITING

THIRD EDITION

AUTHORS
Judy L. Miller
Robert F. Cohen

SERIES EDITORS
Frances Boyd
Carol Numrich

PEARSON
Longman

Dedication

To my parents, Sylvia Sondak and Ben Miller,
and to my daughter, Ariana Jessica Miller.

JLM

To my mother, Lillian Kumock Cohen.

RFC

NorthStar: Reading and Writing Level 5, Third Edition

Copyright © 2009, 2004, 1998 by Pearson Education, Inc.
All rights reserved.

No part of this publication may be reproduced, stored in a retrieval system, or transmitted in any form or by any means, electronic, mechanical, photocopying, recording, or otherwise, without the prior permission of the publisher.

Pearson Education, 10 Bank Street, White Plains, NY 10606

Contributor credit: Terra Brockman, Deborah B. Gordon, and Helen S. Solórzano contributed material to FOCUS ON WRITING in **NorthStar: Reading and Writing Level 5, Third Edition**.

Staff credits: The people who made up the **NorthStar: Reading and Writing Level 5, Third Edition** team, representing editorial, production, design, and manufacturing, are John Barnes, Aerin Csigay, Dave Dickey, Ann France, Melissa Leyva, Sherry Preiss, Robert Ruvo, Debbie Sistino, and Paula Van Ells.

Cover art: Silvia Rojas/Getty Images
Text composition: ElectraGraphics, Inc.
Text font: 11.5/13 Minion
Credits: See page 272.

Library of Congress Cataloging-in-Publication Data

Northstar. Reading and writing. — 3rd ed.
    4 v. ; cm.
  Rev. ed. of: Northstar / Natasha Haugnes, Beth Maher, 2nd. ed. 2004.
  The third edition of the Northstar series has been expanded to 4 separate volumes. Each level is in a separate volume with different contributing authors.
  Includes bibliographical references.
  Contents: Level 2 : Basic Low Intermediate / Beth Maher, Natasha Haugnes — Level 3 : Intermediate / Carolyn Dupaquier Sardinas, Laurie Barton — Level 4 : High Intermediate / Andrew English, Laura Monahon English — Level 5 : Advanced / Robert F. Cohen, Judy L. Miller.
  ISBN-13: 978-0-13-240991-9 (pbk. : student text bk. level 2 : alk. paper)
  ISBN-10: 0-13-240991-7 (pbk. : student text bk. level 2 : alk. paper)
  ISBN-13: 978-0-13-613368-1 (pbk. : student text bk. level 3 : alk. paper)
  ISBN-10: 0-13-613368-1 (pbk. : student text bk. level 3 : alk. paper)
  [etc.]
  1. English language—Textbooks for foreign speakers. 2. Reading comprehension—Problems, exercises, etc. 3. Report writing—Problems, exercises, etc. I. Haugnes, Natasha, 1965– Northstar. II. Title: Reading and writing.
  PE1128.N675 2008
  428.2'4—dc22

                2008024492

ISBN 10: 0-13-233676-6
ISBN 13: 978-0-13-233676-5

Printed in the United States of America
1 2 3 4 5 6 7 8 9 10—CRK—13 12 11 10 09 08

CONTENTS

WELCOME TO NORTHSTAR

THIRD EDITION

NorthStar, now in its third edition, motivates students to succeed in their **academic** as well as **personal** language goals.

For each of the five levels, the two strands—*Reading and Writing* and *Listening and Speaking*—provide a fully integrated approach for students and teachers.

WHAT IS SPECIAL ABOUT THE THIRD EDITION?

NEW THEMES

New themes and **updated content**—presented in a **variety of genres**, including literature and lectures, and in **authentic reading and listening selections**—challenge students intellectually.

ACADEMIC SKILLS

More purposeful **integration of critical thinking** and an enhanced focus on **academic skills** such as inferencing, synthesizing, note taking, and test taking help students develop strategies for **success** in the **classroom** and on **standardized tests.** A culminating **productive task** galvanizes content, language, and **critical thinking skills**.

➤ In the *Reading and Writing* strand, a new, **fully integrated writing section** leads students through the **writing process** with engaging writing assignments focusing on various rhetorical modes.

➤ In the *Listening and Speaking* strand, a **structured approach** gives students opportunities for **more extended and creative oral practice**, for example, presentations, simulations, debates, case studies, and public service announcements.

NEW DESIGN

Full **color pages** with more **photos, illustrations, and graphic organizers** foster student engagement and make the content and activities come alive.

MyNorthStarLab

MyNorthStarLab, an easy-to-use **online learning and assessment program**, offers:

➤ Unlimited access to reading and listening selections and DVD segments.

➤ Focused test preparation to help students succeed on international exams such as TOEFL® and IELTS®. Pre- and post-unit assessments improve results by providing individualized instruction, instant feedback, and personalized study plans.

➤ Original activities that support and extend the *NorthStar* program. These include pronunciation practice using voice recording tools, and activities to build note taking skills and academic vocabulary.

➤ Tools that save time. These include a flexible gradebook and authoring features that give teachers control of content and help them track student progress.

THE NORTHSTAR APPROACH

The *NorthStar* series is based on **current research in language acquisition** and on the **experiences of teachers and curriculum designers**. Five principles guide the *NorthStar* approach.

PRINCIPLES

1 The more profoundly students are stimulated intellectually and emotionally, the more language they will use and retain.

The thematic organization of *NorthStar* promotes intellectual and emotional stimulation. The 50 sophisticated themes in *NorthStar* present intriguing topics such as recycled fashion, restorative justice, personal carbon footprints, and microfinance. The authentic content engages students, links them to language use outside of the classroom, and encourages personal expression and critical thinking.

2 Students can learn both the form and content of the language.

Grammar, vocabulary, and culture are inextricably woven into the units, providing students with systematic and multiple exposures to language forms in a variety of contexts. As the theme is developed, students can express complex thoughts using a higher level of language.

3 Successful students are active learners.

Tasks are designed to be creative, active, and varied. Topics are interesting and up-to-date. Together these tasks and topics (1) allow teachers to bring the outside world into the classroom and (2) motivate students to apply their classroom learning in the outside world.

4 Students need feedback.

This feedback comes naturally when students work together practicing language and participating in open-ended opinion and inference tasks. Whole class activities invite teachers' feedback on the spot or via audio/video recordings or notes. The innovative new MyNorthStarLab gives students immediate feedback as they complete computer-graded language activities online; it also gives students the opportunity to submit writing or speaking assignments electronically to their instructor for feedback later.

5 The quality of relationships in the language classroom is important because students are asked to express themselves on issues and ideas.

The information and activities in *NorthStar* promote genuine interaction, acceptance of differences, and authentic communication. By building skills and exploring ideas, the exercises help students participate in discussions and write essays of an increasingly complex and sophisticated nature.

THE NorthStar UNIT

① FOCUS ON THE TOPIC

This section introduces students to the unifying theme of the reading selections.

> **PREDICT** and **SHARE INFORMATION** foster interest in the unit topic and help students develop a personal connection to it.
>
> **BACKGROUND AND VOCABULARY** activities provide students with tools for understanding the first reading selection. Later in the unit, students review this vocabulary and learn related idioms, collocations, and word forms. This helps them explore content and expand their written and spoken language.

UNIT
10
The End of Poverty

① FOCUS ON THE TOPIC

Ⓐ PREDICT

Look at the title of the unit and the photo collage. What do the photos show? What are some of the differences in the standard of living in developed countries and developing countries? Take five minutes to write down your thoughts about these questions. Share your answers with the class.

231

Ⓑ SHARE INFORMATION

Mickey Mantle credited his skill as a baseball player to the influence of one person. Think of all the people who have influenced your development. What did they contribute to your personality? Was their influence always positive? How old were you when their influence was felt?

Fill in the chart. Then share your answers with a small group.

WHO INFLUENCED YOU?	HOW DID THIS PERSON INFLUENCE YOU?	HOW OLD WERE YOU?
Family member		
Friend		
Teacher or religious leader		
National celebrity (athlete, politician, movie star, performer)		
Other		

Ⓒ BACKGROUND AND VOCABULARY

Choose the word(s) that correctly explain the meaning of the boldfaced word. There can be more than one correct answer. Compare your answers with a partner's.

1. For a long time, he thought that he, too, would die from the **hereditary** disease that killed his father.
   a. inherited   b. genetic

2. Despite **tough** competition, Mantle rose from the lead mines of the West to the heights of fame.
   a. demanding   b. strong

2   UNIT I

② FOCUS ON READING

This section focuses on understanding two contrasting reading selections.

> **READING ONE** is a literary selection, academic article, news piece, blog, or other genre that addresses the unit topic. In levels 1 to 3, readings are based on authentic materials. In levels 4 and 5, all the readings are authentic.
>
> **READ FOR MAIN IDEAS** and **READ FOR DETAILS** are comprehension activities that lead students to an understanding and appreciation of the first selection.

---

② FOCUS ON READING

Ⓐ READING ONE: Gotta Dance

Before you read, discuss the questions with a partner.

Did you ever have a compulsion—something you felt you had to do, no matter what the obstacles or consequences? Did you act on your feelings? Were you glad you did?

GOTTA DANCE[1]
BY JACKSON JODIE DAVISS

1   Maybe I shouldn't have mentioned it to anyone. Before I knew it, it was all through the family, and they'd all made it their business to challenge me. I wouldn't tell them my plan, other than to say I was leaving, but that was enough to set them off. Uncle Mike called from Oregon to say, "Katie, don't do it," and I wouldn't have hung up on him except that he added, "Haven't you caused enough disappointment?" That did it. Nine people had already told me no, and Uncle Mike lit the fire under me[2] when he made it ten. Nine-eight-seven-six-five-four-three-two-one. Kaboom.

2   On my way to the bus station, I stopped by the old house. I still had my key, and I knew no one was home. After ducking my head into each room, including my old one, just to be sure I was alone, I went into my brother's room and set my duffel bag and myself on his bed.

3   The blinds were shut so the room was **dim**, but I looked around at all the things I knew by heart and welcomed the softening effect of the low light. I sat there a very long time in the silence until I began to think I might never rise from that bed or come out of that gray light, so I pushed myself to my feet.

---
[1] **gotta dance:** slang expression for "I have got to dance," "I must dance"
[2] **lit the fire under me:** slang expression for "made me angry," "made me finally take action"

48   UNIT 3

◀ READ FOR MAIN IDEAS

Answer the questions based on your understanding of the reading. Write your answers on a separate piece of paper.

1. What effect did Mickey Mantle's addiction have on:
   • his ability to play baseball?
   • his relationship with family members?
   • his friendships?
2. How did Mickey Mantle feel about his father?

◀ READ FOR DETAILS

Fill in the time line below by creating sentences using the following phrases.

was cured at the Betty Ford Center   joined the Yankees
left baseball   started a campaign for donor awareness
father died   father began teaching him baseball

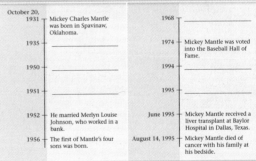

THE LIFE OF MICKEY MANTLE

October 20, 1931	Mickey Charles Mantle was born in Spavinaw, Oklahoma.	1968	
1935		1974	Mickey Mantle was voted into the Baseball Hall of Fame.
1950		1994	
1951		1995	
1952	He married Merlyn Louise Johnson, who worked in a bank.	June 1995	Mickey Mantle received a liver transplant at Baylor Hospital in Dallas, Texas.
1956	The first of Mantle's four sons was born.	August 14, 1995	Mickey Mantle died of cancer with his family at his bedside.

6   UNIT 1

> Following this comprehension section, the **MAKE INFERENCES** activity prompts students to "read between the lines," move beyond the literal meaning, exercise critical thinking skills, and understand the text on a more academic level. Students follow up with pair or group work to discuss topics in the **EXPRESS OPINIONS** section.

READING TWO offers another perspective on the topic and usually belongs to another genre. Again, in levels 1 to 3, the readings are based on authentic materials, and in levels 4 and 5, they are authentic. This second reading is followed by an activity that challenges students to question ideas they formed about the first reading, and to use appropriate language skills to analyze and explain their ideas.

INTEGRATE READINGS ONE AND TWO presents culminating activities. Students are challenged to take what they have learned, organize the information, and synthesize it in a meaningful way. Students practice skills that are essential for success in authentic academic settings and on standardized tests.

B   READING TWO: In Peace, Women Warriors Rank Low

1 *Below is an article about the lives of women soldiers after they return home from a war in Eritrea, a country in East Africa. Before you read the article, discuss the question with a partner.*

How do you think women soldiers feel about their military experience after they return home?

Asmara Journal:
In Peace, Women Warriors Rank Low
By James C. McKinley (from the *New York Times*)

1   SOME DAYS NURIA MOHAMMED SALEH says she actually finds herself missing the war—not the fear and horror, not even the adrenaline kick and camaraderie of soldiering. She misses being treated like a man. Like thousands of other Eritrean women, Mrs. Saleh fought side by side with the men in the rebel army that freed this rocky land from Ethiopian rule in 1991. Like most women who are veterans here, she has found it hard to return to the deeply traditional and patriarchal society[1] she left behind as a teenager.

2   A few years ago, she recalled, she was hammering the enemy with mortar fire. Now she sweeps floors for a dollar a day in an office building near the capital she helped liberate. The only hints of her past are the shrapnel[2] scars around her lips. Mrs. Saleh is one of about 20,000 women who have been discharged from the Eritrean Army in the last two years as part of a larger demobilization of nearly 52,000 troops. Though about 3,000 remain in the army, the vast majority of women were sent home. Some had spent their entire adult lives in the Eritrean People's Liberation Front. Most have little

education, having quit school to join the guerrillas.

3   The Front changed their lives, they said. The rebel commanders were Marxists by training and treated women as equals. The Front's soldiers were taught to ignore sexual, tribal, and religious differences. Women were trained to drive tanks, fight, and handle big guns. Though not many women had the education to become officers, a handful rose to command rebel battalions. Many married fighters from other religions and tribes.

4   Even outside the army in rebel-controlled regions, because the Liberation Front required most men to be in combat, women broke out of traditional molds, working as dentists, medical technicians, administrators, factory workers, mechanics, and teachers, a United Nations report said.

5   But if women who were guerrillas had hoped that fighting and dying in the war would change their status in Eritrean society, they have discovered instead that society's traditions die hard. Several said their families had rejected their mixed marriages and employers had been reluctant to hire them

[1] **patriarchal society:** a social system controlled only by men
[2] **shrapnel:** pieces of artillery, mortar shells, or hand grenades

---

6. Why is the narrator happy now?

_____

_____

C   INTEGRATE READINGS ONE AND TWO

◀ **STEP 1: Organize**

*Review Readings One and Two and complete this grid by putting notes in the appropriate places. If the information is not specified in the text for a particular category, put an **X** in the grid.*

	INSTRUMENT	LOCATION	CLOTHING	AUDIENCE	EFFECT OF MUSIC
Smailovic		Sarajevo / Manchester			
Yo-Yo Ma			formal concert attire	people in concert hall	
Sullivan	piano				soothes, inspires, unites
Salzman		apartment		cat	

◀ **STEP 2: Synthesize**

Work in pairs. Using the notes you took in Step 1, complete the short comparison and contrast essay by filling in the paragraphs with the information needed.

Music is a unifying and healing force for Vedran Smailovic, Yo-Yo Ma, Paul Sullivan, and Mark Salzman. Despite the different environments in which they play, music gives each of them the strength needed to face life's challenges.

Undoubtedly, all four artists would agree that they share an infinite love for their instruments. _____

_____

_____

_____

③ FOCUS ON WRITING

This section emphasizes development of productive skills for writing. It includes sections on vocabulary, grammar, and the writing process.

The **VOCABULARY** section leads students from reviewing the unit vocabulary, to practicing and expanding their use of it, and then working with it—using it creatively in both this section and in the final writing task.

Students learn useful structures for writing in the **GRAMMAR** section, which offers a concise presentation and targeted practice. Vocabulary items are recycled here, providing multiple exposures leading to mastery. For additional practice with the grammar presented, students and teachers can consult the GRAMMAR BOOK REFERENCES at the end of the book for corresponding material in the *Focus on Grammar* and Azar series.

---

③ FOCUS ON WRITING

Ⓐ VOCABULARY

◀ REVIEW

Read the thoughts that may have gone through the mind of Alinka, Eva's younger sister. Complete the thoughts with words and phrases from the box—they are synonyms for the items in parentheses.

asylum	come to terms with their roots	grief
atrocities	dissuade	stoical
beleaguered	fabric	tighten the reins
chaotic	giving vent to	tumultuous

These have been difficult years for my parents. The

_____ of their emotional lives has been made ever so fragile
1. (structure)

because of their own suffering and their firsthand knowledge of the terrible

_____ suffered by so many of their loved ones during World
2. (torment)

War II. My parents wanted to make a new life for us in Canada.

Although they had hoped that their new home in Canada would provide an

_____ for them from their tragic past, my parents' sense of
3. (safe place)

sorrow still dominates them. Despite their _____
4. (self-controlled)

appearance, their every gesture is still _____ by their
5. (troubled)

memories of their _____ past.
6. (violent)

You may think that as the youngest family member of our cluster of four, I

have been untouched by all this. Yet it was not until we moved to Canada that I

realized how very trapped I had been by my parents' _____ . I
7. (sadness)

had never realized how simple life could be. None of my Canadian friends seem to

have a history or to be troubled by the need to _____ . Their
8. (understand their family history)

perpetually happy faces, which my sister sarcastically describes as reflecting not only

"hygienic smiles," but also "hygienic feelings," are a welcome relief to me.

◀ CREATE

Write about an example of truth and lies in your own life, or choose an example from the history of your country. Use at least eight vocabulary words and three words with either negative or positive connotations.

Ⓑ GRAMMAR: Using Double Comparatives to Show Cause-Effect Relationships

1 *Examine the sentence and discuss the questions with a partner.*

The bigger the neocortex, the more deceptive the behavior.

1. How many clauses are in this sentence?
2. What grammatical structure is underlined?
3. Why does the author put the two clauses in juxtaposition in the same sentence?

DOUBLE COMPARATIVES

Double comparatives are sentences that have two clauses, each of which starts with a comparative adjective, noun, or adverb structure. The clauses are separated by a comma and define the logical relationship between ideas with variations of "the more ..., the more," "the less ..., the less," "the more ..., the less," or "the less ..., the more." In most cases, the second clause explains the "effect" of the first. Here are some rules to follow:

1. For a good "balanced" writing style, it is preferable when both sides of the double comparative are "parallel," or written with the same word order.

   The more social scientists study human behavior, the more we understand our social interactions.
   The + comparative + subject + verb + object = The + comparative + subject + verb + object

   The experts agreed that **the more social scientists study human behavior, the more we understand our social interactions.**

2. Sometimes the verb in one clause can be left out.

   The more social the species, the more intelligent it is.
   The more social the species (is), the more intelligent it is.

3. Sometimes both verbs can be left out when the meaning is clear from the sentences that went before.

   (Psychological research is not a waste of money. The university should fund more studies of human behavior. In this field, there can't be too many studies.) **The more, the better.**

4. Notice that a double comparative can never be correct unless the definite article **"the"** accompanies the comparatives in both clauses of the sentence.

Double comparatives are a stylistic tool that writers use to focus the reader's attention more closely on key concepts and the connection between them. However, be careful not to overuse this form.

The **WRITING** section of each unit leads students through the writing process and presents a challenging and imaginative writing task that directs students to integrate the content, vocabulary, and grammar from the unit.

- Students practice a short **pre-writing strategy**, such as freewriting, clustering, brainstorming, interviewing, listing, making a chart or diagram, categorizing, or classifying.

- Then students organize their ideas and write, using a **specific structural or rhetorical pattern** that fits the subject at hand.

- Students then learn **revising techniques** within a sentence-level or paragraph-level activity to help them move towards **coherence and unity** in their writing.

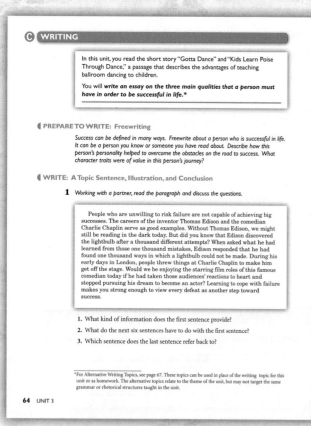

C   WRITING

In this unit, you read the short story "Gotta Dance" and "Kids Learn Poise Through Dance," a passage that describes the advantages of teaching ballroom dancing to children.

You will *write an essay on the three main qualities that a person must have in order to be successful in life.* *

◀ **PREPARE TO WRITE:** Freewriting

Success can be defined in many ways. Freewrite about a person who is successful in life. It can be a person you know or someone you have read about. Describe how this person's personality helped to overcome the obstacles on the road to success. What character traits were of value in this person's journey?

◀ **WRITE:** A Topic Sentence, Illustration, and Conclusion

1 *Working with a partner, read the paragraph and discuss the questions.*

> People who are unwilling to risk failure are not capable of achieving big successes. The careers of the inventor Thomas Edison and the comedian Charlie Chaplin serve as good examples. Without Thomas Edison, we might still be reading in the dark today. But did you know that Edison discovered the lightbulb after a thousand different attempts? When asked what he had learned from those one thousand mistakes, Edison responded that he had found one thousand ways in which a lightbulb could not be made. During his early days in London, people threw things at Charlie Chaplin to make him get off the stage. Would we be enjoying the starring film roles of this famous comedian today if he had taken those audiences' reactions to heart and stopped pursuing his dream to become an actor? Learning to cope with failure makes you strong enough to view every defeat as another step toward success.

1. What kind of information does the first sentence provide?

2. What do the next six sentences have to do with the first sentence?

3. Which sentence does the last sentence refer back to?

*For Alternative Writing Topics, see page 67. These topics can be used in place of the writing topic for this unit or as homework. The alternative topics relate to the theme of the unit, but may not target the same grammar or rhetorical structures taught in the unit.

◀ **REVISE:** Using Special Sentence Structure for Strong Conclusions

A strong conclusion will keep your ideas in the reader's mind and may even change his or her mind about the topic. A conclusion can also give an emotional view of what remains to be done.

Read the conclusion. Is it effective? Why or why not? Share your thoughts with a partner.

> Today's problem of global warming again brings challenges for all the friends of the earth. Is there reason to despair? Absolutely not! We should always keep in mind the example of Rachel Carson and *Silent Spring*. Only then will we realize that science and popular opinion can indeed make a difference. Through Carson's work and her careful reasoning, the environmental protection movement was born. Never before had scientists and ordinary people been able to join together in one movement to defend our planet. This legacy of working together to save our environment gives us hope for tomorrow.

One way to emphasize important ideas is to use sentences with inverted word order.* In sentences beginning with negative or restrictive words such as **never, rarely,** or **only,** the verb is placed before the subject. Because this structure is used to highlight an especially strong point, it should not be overused.

Normal Word Order

We will realize only then that science and popular opinion can indeed make a difference.

Inverted Word Order

Only then will we realize that science and popular opinion can indeed make a difference.

Work with a partner. Make the sentences more emphatic.

1. Scientists and ordinary people had never been able to join together in one movement before. _____

2. I realized what a great leader Carson was only when I read her book. _____
_____

*Note that when inverted word order is used, auxiliary verb forms are needed, as in "question formats":

	Normal Word Order		Inverted Word Order
(Present Tense)	I **realize** only when . . .	→	Only when . . . **do I realize**
	He/she **realizes** only when . . .	→	Only when . . . **does he/she realize**
(Past Tense)	I **realized** only when . . .	→	Only when . . . **did I realize**
(Future Tense)	I **will realize** only when . . .	→	Only when . . . **will I realize**

In the final phase of the writing process, students **edit** their work with the help of a **checklist** that focuses on mechanics, completeness, enhancing style, and incorporating the vocabulary and grammar from the unit.

ALTERNATIVE WRITING TOPICS are provided at the end of the unit. They can be used as *alternatives* to the final writing task, or as *additional* assignments. RESEARCH TOPICS tied to the theme of the unit are organized in a special section at the back of the book.

COMPONENTS

TEACHER'S MANUAL WITH ACHIEVEMENT TESTS

Each level and strand of *NorthStar* has an accompanying Teacher's Manual with step-by-step **teaching suggestions**, including unique guidance for using *NorthStar* in secondary classes. The manuals include time guidelines, expansion activities, and techniques and instructions for using MyNorthStarLab. Also included are reproducible unit-by-unit achievement **tests** of **receptive** and **productive** skills, **answer keys** to both the student book and tests, and a unit-by-unit **vocabulary** list.

EXAMVIEW

NorthStar ExamView is a stand-alone CD-ROM that allows teachers to **create and customize** their own *NorthStar* tests.

DVD

The *NorthStar* DVD has **engaging**, **authentic video clips**, including animation, documentaries, interviews, and biographies, that correspond to the themes in *NorthStar*. Each theme contains a three- to five-minute segment that can be used with either the *Reading and Writing* strand or the *Listening and Speaking* strand. The video clips can also be viewed in MyNorthStarLab.

COMPANION WEBSITE

The companion website, www.longman.com/northstar, includes resources for teachers, such as the **scope and sequence**, **correlations** to other Longman products and to state standards, and **podcasts** from the *NorthStar* authors and series editors.

MyNorthStarLab

PEARSON LONGMAN **mynorthstarlab** | AVAILABLE WITH the new edition of **NORTHSTAR**

NorthStar is now available with **MyNorthStarLab**—an easy-to-use **online** program **for students and teachers** that saves time and improves results.

> **STUDENTS** receive **personalized instruction** and **practice** in all four skills. Audio, video, and test preparation are all in **one** place—available **anywhere, anytime**.

> **TEACHERS** can take advantage of many resources including online **assessments**, a flexible **gradebook**, and **tools for monitoring student progress**.

CHECK IT OUT! GO TO www.mynorthstarlab.com FOR A PREVIEW!

TURN THE PAGE TO SEE KEY FEATURES OF **MyNorthStarLab**.

MyNorthStarLab

MyNorthStarLab supports students with **individualized instruction**, **feedback**, and **extra help**. A wide array of resources, including a flexible **gradebook**, helps teachers manage student progress.

The MyNorthStarLab **WELCOME** page **organizes assignments and grades**, and **facilitates communication** between students and teachers.

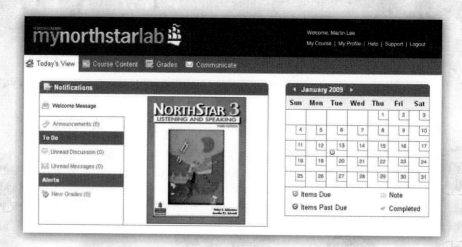

For each unit, MyNorthStarLab provides a **READINESS CHECK**.

➤ Activities **assess** student knowledge **before** beginning the unit and **follow up** with individualized instruction.

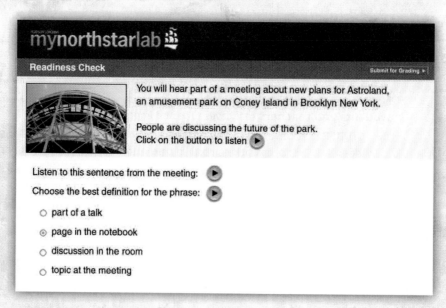

Student book material and **new** practice activities are available to students online.

➤ Students benefit from virtually unlimited **practice anywhere, anytime**.

Interaction with **Internet** and **video** materials will:

➤ Expand students' knowledge of the topic.

➤ Help students practice new vocabulary and grammar.

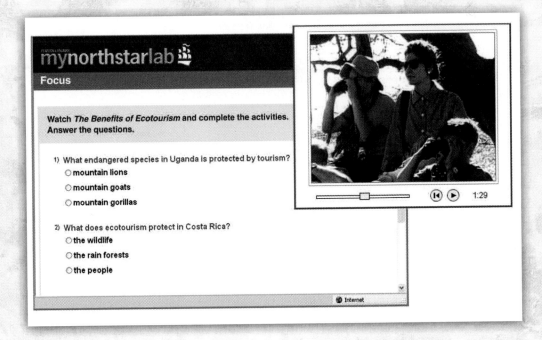

INTEGRATED SKILL ACTIVITIES in MyNorthStarLab challenge students to bring together the **language skills** and **critical thinking skills** that they have practiced throughout the unit.

Integrated Task - Read, Listen, Write | Submit for Grading ▶

THE ADVENTURE OF A LIFETIME

We at the Antarctic Travel Society encourage you to consider an excited guided tour of Antarctica for your next vacation.

The Antarctic Travel society carefully plans and operates tours of the Antarctic by ship. There are three trips per day leaving from ports in South America and Australia. Each ship carries only about 100 passengers at a time. Tours run from November through March to the ice-free areas along the coast of Antarctica.

In addition to touring the coast, our ships stop for on-land visits, which generally last for about three hours. Activities include guided sightseeing, mountain climbing, camping, kayaking, and scuba diving. For a longer stay, camping trips can also be arranged.

Our tours will give you an opportunity to experience the richness of Antarctica, including its wildlife, history, active research stations, and, most of all, its natural beauty.

Tours are supervised by the ship's staff. The staff generally includes experts in animal and sea life and other Antarctica specialists. There is generally one staff member for every 10 to 20 passengers. Theses trained and responsible individuals will help to make your visit to Antarctica safe, educational, and unforgettable.

READ, LISTEN AND WRITE ABOUT TOURISM IN ANTARCTICA
Read.
Read the text. Then answer the question.

According to the text, how can tourism benefit the Antartic?

▶ **Listen.**
Click on the Play button and listen to the passage.
Use the outline to take notes as you listen.

Main idea:

Seven things that scientists study:

The effects of tourism:

Write.
Write about the potential and risks in Antarctica.
Follow the steps to prepare.

Step 1
• Review the text and your outline from the listening task.
• Write notes about the benefits and risks of tourism.

Step 2
Write for 20 minutes. Leave 5 minutes to edit your work.

The MyNorthStarLab **ASSESSMENT** tools allow instructors to customize and deliver achievement tests online.

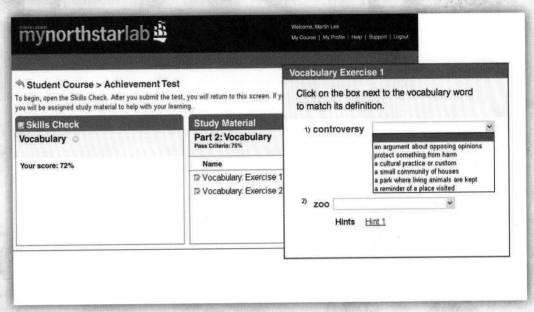

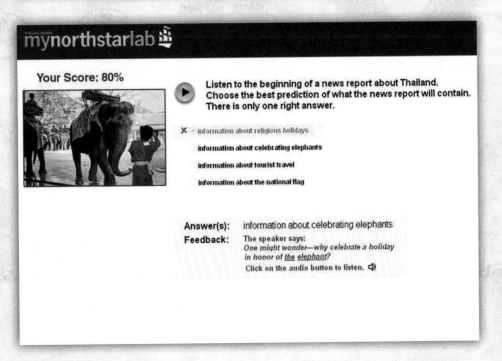

SCOPE AND SEQUENCE

UNIT	CRITICAL THINKING	READING

1 Mickey's Team
 	
Theme: Addiction
Reading One: *My Time in a Bottle*
  An autobiographical text
Reading Two: *Addiction*
  An excerpt from a psychology text
	Infer characters' motivations
	Classify information
	Hypothesize unreal situations
	Evaluate personal experiences
	Support answers with evidence from the text
	Identify the logic of an argument
	Identify an author's biases
		Make predictions
		Read for main ideas and details
		Infer information not explicit in the reading
		Order information according to a timeline
		Organize and synthesize information from two texts

2 Lies and Truth
 	
Theme: Lying
Reading One: *Looking for the Lie*
  A news article
Reading Two: *There Is Such a Thing as Truth*
  A personal essay
	Interpret a cartoon
	Recognize personal attitudes and values
	Hypothesize another's point of view
	Relate the theme to personal experience
	Consider advantages and disadvantages
	Infer word meaning from context
		Predict content of the reading
		Identify main ideas and details
		Contrast a common theme in two texts
		Organize and synthesize information from two texts

3 The Road to Success
 	
Theme: Personality
Reading One: *Gotta Dance*
  A short story
Reading Two: *Kids Learn Poise Through Dance*
  An article
	Interpret a photograph
	Identify personality traits
	Analyze character and motivation in fiction
	Infer information not explicit in the text
	Categorize information
	Support answers with information from the text
		Make predictions
		Summarize main ideas
		Read for details
		Locate information in the text
		Relate text to personal value
		Identify connecting themes between texts

4 Silent Spring
 	
Theme: Trends
Reading One: *A Fable for Tomorrow*
  An excerpt from a book
Reading Two: *The Story of Silent Spring*
  An essay
	Identify and interpret trends
	Examine imagery in a text
	Analyze author's purpose
	Hypothesize another's point of view
	Relate text to broader historical context
		Make predictions
		Identify the historic context of a book
		Summarize main ideas
		Scan for details
		Identify cause and effect
		Recognize the organization of a text
		Organize and synthesize information from two texts

WRITING	VOCABULARY	GRAMMAR
Develop the elements of character, technique, and theme in autobiographical writing Write a paragraph Combine sentences using past unreal conditionals Take notes to prepare for writing Use quotations	Find and use synonyms Use context clues to find meaning Recognize suffixes	Past unreal conditionals
Write a comparison and contrast paragraph Use double comparatives Write an opinion essay Develop thesis statements and introductory paragraphs Develop an introductory hook	Find and use synonyms Use context clues to find meaning Recognize positive and negative connotations	Double comparatives
Write an opinion statement Write a dialogue Use adjective clauses Develop a paragraph with a topic sentence, illustrations, and a conclusion Write an essay with unified paragraphs	Find collocations Use hyphenated adjectives Use idiomatic expressions	Identifying and nonidentifying adjective clauses
Write an interview Write a paragraph analysis Use discourse connectors and adverb clauses Take notes to prepare for writing Develop a logical organizational pattern Write a cause-and-effect essay	Recognize prefixes and suffixes Use context clues to find meaning	Adverb clauses and discourse connectors to express cause and effect

SCOPE AND SEQUENCE

UNIT	CRITICAL THINKING	READING

5 **What Is Lost in Translation?**
 	
Theme: Cross-cultural insights
Reading One: *Lost in Translation*
  An excerpt from a memoir
Reading Two: *In One School, Many Sagas*
  An article
	Recognize personal assumptions and biases
	Infer characters' attitudes and feelings
	Infer word meaning from context
	Compare and contrast cultural customs
	Hypothesize another's point of view
	Categorize information
		Predict content
		Read for main ideas and details
		Identify an author's point of view
		Organize and synthesize information from three different texts
		Compare and contrast two readings
		Recognize the organization of a text

6 **The Landscape of Faith**
 	
Theme: Religion
Reading One: *Peace Prevails*
  A newspaper interview
Reading Two: *Religion*
  An encyclopedia definition
	Compare religious backgrounds
	Hypothesize another's point of view
	Classify information
	Support answers with information from the text
	Infer word meaning from context
	Relate text to personal values
		Make predictions
		Summarize main ideas
		Read for details
		Relate supporting details to main ideas
		Organize and synthesize information from two texts

7 **In Business, Size Matters**
 	
Theme: Business
Reading One: *Howard Schultz's Formula for Starbucks*
  A magazine article
Reading Two: *Swiping at Industry*
  A newspaper article
	Interpret a cartoon
	Analyze information to form a recommendation
	Hypothesize another's point of view
	Infer word meaning from context
	Categorize ideas
	Evaluate advantages and disadvantages
	Recognize the organization of a text
		Make predictions
		Read for main ideas
		Scan for details
		Infer information not explicit in the text
		Identify connecting themes between texts

WRITING	VOCABULARY	GRAMMAR
Write a comparison and contrast essay Write statements of comparison and contrast Take notes in outline form Develop an outline Develop a logical organizational pattern Combine sentences for variety and polish	Use context clues to find meaning Recognize suffixes	Adverb clauses of comparison and contrast
Write an opinion paragraph Write summary statements Paraphrase quotations Write an interview Develop definitions Develop an outline Write a definition essay	Find and use synonyms Use context clues to find meaning Analyze analogies Categorize words	Definite and indefinite articles Count and non-count nouns
Summarize questionnaire data Write a report offering advice Write an interview Take notes to prepare for writing Examine and develop thesis statements Write an essay showing advantages and disadvantages Compose transitional sentences	Find and use synonyms Use context clues to find meaning Use idiomatic expressions	Infinitives and gerunds

SCOPE AND SEQUENCE

UNIT	CRITICAL THINKING	READING
8 **When the Soldier Is a Woman . . .** **Theme:** The Military **Reading One:** Women at War A series of letters **Reading Two:** In Peace, Women Warriors Rank Low A newspaper article	Recognize personal values Make generalizations Support opinions with information from the text Infer an author's attitude and feelings Compare and contrast experiences Evaluate characters' motivations Relate broad themes to specific situations	Predict content Identify main ideas Locate specific information in the text Identify connecting themes between texts Organize and synthesize information from two texts
9 **The Cellist of Sarajevo** **Theme:** The arts **Reading One:** The Cellist of Sarajevo A magazine article **Reading Two:** The Soloist An excerpt from a novel	Interpret a photograph Compare tastes and preferences Compare and contrast two artists' careers Theorize characters' motivations Analyze descriptive language Infer information not explicit in the text Recognize the organization of a text	Interpret a quotation Make predictions Identify main ideas Locate details in the text Identify similarities and differences between texts Organize and synthesize information from two texts
10 **The End of Poverty** **Theme:** Poverty **Reading One:** Can Extreme Poverty Be Eliminated? An essay **Reading Two:** Making Ends Meet A book review excerpt	Interpret photographs Analyze statistics Analyze an author's purpose Propose solutions to a problem Evaluate an author's arguments Develop a logical argument for and against an issue	Make predictions Read for main ideas Scan for supporting details Restate arguments in the text Organize and synthesize information from two texts

WRITING	VOCABULARY	GRAMMAR
Write a personal letter Write a summary Construct a dialogue Take notes to prepare for writing Write an essay response Write an introductory paragraph Embed quotations in a written work	Categorize vocabulary Recognize suffixes Use idiomatic expressions	Direct and indirect speech
Write a comparison and contrast essay Summarize the reading Evaluate passive voice usage Develop an outline Analyze descriptive language Use descriptive and figurative language	Use context clues to find meaning Categorize vocabulary Use participles as adjectives	The passive voice
Write compare and contrast paragraphs Construct a dialogue Write short argumentative statements Develop a logical organizational pattern Write an argumentative essay Refute opposing points of view Compose statements of concession	Find and use synonyms Use context clues to find meaning Use idiomatic expressions Recognize positive and negative connotations	Noun clauses in apposition

ACKNOWLEDGMENTS

This project would have never come to fruition without the kind support and sincere dedication of many people.

As in the past, our greatest debt is to our wonderful editor and friend, Carol Numrich, whose expertise, optimism, and creative insight have guided us throughout every stage of the writing process. We are also grateful to Frances Boyd, whose expression of confidence in our work has continued to be a great source of encouragement.

In addition, we would like to thank Debbie Sistino for her coordination of this effort and her sound guidance every step of the way, John Barnes for his meticulous and expert work in the development phase of this edition, and Robert Ruvo for his contribution as production editor.

Finally, our heartfelt thanks go to our colleagues at the American Language Program at Columbia University and the Department of Language and Cognition at Eugenio María de Hostos Community College, and to our students, who are our inspiration.

Judy L. Miller and *Robert F. Cohen*

Reviewers

For the comments and insights they graciously offered to help shape the direction of the Third Edition of *NorthStar,* the publisher would like to thank the following reviewers and institutions.

Gail August, Hostos Community College; **Anne Bachmann**, Clackamas Community College; **Aegina Barnes**, York College, CUNY; **Dr. Sabri Bebawi**, San Jose Community College; **Kristina Beckman**, John Jay College; **Jeff Bellucci**, Kaplan Boston; **Nathan Blesse**, Human International Academy; **Alan Brandman**, Queens College; **Laila Cadavona-Dellapasqua**, Kaplan; **Amy Cain**, Kaplan; **Nigel Caplan**, Michigan State University; **Alzira Carvalho**, Human International Academy, San Diego; **Chao-Hsun (Richard) Cheng**, Wenzao Ursuline College of Languages; **Mu-hua (Yolanda) Chi**, Wenzao Ursuline College of Languages; **Liane Cismowski**, Olympic High School; **Shauna Croft**, MESLS; **Misty Crooks**, Kaplan; **Amanda De Loera**, Kaplan English Programs; **Jennifer Dobbins**, New England School of English; **Luis Dominguez**, Angloamericano; **Luydmila Drgaushanskaya**, ASA College; **Dilip Dutt**, Roxbury Community College; **Christie Evenson**, Chung Dahm Institute; **Patricia Frenz-Belkin**, Hostos Community College, CUNY; **Christiane Galvani**, Texas Southern University; **Joanna Ghosh**, University of Pennsylvania; **Cristina Gomes**, Kaplan Test Prep; **Kristen Grinager**, Lincoln High School; **Janet Harclerode**, Santa Monica College; **Carrell Harden**, HCCS, Gulfton Campus; **Connie Harney**, Antelope Valley College; **Ann Hilborn**, ESL Consultant in Houston; **Barbara Hockman**, City College of San Francisco; **Margaret Hodgson**, NorQuest College; **Paul Hong**, Chung Dahm Institute; **Wonki Hong**, Chung Dahm Institute; **John House**, Iowa State University; **Polly Howlett**, Saint Michael's College; **Arthur Hui**, Fullerton College; **Nina Ito**, CSU, Long Beach; **Scott Jenison**, Antelope Valley College; **Hyunsook Jeong**, Keimyung University; **Mandy Kama**, Georgetown University; **Dale Kim**, Chung Dahm Institute; **Taeyoung Kim**, Keimyung University; **Woo-hyung Kim**, Keimyung University; **Young Kim**, Chung Dahm Institute; **Yu-kyung Kim**, Sunchon National University; **John Kostovich**, Miami Dade College; **Albert Kowun**, Fairfax, VA; **David Krise**, Michigan State University; **Cheri (Young Hee) Lee**, ReadingTownUSA English Language Institute; **Eun-Kyung Lee**, Chung Dahm Institute; **Sang Hyock Lee**, Keimyung University; **Debra Levitt**, SMC; **Karen Lewis**, Somerville, MA; **Chia-Hui Liu**, Wenzao Ursuline College of Languages; **Gennell Lockwood**, Seattle, WA; **Javier Lopez Anguiano**, Colegio Anglo Mexicano de Coyoacan; **Mary March**, Shoreline Community College; **Susan Matson**, ELS Language Centers; **Ralph McClain**, Embassy CES Boston; **Veronica McCormack**, Roxbury Community College; **Jennifer McCoy**, Kaplan; **Joseph McHugh**, Kaplan; **Cynthia McKeag Tsukamoto**, Oakton Community College; **Paola Medina**, Texas Southern University; **Christine Kyung-ah Moon**, Seoul, Korea; **Margaret Moore**, North Seattle Community College; **Michelle Moore**, Madison English as a Second Language School; **David Motta**, Miami University; **Suzanne Munro**, Clackamas Community College; **Elena Nehrbecki**, Hudson County CC; **Kim Newcomer**, University of Washington; **Melody Nightingale**, Santa Monica College; **Patrick Northover**, Kaplan Test and Prep; **Sarah Oettle**, Kaplan, Sacramento; **Shirley Ono**, Oakton Community College; **Maria Estela Ortiz Torres**, C. Anglo Mexicano de Coyoac'an; **Suzanne Overstreet**, West Valley College; **Linda Ozarow**, West Orange High School; **Ileana Porges-West**, Miami Dade College, Hialeah Campus; **Megan Power**, ILCSA; **Alison Robertson**, Cypress College; **Ma. Del Carmen Romero**, Universidad del Valle de Mexico; **Nina Rosen**, Santa Rosa Junior College; **Daniellah Salario**, Kaplan; **Joel Samuels**, Kaplan New York City; **Babi Sarapata**, Columbia University ALP; **Donna Schaeffer**, University of Washington; **Lynn Schneider**, City College of San Francisco; **Errol Selkirk**, New School University; **Amity Shook**, Chung Dahm Institute; **Lynn Stafford-Yilmaz**, Bellevue Community College; **Lynne Ruelaine Stokes**, Michigan State University; **Henna Suh**, Chung Dahm Institute; **Sheri Summers**, Kaplan Test Prep; **Martha Sutter**, Kent State University; **Becky Tarver Chase**, MESLS; **Lisa Waite-Trago**, Michigan State University; **Carol Troy**, Da-Yeh University; **Luci Tyrell**, Embassy CES Fort Lauderdale; **Yong-Hee Uhm**, Myongii University; **Debra Un**, New York University; **José Vazquez**, The University of Texas Pan American; **Hollyahna Vettori**, Santa Rosa Junior College; **Susan Vik**, Boston University; **Sandy Wagner**, Fort Lauderdale High School; **Joanne Wan**, ASC English; **Pat Wiggins**, Clackamas Community College; **Heather Williams**, University of Pennsylvania; **Carol Wilson-Duffy**, Michigan State University; **Kailin Yang**, Kaohsing Medical University; **Ellen Yaniv**, Boston University; **Samantha Young**, Kaplan Boston; **Yu-san Yu**, National Sun Yat-sen University; **Ann Zaaijer**, West Orange High School

Mickey's Team

①FOCUS ON THE TOPIC

A PREDICT

Look at the photo of Mickey Mantle, a famous baseball player elected to the Baseball Hall of Fame. What do you already know about Mickey Mantle? What do you already know about the kinds of personal problems that famous people often have? Discuss your ideas with a partner.

B SHARE INFORMATION

Mickey Mantle credited his skill as a baseball player to the influence of one person. Think of all the people who have influenced your development. What did they contribute to your personality? Was their influence always positive? How old were you when their influence was felt?

Fill in the chart. Then share your answers with a small group.

WHO INFLUENCED YOU?	HOW DID THIS PERSON INFLUENCE YOU?	HOW OLD WERE YOU?
Family member		
Friend		
Teacher or religious leader		
National celebrity (athlete, politician, movie star, performer)		
Other		

C BACKGROUND AND VOCABULARY

Choose the word(s) that correctly explain the meaning of the boldfaced word. There can be more than one correct answer. Compare your answers with a partner's.

1. For a long time, he thought that he, too, would die from the **hereditary** disease that killed his father.

    a. inherited   **b.** genetic

2. Despite **tough** competition, Mantle rose from the lead mines of the West to the heights of fame.

    a. demanding   **b.** strong

3. Mickey Mantle was one of the greatest and most popular baseball players in American history. When he died, baseball fans were **devastated**.

   a. heartsick   **b.** worried

4. Mickey Mantle was a "natural," a player whose talent seemed to come from an inner grace, but he suffered many painful injuries and long periods of **depression**.

   a. melancholy   **b.** sorrow

5. Mantle drank to deaden the pain of his injuries and to **avoid** thinking about his father's early death.

   a. escape   **b.** stop

6. There was nothing **controversial** about his career: everyone agreed he was a wonderful athlete and a powerful player, winning championship after championship for the New York Yankees.

   a. debatable   **b.** argumentative

7. Even today fans still **choke up** and shed a tear for Mickey Mantle, symbol of the hope, prosperity, and confidence of America in the 1950s and '60s.

   a. are unable to speak   **b.** are unable to breathe

8. Mantle also **blamed** himself for neglecting his children during his long career.

   a. praised   **b.** condemned

9. During his retirement, he stopped drinking and became **sober** after a period of time in a treatment center.

   a. abstinent   **b.** intoxicated

10. When Mantle developed liver disease later in life, he needed a new liver from a **donor**.

    a. receiver   **b.** supplier

11. At the end of his life, he became a spokesperson for organ donation with the **slogan** "Be a hero, be a donor."

    a. motto   **b.** memorandum

Ⓐ READING ONE: My Time in a Bottle

Before you read, discuss the question with a partner.

What effect can a parent's addiction have on a child?

MY TIME IN A BOTTLE

Mickey Mantle

By Mickey Mantle
(from *Sports Illustrated*)

1 IF ALCOHOLISM IS **HEREDITARY**, if it's in the genes, then I think mine came from my mother's side of the family. Her brothers were all alcoholics. My mother, Lovell, and my father, Mutt, weren't big drinkers. Dad would buy a pint of whiskey on Saturday night and put it in the icebox. Then every night when he came home from working eight hours in the lead mines of Oklahoma, he'd head for the icebox and take a swig[1] of whiskey.

2 My dad loved baseball, played semi-professional ball on the weekends, and was a tremendous St. Louis Cardinals fan. In fact, he named me after Mickey Cochrane, the Hall of Fame catcher for Philadelphia and Detroit who was a great hitter. Dad had high hopes for me. He thought I could be the greatest ballplayer who ever lived, and he did everything to help me realize his dream.

3 Even though he was dog tired after long days at the mine, Dad would still pitch batting practice to me in the backyard when he got home from work, beginning from the time I was four years old. My mother would call us to dinner, but the meal would wait until Dad was finished instructing me from the right and left sides of the plate. Dad was a **tough** man. If I'd done something wrong, he could just look at me—he didn't have to say anything—and I'd say, "I won't do it no more, Dad." I loved my father, although I couldn't tell him that, just like he couldn't tell me.

4 I joined the Yankees at 19. The following spring, when Dad died of Hodgkin's disease[2] at age 39, I was **devastated**, and that's when I started drinking. I guess alcohol helped me escape the pain of losing him.

5 God gave me a great body to play with, and I didn't take care of it. And I blame a lot of it on alcohol. Everyone likes to make the excuse that injuries shortened my career. Truth is, after I'd

---

[1] **swig:** a gulp of a liquid, usually alcohol

[2] **Hodgkin's disease:** a cancer of the blood characterized by enlargement of the spleen, lymph nodes, and liver. It is hereditary. For a long time, Mickey Mantle thought he would develop the disease. One of his sons had it and died around the same age as Mantle's father.

had a knee operation, the doctors would give me rehab[3] work to do, but I wouldn't do it. I'd be out drinking. . . . Everything had always come naturally to me. I didn't work hard at it.

6   After I retired at 37, my drinking got really bad. I went through a deep **depression**. Billy Martin, Whitey Ford, Hank Bauer, Moose Skowron [my Yankee teammates], I left all those guys and I think it left a hole in me.... We were as close as brothers. I haven't met anyone else I've felt as close to.

7   I never thought about anything serious in my life for a continuous period of days and weeks until I checked into the Betty Ford Center.[4] I've always tried to **avoid** anything emotional, anything **controversial**, anything serious, and I did it through the use of alcohol. Alcohol always protected me from reality.

8   You are supposed to say why you ended up at the Center. I said I had a bad liver and I was depressed. Whenever I tried to talk about my family, I got all **choked up**. One of the things I really messed up, besides baseball, was being a father. I wasn't a good family man. I was always out, running around with my friends. My son Mickey Jr. could have been a wonderful athlete. If he had had my dad, he could have been a major league baseball player. My kids never **blamed** me for not being there. They don't have to. I blame myself.

9   During my time at the Betty Ford Center, I had to write my father a letter and tell him how I felt about him. It only took me ten minutes to write the letter, and I cried the whole time, but after it was over, I felt better. I said that I missed him, and I wish he could have lived to see that I did a lot better than my first season with the Yankees. I told him I had four boys—he died before my first son, Mickey Jr., was born—and I told him I loved him. I would have been better off if I could have told him that a long time ago.

10   Dad would have been proud of me today, knowing that I've completed treatment at Betty Ford and have been **sober** for three months. But he would have been mad that I had to go there in the first place.

11   For all those years I lived the life of someone I didn't know: a cartoon character. From now on, Mickey Mantle is going to be a real person.

Epilogue

12   As one of Mickey Mantle's last wishes, he wanted to establish a **donor** awareness program, called "Mickey's Team," at Baylor Hospital in Texas, where he received a liver transplant. He planned to tape a series of public service announcements for the program and even invented a **slogan** before he died: "Be a hero, be a donor." Mickey's painful problems have inspired a twofold increase in the number of people requesting donor cards. "That program," says Mickey Jr., "will probably be the biggest thing he's going to be known for." (Richard Jerome et al., "Courage at the End of the Road," *People*)

---

[3] **rehab, rehabilitation:** training to restore a person to good physical condition

[4] **Betty Ford Center:** a live-in treatment center for drug and alcohol addiction located in Rancho Mirage, California. It is named in honor of the wife of former U.S. president Gerald Ford, and many celebrities have been helped there.

◖ READ FOR MAIN IDEAS

Answer the questions based on your understanding of the reading. Write your answers on a separate piece of paper.

1. What effect did Mickey Mantle's addiction have on:
   - his ability to play baseball?
   - his relationship with family members?
   - his friendships?

2. How did Mickey Mantle feel about his father?

◖ READ FOR DETAILS

Fill in the time line below by creating sentences using the following phrases.

was cured at the Betty Ford Center	joined the Yankees
left baseball	started a campaign for donor awareness
father died	father began teaching him baseball

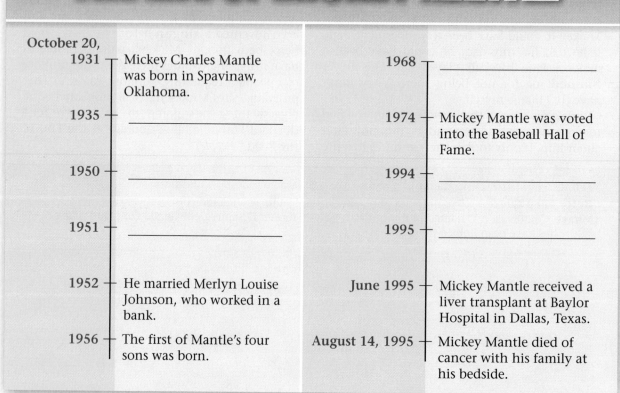

THE LIFE OF MICKEY MANTLE

October 20, 1931 — Mickey Charles Mantle was born in Spavinaw, Oklahoma.	**1968** — _____
1935 — _____	**1974** — Mickey Mantle was voted into the Baseball Hall of Fame.
1950 — _____	**1994** — _____
1951 — _____	**1995** — _____
1952 — He married Merlyn Louise Johnson, who worked in a bank.	**June 1995** — Mickey Mantle received a liver transplant at Baylor Hospital in Dallas, Texas.
1956 — The first of Mantle's four sons was born.	**August 14, 1995** — Mickey Mantle died of cancer with his family at his bedside.

6 UNIT I

◖ MAKE INFERENCES

1 *Working with a partner, circle the choice that best completes each sentence. Refer to Reading One to support your choices.*

1. Mickey Mantle's father _____
   a. caused Mickey's drinking problem.
   b. may have influenced Mickey's drinking problem.
   c. had nothing to do with Mickey's drinking problem.

2. Mantle's father pitched batting practice to Mickey even when he was dog tired because _____
   a. he felt Mickey didn't practice enough on his own.
   b. he was an experienced ball player and always wanted to play.
   c. he wanted Mickey to become the player he himself hadn't been.

3. The main reason for Mickey's shortened career was _____
   a. the fact that he was an alcoholic.
   b. the fact that he was injured so frequently.
   c. the fact that Mickey did not work hard enough.

4. Mickey probably sees himself as a cartoon character because _____
   a. he was always drunk.
   b. he didn't keep his Yankee teammates as friends.
   c. he always tried to avoid anything serious.

5. Mickey set up "Mickey's Team" because _____
   a. he wanted to be a hero.
   b. he wanted to be remembered.
   c. he wanted to help others.

6. Mickey Mantle wrote a letter to his father because _____
   a. he hadn't expressed his feelings to his father.
   b. his father hadn't seen his children.
   c. he missed his father.

2 *Discuss the questions with a partner and write your answers in the space provided.*

1. Why did Mickey Mantle become addicted?

_____

_____

_____

_____

2. Why did Mickey Mantle say that it would have been better for him if he had told his father he loved him a long time ago?

_____

_____

_____

_____

3. Did Mickey Mantle think that his life was a success?

_____

_____

_____

_____

◀ **EXPRESS OPINIONS**

Discuss the questions in a small group. Share your group's conclusions with the rest of the class.

1. Do you think Mickey Mantle was a hero? In your opinion, what makes a person a hero?

2. In your opinion, should anyone get priority for organ transplants? If so, who? Important people, young people, people with money? The sickest people or the people who can best survive a transplant?

B **READING TWO: Addiction**

1 *Below is a passage from a psychology text on addiction. Before you read the passage, answer the question. When you have finished, share your answer with a partner.*

Why do people become addicted to playing video games, watching television, gambling, or eating?

PSYCHOLOGY TODAY

ADDICTION

1   Addiction is one of the toughest problems facing our culture today. Growing problems within the family as well as many other cultural stressors make addiction a national and international problem that is growing rapidly. Contrary to some popular thought, people do not become addicted just because certain behaviors or substances cause pleasure. There are usually reasons why an addiction happens, and these same reasons make an addiction difficult to stop.

Key Elements of Addiction

2   Addiction has two elements that must be understood. The first is tolerance. A person is drawn to addictive behavior or to a substance because of the way they affect his or her emotions. They enhance some feelings and deaden others. Emotional pain is reduced momentarily, and the person hopes that it will not return. But it invariably does. Tolerance means that over time, more and more of the behavior or substance is required to produce the desired effect until the situation becomes hazardous. In the case of eating, spending, or gambling, more and more intense experiences are required for satisfaction. Eventually, even those fail. In the case of chemical addictions, one may become impaired, or an overdose may result in death. There is also the risk of arrest, the loss of a job, or divorce.

3   The second element that is important to understand is withdrawal. Withdrawal means that an individual has a very painful physical and/or emotional reaction when the substance or behavior is stopped. After a person has become adjusted to a certain level of a chemical substance in the blood or an experience or behavior, removal of this stimulation affects the emotional and biochemical balance that has been established. Complete withdrawal can last two years or more and has emotional and physiological effects that are very difficult to endure.

Factors That Influence Addiction

4   There is often a genetic inclination toward one type of addiction or another. This is not to say that heredity alone is sufficient to cause an addiction, but that the specific nature of the addiction may well be influenced by genetics. For instance, an alcoholic often has alcoholic parents or grandparents and may also have an unusually strong "positive" response to alcohol.

5   Trauma can also shape and foster addiction. Chemical substance abusers may have a history of emotional trauma in childhood, or post traumatic stress, such as that found among war veterans.

6   Another important factor in addiction is shame. Shame is a very powerful feeling that we have when we feel that we don't measure up to certain standards. It often masquerades as other feelings, but it is commonly found in addicts both as a cause and a result of the addiction. Shame spirals upward as an addiction progresses.

7   One last contributor to addiction is anxious depression, the type of depression in which pressure makes the next two hours seem like the most important time of your life. It is an agitated feeling, very different from the melancholy depression that causes a person to sit in bed all day unable to get up or get dressed.

Recovery

8   Recovery from any addiction is not easily achieved. The emotional issues that helped to cause the addiction initially have to be addressed, and the damage to the person's life caused by the addiction must be gradually healed as much as possible. It is hard, demanding work, but the rewards are great.

2 *Working with a partner, read each statement and decide if it is **T** (true) or **F** (false). If it is false, correct it. Find support for your answers in the reading passage.*

    <u> F </u>   **1.** Addictive personalities are easily cured.

                 <u>This is false because the recovery process is very complex.</u>

    <u>   </u>   **2.** If you have too many nights out having fun, you can become addicted.

              <u>   </u>

    <u>   </u>   **3.** Getting used to a drug and eventually needing more and more of it in order to enjoy its effects is an example of tolerance.

              <u>   </u>

    <u>   </u>   **4.** If you become addicted, you are not really responsible. Blame your genes.

              <u>   </u>

    <u>   </u>   **5.** Addiction is a cure for emotional pain.

              <u>   </u>

C INTEGRATE READINGS ONE AND TWO

◀ STEP 1: Organize

Reading Two was about the causes of addictions, the way an addiction gradually takes hold, and the problems people face when they try to be cured of an addiction. Reread Reading One and fill in the chart on the next page to give examples from Mickey Mantle's life about his addiction. Put notes in the appropriate boxes. When you are finished, share your notes with a partner.

FEATURES OF ADDICTION	EXAMPLES FROM MICKEY MANTLE'S LIFE
Tolerance	
Withdrawal	
Genetic Disposition	
Trauma	
Shame	
Depression	
Recovery	

◀ **STEP 2: Synthesize**

You are a journalist writing a feature article about different celebrities with addictions. Using the chart you completed in Step 1, on a separate piece of paper, write a paragraph about Mickey Mantle. Start your paragraph with this topic sentence: "Mickey Mantle had the classic addictive personality."

③ FOCUS ON WRITING

Ⓐ VOCABULARY

◀ **REVIEW**

Imagine that the letter on the next page was the one Mickey Mantle wrote at the Betty Ford Center to his long-dead father. Fill in each blank with one of the words from the box on the next page.

avoided	depressed	failed	sober
blame	~~devastated~~	instruction	tolerance
choked up	enhanced	recovered	tough

Dear Dad,

Your death really **(1.)** _devastated_ me. I don't think I have ever **(2.)** _____ from the pain and the fact that I never managed to tell you how much I loved you. The hardest thing I ever had to do was to say good-bye to you.

How do I account for my success? I owe it all to your patient **(3.)** _____ in baseball, your faith in me, and your love. If you had lived, you would have seen my four beautiful sons. You would have shared my fame, and your presence would have added to and **(4.)** _____ my success. You would have seen me realize those dreams we had so long ago.

More than anything else in the world, I wanted you to be proud of me. When I lost you, I lost my guide, my anchor in life. You were such a responsible person, but I **(5.)** _____ to follow your example. You had no **(6.)** _____ for wrong behavior, but I became very **(7.)** _____ after your death. Despite all the success, I lost my way for a long time, but I have beaten my addiction and now I am always **(8.)** _____. Whatever happens, I am determined to use the rest of my life to make things up to my family.

Even though I was elected to the Baseball Hall of Fame, I was not the great father to my sons during their childhood that you were to me during mine. I can't deny that in their own ways, my kids bear the scars of my neglect. I get all **(9.)** _____ when I think about all this because they don't **(10.)** _____ me for my failures as a parent. I only wish that I had been there for my kids in the same way that you were always there for me. You were **(11.)** _____ on me, but you always wanted the best. Perhaps I could have **(12.)** _____ some of this suffering if, years ago, I had had the courage to tell you how much I loved you.

Your loving son,
Mickey

1 *Working in a small group, fill in the chart with the correct forms of the words. Use your dictionary if necessary. (An X indicates that there is no commonly used word).*

NOUN	VERB	ADJECTIVE	ADVERB
1.	avoid		
2.	blame		X
3. depression			
4.		devastated	
5.	enhance		X
6. recovery			X
7.	fail		X
8.	X	sober	
9. tolerance			
10.		tough	X

A suffix comes at the end of the word. When you recognize certain suffixes, you will be able to understand what part of speech a word belongs to and where the word can be used in the structure of a sentence.

2 *Complete the sentences with information from the chart above. Then check your answers with a partner's.*

1. Common suffixes for _____ are *-ance, -ety (-ity), -ment, -ness, -tion (-sion),* and *-ure.*

2. The endings *-able, -ed,* and *-ing* are common suffixes for _____.

3. To create an adverb from an adjective, all you have to do is to add the suffix

_____. When you do so, sometimes the last letter (-*e*) of the

adjective is dropped.

4. Common suffixes for _____ are -*ate* and -*en*.

◖ **CREATE**

Read the beginning of a paragraph about why Mickey Mantle felt better about himself at the end of his life. Use at least seven more words from the list below to complete the paragraph. Be sure to use the correct form of each word as shown in the chart in Expand. Then read your writing to a partner.

avoid	depressed	fail	~~sobriety~~
blame	devastate	instruct	tolerate
choked up	enhance	recover	tough

How Mickey Mantle Changed

    At the end of his life, Mickey Mantle was more in touch with his feelings than he had ever been before. He had overcome his addiction to alcohol and was able to stay *sober* . _____

_____

_____

_____

_____

_____

_____

B **GRAMMAR: Using Past Unreal Conditionals to Evaluate the Effect of Past Actions**

1 *Examine the sentence and discuss the questions with a partner.*

If I had done the physical rehab work after my injuries, I would have been able to play baseball after age 37.

  1. Did Mickey Mantle do the physical rehab work after his injuries?

  2. Was he able to play baseball after age 37?

  3. How are these two ideas connected in the sentence above?

PAST UNREAL CONDITIONALS

A **past unreal conditional** is used to express past untrue or past imagined situations and their result. A past unreal conditional statement can be used to explain why things happened the way they did or to express a regret about the past. A past unreal conditional statement is formed by combining an *if-clause* and a **result clause**. Both clauses have to be stated in terms that are opposite to what really happened.

Reality	Mickey Mantle didn't do the rehab work after his injuries; therefore, he wasn't able to play baseball after the age of 37.
Past unreal conditional	If Mickey Mantle had done the rehab work after his injuries, he would have been able to play baseball after the age of 37.

Formation
To form a past unreal conditional statement, use **had** (not) + past participle in the *if*-clause and **would, might, could** (not) + **have** + past participle in the result clause.

If-clause	**If** Mickey Mantle **had done** the rehab work,
Result clause	he **would have been** able to play baseball after the age of 37.

If-clause	**If** Mantle **hadn't been** out drinking with his friends all the time,
Result clause	he **would have had** time to do the rehab work.

GRAMMAR TIP: Using *could have* or *might have* in the result clause shows more doubt about the conclusion.

2 *Combine the ideas in these sentences by using the past unreal conditional. Remember that these conditional sentences must express the opposite of what really happened.*

1. Mickey Mantle needed a transplant.

   There has been a twofold increase in the number of people requesting donor cards from Baylor Hospital.

   If Mickey Mantle hadn't needed a transplant, there might not have been a twofold increase in the number of people requesting donor cards from Baylor Hospital.

2. Mickey Mantle's father trained his son to play baseball from the age of four. Mickey became a champion.

   _____

   _____

   _____

3. Mickey Mantle centered his social life on alcohol.

He neglected his wife and sons.

_____

_____

_____

4. Mickey Mantle's father died in 1952.

He never saw Mickey Mantle become a champion.

_____

_____

_____

5. Mantle went to the Betty Ford Center the year before he died.

He reconciled with his family at the end of his life.

_____

_____

_____

3 *Using the information from the readings, write your own past unreal conditionals about the themes below in Mickey Mantle's life. When you write your sentences, try to use the vocabulary words you have studied in this unit.*

   1. Mickey's transplant

   If Mickey Mantle had been sober all his life, he wouldn't have needed

   a liver transplant.

   2. Mickey's relationship with his father

   _____

   _____

   3. Mickey's relationship with his sons

   _____

   _____

   4. Mickey's addiction to alcohol

   _____

   _____

In this unit, you read an excerpt from an autobiographical article by Mickey Mantle and a passage about the nature of addictions.

You will **write an autobiographical narrative about a problem that you had to deal with and how you tried to overcome it.***

PREPARE TO WRITE: Notetaking

1 *Jot down notes of the different times you have faced a personal struggle or challenge in your life. Your notes can be in words, numbers, pictures, or in whatever other symbols that help you to respond most comfortably to the task.*

2 *Think of what you tried to do to resolve the specific problem(s). Were you able to find solutions? Why or why not? Which situation was the most significant in your life? As you write your notes, do not worry about grammar or formal structure. Just express your ideas as they occur to you.*

3 *Share your notes with a partner. Compare insights and decide which particular experience would be the best one to write about in an autobiographical narrative.*

WRITE: An Autobiographical Narrative

1 *Working with a partner, reread the paragraph from "My Time in a Bottle" and discuss the questions.*

> "Even though he was dog tired after long days at the mine, Dad would still pitch batting practice to me in the backyard when he got home from work, beginning from the time I was four years old. My mother would call us to dinner, but the meal would wait until Dad was finished instructing me from the right and left sides of the plate. Dad was a tough man. If I'd done something wrong, he could just look at me—he didn't have to say anything—and I'd say, 'I won't do it no more, Dad.' I loved my father, although I couldn't tell him that, just like he couldn't tell me."

1. Who is being described here?
2. Who is the narrator (the person who is telling the story)?
3. During which period in the narrator's life does the action take place?
4. What verb tenses are used?
5. What statement refers to an issue that caused the author a lot of pain?

---

*For Alternative Writing Topics, see page 22. These topics can be used in place of the writing topic for this unit or as homework. The alternative topics relate to the theme of the unit, but may not target the same grammar or rhetorical structures taught in the unit.

The person being described here is Mickey Mantle's father. Because the passage is written in the first-person narrative (as shown by the use of the pronoun *I* and the possessive adjective *my*), it is clear to the reader that the narrator is Mickey Mantle himself. The verbs are all in a past tense form (the simple past: "he was dog tired"; the habitual past: "My mother would call"), and the actions that are being described here all refer to the period in the author's childhood starting at age four. The statement at the very end, "I loved my father, although I couldn't tell him that, just like he couldn't tell me," makes us aware of an issue that bothered Mantle a lot.

What we can appreciate in this paragraph are the three major "elements" of autobiography: **character, technique,** and **theme.**

Character

Authors of autobiographies provide details about themselves and people around them, and about their reactions to the events in their lives. From the comfortable distance created by the passage of time, the narrators create self-portraits and portraits of the principal players in their lives. Through the portraits, we discover each writer's character or system of values. We learn how the writer views various character traits (such as generosity, sensitivity, meanness, happiness, and sadness) by examining how such traits were reflected in the author's own behavior and that of others. In addition, we learn why the autobiographer believes the individuals being described became the way they were and how the writer's present values may now be different from his or her past values.

In the example paragraph, the author provides details about himself and his father. He writes, "Dad was a tough man," and explains further that his father "could just look at [him]" to get him to do what he wanted. The great influence the author's father had on his character development is thus revealed in these few words.

2 *Write short answers to the questions and discuss your answers with a partner.*

1. What did you learn about the character of Mickey Mantle's father in the example paragraph?

2. By reading Mantle's portrait of his father, we learn about the values Mickey Mantle respected. What are these values?

3. Look at the rest of "My Time in a Bottle." Does Mickey Mantle claim he kept to these values? Underline the sentences where you find the answer.

3 *Discuss the questions with a partner.*

1. Suppose that in the example paragraph Mickey Mantle had written, "Every day after work my father practiced pitching balls to me before sitting down to dinner." Would this have been an interesting sentence or a dull one? Why?

2. Underline the descriptive words Mantle uses to tell about his father's days. Why are these words effective? What do they communicate?

3. Underline the sentence where Mantle offers a direct quotation of his own words. Why does he do this? What is wrong with the grammar of the sentence?

4 *Write short answers to the questions and compare them with a partner's.*

1. What is the main theme of the paragraph we examined? Underline the sentence that you think is the most significant.

2. Is there anything in this paragraph that shows the weakness or vulnerability of the narrator?

3. Does this make us feel closer to the narrator? Why or why not?

5 *Write a first draft. Discuss a problem that you had and how you overcame it. Use the first-person narrative and the past tense. Express yourself in interesting and descriptive language. Pay careful attention to the main elements of an autobiographical narrative—character, technique, and theme.*

You can:

a. describe your personality as it was during a particular period or at the time of a special event in your life

b. consider how that period or special event affected you and how it may have caused your system of values to change or remain the same

c. describe any individuals who had a great influence on you at the time

d. share with the reader the issue that was most on your mind at that time

e. discuss whether there was anything you should have done differently

Refer to the notes that you wrote at the beginning of this section to see if you can expand upon one of the ideas that you mentioned there.

◀ REVISE: Using Quotes for Interest and Authenticity

Direct quotations attract the reader to the writing in an autobiographical narrative. Without direct quotations, the writing may seem dull and unreal.

You must use quotation marks when you use the exact words that a person has said or written. You place the second quotation mark after a period, comma, question mark, or exclamation point.

Mickey Mantle wrote, "Dad was a tough man."
"Dad was a tough man," said Mickey Mantle.

1 *Working with a partner, rewrite the direct quotations with the correct punctuation.*

  1. Beginner's luck they said.

   "Beginner's luck," they said.

  2. I'm only playing for $50 a night. It's nothing. I can control it I would say to him.

  3. But he adds it's up to you to do the hard work of healing.

  4. Just lend me your ATM card I'd say.

  5. They'd say over and over again you're becoming an addict.

  6. get help as soon as you can I tell them.

2 *Read the autobiographical paragraph. Working with a partner, decide where each of the quotations on page 20 should be inserted in the paragraph. Place the number of each sentence on the appropriate line.*

> Gambling is not a pastime for me; it's a compulsion. It took me many years to recognize my addiction. The first time I went to a casino, I played my $35 into $10,000. __1__ The next night, I lost it all. In senior year, I frequently begged my college roommate for his credit card. _____ When I got my first job, I assured my uncle I was not an addict. _____ My friends also tried to warn me of the dangers. _____ But I wouldn't listen. Like all addicts, I needed more and more intense experiences, risking more and more money until I lost my job and my self-respect. Today, I am in a recovery program. My doctor suggests that losing my parents in a car accident when I was ten made me psychologically vulnerable. _____ What do I say to others who risk addiction? _____.

After you have finished, reread the paragraph with the direct quotations in place. Discuss with your partner why the paragraph is now better than it was without the quotations.

3 *Look at the first draft of your narrative. Have you used direct quotations correctly? Have you also used other effective stylistic devices, such as questions and interesting language and imagery?*

◀ **EDIT: Writing the Final Draft**

Write your final draft. Carefully edit it for grammatical and mechanical errors. Make sure you used some of the vocabulary and grammar from the unit. Use the checklist to help you write the final draft. Then neatly write or type your narrative.

✓ FINAL DRAFT CHECKLIST

- ○ Does your narrative give a clear picture of the problem?
- ○ Are the three main elements of autobiographical narratives—character, technique, and theme—properly addressed?
- ○ Do you use correct punctuation for the direct quotations that are included?
- ○ Is the past unreal conditional used correctly to evaluate the consequence of past actions on your life?
- ○ Has vocabulary from the unit been used?

ALTERNATIVE WRITING TOPICS

Write an essay on one of the topics. Use the vocabulary and grammar from the unit.

1. Imagine that you are a character from Mickey Mantle's childhood: a brother, a sister, a parent, a friend. Write a paragraph from that person's point of view. For example, you may want to describe how a younger brother could have been jealous of the daily sessions Mantle had with his father. You could begin the paragraph this way: "Every day was the same. I sat alone while my father spent all his free time with my brother."

2. Write a letter to someone who has been very important to you in your life. Mickey Mantle wrote one to his father, but the person you choose can still be alive today. If you hadn't had that person in your life, what would have happened to you? Would your life have been different? How?

3. Choose a famous sports hero, celebrity, or national leader. Make sure you know a lot about this person's life. Put yourself in the individual's shoes, and write an imaginary autobiography from the person's point of view. Discuss the influence of the person's early life, the contributions he or she made, and the contradictions between the person's public and private life. What are the individual's strengths and weaknesses? What would the person's life have been like if his or her career hadn't been successful? If he or she hadn't made some mistakes? If certain people hadn't been there to help?

4. Some people think that alcoholics should not be eligible for organ transplants. They say that if alcoholics hadn't abused their bodies, they wouldn't have gotten so sick. Other people feel that it is unfair to deny lifesaving help to another human being. Still other people are worried about society's limited number of donor organs and limited economic resources. What do you think?

RESEARCH TOPICS, see page 261.

Lies and Truth

①FOCUS ON THE TOPIC

Ⓐ PREDICT

Why do people lie? Should we be honest all the time? Take ten minutes to write about the questions.

Do you agree with these quotes? Is it possible to tell when someone is lying?

> "A liar chatters with his fingertips; betrayal oozes out of him at every pore."
> —Sigmund Freud
>
> "The mouth may lie, but the face it makes nonetheless tells the truth."
> —Friedrich Nietzsche

Interview a partner about experiences with lying.

1. How do you know when someone is lying to you?

2. Is it easier to tell if someone is lying in person or in writing?

3. When a person lies to you, do you usually confront the person and say, "You're lying," or do you do nothing at all? Explain.

4. In what kinds of situations have you been forced to lie? If your lies were discovered, what happened?

C BACKGROUND AND VOCABULARY

Write your own synonym for the boldfaced words. Use the context of the sentences to help determine the meaning of the word. Use a dictionary to check your work.

1. Many psychological experiments have been conducted to see if there are ways that people can successfully **spot** liars. _____

2. As children, we are taught to tell the truth and not to use **deception** with other people. _____

3. In everyday life, people may feel a sense of **betrayal** when someone lies to them and breaks their trust. _____

4. People sometimes tell "white lies" to be kind, not to be **malicious**.

   _____

5. According to a Cornell University study, it seems that students are more likely to engage in **outright** lying on the telephone (37 percent) or in instant messages (21 percent) than in e-mails (14 percent). _____

6. The man was a cold and **cunning** liar who took advantage of lonely people by tricking them out of their money. _____

7. **Empirical** evidence from brain scans indicates that lying leads to more brain activity than telling the truth, although there is no accepted theory to explain these results. _____

8. The **quest** for the perfect way to detect liars has been unsuccessful so far.

_____

9. Severe mental illness creates **delusions** that seem completely real to the patient; in this case, the patient may not be aware that he is lying.

_____

10. There is no completely accurate way of detecting lies, and even lie detectors are not **foolproof**. _____

11. Some people regret that we are **plagued by** liars who refuse to speak the truth, but others feel that certain types of lying may be necessary.

_____

②FOCUS ON READING

Ⓐ READING ONE: Looking for the Lie

Before you read, discuss the question with a partner.

What do you think would happen in a society if no one could tell lies?

Looking for the Lie

(New York Times Magazine, 02/05/06)
By Robin Marantz Henig

Trying to catch a liar

1   **W**HEN people hear that I'm writing an article about deception, they're quick to tell me how to catch a liar. Liars always look to the left, several friends say; liars always cover their mouths, says a man sitting next to me on a plane. Beliefs about lying are plentiful and often contradictory: depending on whom you choose to believe, liars can be detected because they fidget a lot, hold very still, cross their legs, cross their arms, look up, look down, make eye contact, or fail to make eye contact. Freud thought anyone could **spot deception** by paying close enough attention, since the liar, he wrote, "chatters with his fingertips; **betrayal** oozes out of him at every pore." Nietzsche wrote that "the mouth may lie, but the face it makes nonetheless tells the truth."

2   The idea that liars are easy to spot is still with us. Just last month, Charles Bond, a psychologist at Texas Christian University, reported that among 2,520 adults surveyed in 63 countries, more than 70 percent believe that liars avert their gazes[1]. The majority believe that liars squirm, stutter, touch or scratch themselves or tell longer stories than usual. The liar stereotype exists in just about every culture, Bond wrote, and its persistence "would be less puzzling if we had more reason to imagine that it was true." What is true, instead, is that there are as many ways to lie as there are liars; there's no such thing as a dead giveaway[2].

3   Most people think they're good at spotting liars, but studies show otherwise. A very small minority of people, probably fewer than 5 percent, seem to have some innate ability to sniff out deception with accuracy. But, in general, even professional lie-catchers, like judges and customs officials, perform, when tested, at a level not much better than chance. In other words, even the experts would have been right almost as often if they had just flipped a coin. Most of the mechanical devices now available, like the polygraph, detect not the lie but anxiety about the lie. The polygraph measures physiological responses to stress, like increases in blood pressure, respiration rate and electrodermal skin response. So it can miss the most dangerous liars: the ones who don't care that they're lying or have been trained to lie. It can also miss liars with nothing to lose if they're detected, the true believers willing to die for the cause.

4   Serious lies can have a range of motives and implications. They can be **malicious**, like lying about a rival's behavior in order to get him fired, or merely strategic, like not telling your wife about your mistress. Not every one of them is a lie that needs to be uncovered. "We humans are active, creative mammals who can represent what exists as if

---

[1] **avert their gazes:** look away
[2] **dead giveaway:** something that reveals you have lied or done something wrong

it did not and what doesn't exist as if it did," wrote David Nyberg, a visiting scholar at Bowdoin College, in *The Varnished Truth*. "Concealment, obliqueness, silence, **outright** lying—all help to keep Nemesis at bay[3]; all help us abide too-large helpings of reality." Learning to lie is an important part of maturation. What makes a child able to tell lies, usually at about age 3 or 4, is that he has begun developing a theory of mind, the idea that what goes on in his head is different from what goes on in other people's heads.

5   Deception is, after all, one trait associated with the evolution of higher intelligence. According to the Machiavellian[4] Intelligence Hypothesis, developed by Richard Byrne and Andrew Whiten, two Scottish primatologists at the University of St. Andrews in Fife, the more social a species, the more intelligent it is. This hypothesis holds that as social interactions became more and more complex, our primate ancestors evolved so they could engage in the trickery, manipulation, skullduggery[5], and sleight of hand[6] needed to live in larger social groups, which helped them to avoid predators and survive.

6   "All of a sudden, the idea that intelligence began in social manipulation, deceit, and **cunning** cooperation seems to explain everything we had always puzzled about," Byrne and Whiten wrote. In 2004, Byrne and another colleague, Nadia Corp, looked at the brains and behavior of 18 primate species and found **empirical** support for the hypothesis: the bigger the neocortex, the more deceptive the behavior.

7   "Lying is just so ordinary, so much a part of our everyday lives and everyday conversations, that we hardly notice it," said Bella DePaulo, a psychologist at the University of California, Santa Barbara. "And in many cases it would be more difficult, challenging and stressful for people to tell the truth than to lie."

8   DePaulo said that her research led her to believe that not all lying is bad, that it often serves a perfectly respectable purpose; in fact, it is sometimes a nobler, or at least kinder, option than telling the truth. "I call them kindhearted lies, the lies you tell to protect someone else's life or feelings," DePaulo said. A kindhearted lie is when a genetic counselor says nothing when she happens to find out, during a straightforward test for birth defects, that a man could not have possibly fathered his wife's new baby. It's when a neighbor lies about hiding a Jewish family in Nazi-occupied Poland. It's when a doctor tells a terminally ill patient that the new chemotherapy might work. And it's when a mother tells her daughter that nothing bad will ever happen to her.

9   The Federal government has been supporting research recently to look for machines that detect the brain tracings of deception. But the **quest** might be doomed to failure, since it might turn out to be all but impossible to tell which tracings are signatures of truly dangerous lies, and which are the images of lies that are harmless and kindhearted, or self-serving without being dangerous. Alternatively, the quest could turn out to be more successful than we really want, generating instruments that can detect deception not only as an antiterrorism device but also in situations that have little

---

[3] **keep Nemesis at bay:** escape revenge (Nemesis was the ancient Greek goddess of rightful punishment)
[4] **Machiavellian:** named after Niccolo Machiavelli (1469–1527), an Italian political philosopher; in common language, we call something Machiavellian when it uses deceitful methods for selfish reasons
[5] **skullduggery:** dishonest behavior
[6] **sleight of hand:** the use of tricks and lies to achieve something

(continued on next page)

to do with national security: job interviews, tax audits, classrooms, boardrooms, bedrooms.

10   But it would be destabilizing indeed to be stripped of the half-truths and **delusions** on which social life depends. As the great physician-essayist Lewis Thomas once wrote, a **foolproof** lie-detection device would turn our quotidian lives upside down: "Before long, we would stop speaking to each other, television would be abolished as a habitual felon, politicians would be confined by house arrest and civilization would come to a standstill." It would be a mistake to bring such a device too rapidly to market, before considering what might happen not only if it didn't work—which is the kind of risk we are accustomed to thinking about—but also what might happen if it did. Worse than living in a world **plagued by** uncertainty, in which we can never know for sure who is lying to whom, might be to live in a world plagued by its opposite: certainty about where the lies are, thus forcing us to tell one another nothing but the truth.

■

◖ READ FOR MAIN IDEAS

Underline three sentences in the text that express the three main points the author is presenting. Share your answers with a partner.

◖ READ FOR DETAILS

*Working with a partner, read each statement and decide if it is **T** (true) or **F** (false). If it is false, correct it.*

_____ **1.** Most people believe that liars avert their glances.

_____ **2.** About 20% of people have a natural ability to detect liars.

_____ **3.** Psychologists are better than ordinary people at detecting liars.

_____ **4.** Polygraphs can detect lies.

_____ **5.** Some experts like David Nyberg and Bella DePaulo think that lying is a necessary way for us to cope with reality.

_____ **6.** According to the Machiavellian Intelligence Hypothesis, intelligence evolved in order to increase the ability to deceive.

_____ **7.** Learning to lie is a sign that something has gone wrong in a child's development.

_____ **8.** Many experts believe that people would feel more secure if everyday lies were uncovered.

_____ **9.** According to the text, doctors shouldn't lie to their patients and parents should never lie to their children.

_____ **10.** An antiterrorism device could also detect lies told at work, school, and home.

_____ **11.** Lewis Thomas was an advocate for a foolproof lie-detection device.

MAKE INFERENCES

1 *Examine the quotes from Reading One. Choose the answer that best explains what the person intended to say.*

1. "The liar stereotype exists in just about every culture . . . and its persistence 'would be less puzzling if we had more reason to imagine that it was true.' "
   a. The liar stereotype is widespread and true.
   b. The liar stereotype is widespread and false.

2. "We humans are active, creative mammals who can represent what exists as if it did not and what doesn't exist as if it did."
   a. Humans are able to use rational thought.
   b. Humans have imagination.

3. "Concealment, obliqueness, silence, outright lying—all help to hold Nemesis at bay; all help us abide too-large helpings of reality."
   a. Too much reality is bad for us.
   b. Too much lying is bad for us.

4. "Before long, we would stop speaking to each other, television would be abolished as a habitual felon, politicians would be confined by house arrest and civilization would come to a standstill."
   a. Social interaction is built on truth.
   b. Social interaction is built on lies.

2 *How would the experts in this article categorize the lies listed below: malicious lies, selfish lies that are not dangerous, or lies of kindness? Work with a partner and look back to the reading and provide evidence for your decisions.*

a. a woman lies to her husband about her previous boyfriends

b. parents don't tell their children they are adopted

c. a man refuses to tell where he has hidden weapons he bought

d. an accountant hides the corruption of the company from the shareholders

e. a man tells his friend she looks good when she doesn't

EXPRESS OPINIONS

Discuss the questions in a small group. Share your group's conclusions with the rest of the class.

1. Can we ever feel secure if there is no real way to detect liars? Why or why not?

2. Should a nation's security depend on its ability to have access to information about every aspect of people's lives? Why or why not?

3. Explain what Robin Marantz Henig means when she writes: "It would be destabilizing indeed to be stripped of the half-truths and delusions on which social life depends." Do you agree or disagree with her? Why?

1 *Below is a passage entitled "There is Such a Thing as Truth." The writer is an Academy Award-winning documentary filmmaker whose works include* The Thin Blue Line, A Brief History of Time, *and* The Fog of War: Eleven Lessons from the Life of Robert S. McNamara. *He is also the director of a number of critically acclaimed television programs. Before you read the passage, answer the questions.*

Is it always possible to discover the truth? Is there one truth, or does it depend on each person's opinion?

There Is Such a Thing as Truth

by Errol Morris (*This I Believe* series on npr.org)

1 I believe in truth. And in the pursuit of truth. When I was 10 years old, I asked a neighborhood kid who was older than me, "Which city is further west: Reno, Nevada, or Los Angeles?" The correct answer is Reno, Nevada. But he was convinced it was the other way around.

2 He was so convinced that Los Angeles was west of Reno that he was willing to bet me two bucks[1]. So I went into the house to get my Rand McNally atlas. The kid looked at the atlas and said, "The map is drawn funny." It wasn't. Was his argument that the map didn't preserve east, west, north and south? What kind of map would that be? I showed him if you trace down the 120-degree west line of longitude—which runs almost directly through Reno, Nevada—you end up in the Pacific Ocean, somewhere west of Los Angeles.

3 He replied that lines of longitude don't cross the ocean. What? I told him that the lines of longitude were there to indicate how far west or east some location was, regardless of whether it was on land or on sea. There was one insurmountable problem, however. He was bigger than I was.

4 I drew a number of conclusions from this story. There is such a thing as truth, but we often have a vested interest[2] in ignoring it or outright denying it. Also, it's not just thinking something that makes it true. Truth is not relative. It's not subjective. It may be elusive or hidden. People may wish to disregard it. But there is such a thing as truth and the pursuit of truth: trying to figure out what has really happened, trying to figure out how things really are.

5 Almost 15 years ago, I stumbled on[3] a story about an innocent man, a man who had been sentenced to die in the Huntsville, Texas, electric chair. And through hard work, luck and a certain amount of pathological obsession, I was able to make the movie *The Thin Blue Line* and to help get him out of prison.

6 What kept me going was the belief that there had to be answers to the questions "Did he do it?" "Was he guilty or innocent?" "If he didn't do it, who did?" and that I could find an answer to these questions through investigating.

7 It's not that we find truth with a big "T." We investigate and sometimes we find things out

---

[1] **a buck:** a dollar
[2] **a vested interest in (something):** a selfish motive
[3] **stumbled on:** discovered by accident

and sometimes we don't. There's no way to know in advance. It's just that we have to proceed as though there are answers to questions. We must proceed as though, in principle, we can find things out—even if we can't. The alternative is unacceptable.

8   I will never know whether the neighborhood kid really didn't understand the logic of my argument about Reno, Nevada. Or whether he understood it completely and just didn't want to admit it. Or whether he understood it and just didn't want to pay up. I'll never know.

9   All I know is I never got my two dollars.

2 *Based on what you have read in "There Is Such a Thing as Truth," answer the questions about the text. When you are finished, compare your answers with a partner's.*

1. Why was the neighborhood child wrong? Why couldn't Morris get the child to admit he was wrong?

   _____

   _____

2. What was Errol Morris's film *The Thin Blue Line* about?

   _____

   _____

3. How does the subject matter of the film relate to the childhood story of the map?

   _____

   _____

4. What is Errol Morris's view of truth?

   _____

   _____

5. What advice does he give? Are we always successful in getting the truth to be heard by those who have power?

   _____

   _____

C INTEGRATE READINGS ONE AND TWO

STEP 1: Organize

Write the main ideas from each reading. Express them in your own words. Compare your answers with a partner's.

Reading 1

That there is no foolproof way to detect liars may be a good thing.

Learning to lie is an important part of intelligence and growing up.

_____
_____

_____
_____

Reading 2

We must try to discover the truth.

_____
_____

People ignore the truth because it serves their selfish interests.

Society needs truth to protect those with less power.

STEP 2: Synthesize

Write a one-paragraph summary to contrast the main ideas of the two readings.

3 FOCUS ON WRITING

A VOCABULARY

REVIEW

Read the selection on the next page. Fill in each blank with the word from the box that matches the definition under the blank.

betrayal	elusive	insurmountable	quest
deception	empirical	outright	regardless of
delusions	foolproof	plagued by	

Truth and History

Strangely, a nation first has to remember something before it can begin to forget it. Only when nations turn away from their subjective _____ 1. (false beliefs) about the past can they join with others in peaceful union. The European Union is a convincing example. The nations of Europe fought against each other in two worldwide conflicts in the 20th century. Only after Germans faced the enormity of their past could they stop being _____ it. _____ the 2. (tormented by) 3. (Despite) difficulty, until the French understood their role in World War II, they could not move on. In fact, each nation in Europe, to one degree or another, had to overcome the almost _____ obstacles of its own past in order to build a strong 4. (overwhelming) European Union.

The instrument used in this _____ for truth was not personal 5. (search) memory but history: the _____, professional study of the past, based 6. (objective) on facts, proof, and evidence. Historians believe in the pursuit of truth no matter how _____ it may be. But history is not comfortable reading because 7. (difficult to find) it shows us how we may be lying to ourselves about the past. It reveals the myths and even _____ lies we invent about our countries to be a 8. (complete) _____ of the truth. But without a powerful desire for truth among 9. (breach) ordinary citizens, history books can become a simple instrument for political

_____. 10. (trickery) The new Europe, "bound together," as the historian Tony Judt has written, "by the signs and symbols of its terrible past, is a remarkable achievement," but there is no _____ way to keep the lessons of the past alive unless they are 11. (sure and certain) taught to the coming generations.

Negative and Positive Connotations of Words

*The two words in each pair are related in meaning. However, one word has a more positive meaning (or connotation), while the other has a more negative meaning (or connotation). Put a **P** next to the word with the more positive connotation or an **N** next to the word with the more negative connotation.*

1. __N__ **a.** manipulate   __P__ **b.** persuade
2. ____ **a.** creativity   ____ **b.** trickery
3. ____ **a.** sleight of hand   ____ **b.** magic
4. ____ **a.** artful   ____ **b.** deceptive
5. ____ **a.** false stories   ____ **b.** tall tales
6. ____ **a.** cover up   ____ **b.** throw a veil over (something)

Circle the word or phrase that best completes each sentence.

1. Using reason, facts, and proof, professional historians try to (*manipulate / persuade*) people to recognize unpopular truths.

2. Some political leaders (*manipulate / persuade*) others by playing on their fears and ignorance.

3. Teachers have to be very (*deceitful / artful*) in devising history lessons that are interesting to their students.

4. Truth be told, many students dislike discussing history because politicians can be very (*deceitful / artful*) in changing history to suit their purposes.

5. Some people prefer to (*throw a veil over / cover up*) the past for selfish reasons because they have a vested interest in keeping silent about their own role.

6. Victims may also keep silent and (*throw a veil over / cover up*) the past, but for them, it's because the past is too painful and heartbreaking to discuss.

7. Computer animators use their (*creativity / trickery*) to make the writers' stories come alive.

8. A leader used lies and (*creativity / trickery*) to convince us to follow his plan.

9. At bedtime, parents read their children many (*tall tales / false stories*) about mythical creatures and animals that talk.

10. A man came into the police station and told a (*tall tale / false story*) to the police to hide his crime.

CREATE

Write about an example of truth and lies in your own life, or choose an example from the history of your country. Use at least eight vocabulary words and three words with either negative or positive connotations.

B GRAMMAR: Using Double Comparatives to Show Cause-Effect Relationships

1 *Examine the sentence and discuss the questions with a partner.*

The bigger the neocortex, the more deceptive the behavior.

1. How many clauses are in this sentence?

2. What grammatical structure is underlined?

3. Why does the author put the two clauses in juxtaposition in the same sentence?

DOUBLE COMPARATIVES

Double comparatives are sentences that have two clauses, each of which starts with a comparative adjective, noun, or adverb structure. The clauses are separated by a comma and define the logical relationship between ideas with variations of **"the more . . . , the more," "the less . . . , the less," "the more . . . , the less,"** or **"the less . . . , the more."** In most cases, the second clause explains the "effect" of the first. Here are some rules to follow:

1. For a good "balanced" writing style, it is preferable when both sides of the double comparative are "parallel," or written with the same word order.

   The more social scientists study human behavior, the more we understand our social interactions.
   The + comparative + subject + verb + object = The + comparative + subject + verb + object

   The experts agreed that **the more social scientists study human behavior, the more we understand our social interactions.**

2. Sometimes the verb in one clause can be left out.

   The more social the species, the more intelligent it is.
   The more social the species (is), the more intelligent it is.

3. Sometimes both verbs can be left out when the meaning is clear from the sentences that went before.

   (Psychological research is not a waste of money. The university should fund more studies of human behavior. In this field, there can't be too many studies.) **The more, the better.**

4. Notice that a double comparative can never be correct unless the definite article **"the"** accompanies the comparatives in both clauses of the sentence.

Double comparatives are a stylistic tool that writers use to focus the reader's attention more closely on key concepts and the connection between them. However, be careful not to overuse this form.

2 *Working with a partner, write **C** next to the sentences that are correct and **I** next to those that are incorrect. Correct the incorrect sentences.*

_____ **1.** The most informed we are, the more we can protect ourselves.

_____ **2.** The more we investigate a problem, the closer we come to finding the solution.

_____ **3.** The more I think about it, the least sure I become.

_____ **4.** The bigger the deception, the greatest the challenge.

3 *The following refers to the story of Erin Brockovich, who became famous for uncovering the truth of a company's lie about pollution in the biggest class action lawsuit in American history. Use the cues to rewrite the underlined sentences or parts of sentences with a double comparative. You may have to change the word order and leave out or change some words.*

1. Pacific Gas and Electric Company was anxious to buy up the property of residents in Hinkley, California. Many residents did not want to sell their property, but the company insisted that <u>they sell very soon. Otherwise, they would receive less money.</u>

Cue: *the longer . . . the less* OR *the sooner . . . the more*

The company insisted that the longer they waited to sell, the less money

they would receive. OR The sooner they sold their land to the company,

the more money they would receive.

2. Working as a file clerk for the law firm of Masry and Vititoe, Erin Brockovich examined many documents. <u>After reading document after document, she found proof</u> that the company had been lying about the pollution of the town's drinking water.

Cue: *The more . . . the more*

_____

_____

that the company had been lying about the pollution of the town's drinking water.

3. The company told the people that only harmless chromium 3 leaked from their factory into the water. In fact, it was harmful chromium 6. Based on scientific evidence, it was clear that <u>there was a direct relationship between frequent exposure to chromium 6 and harm to people's health.</u>

Cue: *the greater/the more . . . the more*

Based on scientific evidence, it was clear that _____

_____

_____

4. Not only could chromium 6 cause all kinds of illnesses, but it could also affect people's DNA and the heredity of future generations. <u>As Erin showed her boss, Ed Masry, the vast mountain of evidence, he became convinced</u> that she had uncovered an insidious lie.

   Cue: *The more . . . the more*

   _____

   _____

   _____ that she had uncovered an insidious lie.

5. Unfortunately, <u>as Hinkley residents continued to drink the water, their health became worse.</u>

   Cue: *the more . . . the sicker*

   Unfortunately, _____

   _____

   _____

6. At first, people hesitated to file the legal papers against the company because they depended on it for a lot of financial assistance. Obviously, <u>when people depend a lot on others for money, they are not so willing</u> to displease them.

   Cue: *the more . . . the less*

   Obviously, _____

   _____

   _____ to displease them.

7. However, Erin Brockovich eventually convinced them. <u>As people got to know her better, they trusted her.</u>

   Cue: *The more / The better . . . the more*

   _____

   _____

   _____

8. The law firm itself was not sure it wanted so many people in the legal suit. But it soon realized that <u>its success in court would depend greatly on how many people joined the suit.</u>

   Cue: *the more . . . the greater*

   But it soon realized that _____

   _____

   _____

9. The result was that Erin Brockovich and Ed Masry were able to win a settlement of over $333 million for more than 630 families. Now, with her own consulting company, Erin Brockovich continues to fight for the disadvantaged. She is convinced that <u>when we dig more and more for the truth, we are able to uncover the lies</u> that prevent us from living quality lives.

Cue: *the more . . . the more*

She is convinced that _____

_____

_____ that prevent us from living quality lives.

Ⓒ WRITING

In this unit, you read "Looking for the Lie" and "There is Such a Thing as Truth," two essays discussing the place of truth and lies in our life.

You will **write an opinion essay in response to this question: Should we always tell the truth?***

◖ PREPARE TO WRITE: Brainstorming

Working in a small group, brainstorm the advantages and disadvantages of always telling the truth.

Advantages of Always Telling the Truth

1.

2.

3.

4.

5.

Disadvantages of Always Telling the Truth

1.

2.

3.

4.

5.

---

*For Alternative Writing Topics, see page 44. These topics can be used in place of the writing topic for this unit or as homework. The alternative topics relate to the theme of the unit, but may not target the same grammar or rhetorical structures taught in the unit.

◀ WRITE: An Introductory Paragraph with a Thesis Statement

1 *Working with a partner, reread the introductory paragraph and discuss the questions.*

> Is honesty the best policy? We are taught that it is when we are little. However, most of us soon learn that social life is full of lies. Telling the truth all the time just doesn't seem possible. Some people, like Robin Marantz Henig in her article "Looking for the Lie," believe that if we told the truth all the time the whole structure of our social relationships would crumble. Others, like Errol Morris in his essay "There is Such a Thing as Truth," point out that we sometimes have a duty to discover the truth and that ignoring "lies" may cause great harm. We are often tempted to tell the so-called "kindhearted" lies either because we want to avoid hurting others or because we do not like confrontation or conflict. However, this is just taking the easy way out. It is important for us to be honest with others because by being truthful, we stop living a lie in our own life, we show respect for others, and we create the conditions for meaningful relationships.

1. How does the writer attract the reader's attention in the first sentence?

2. How do you think the ideas develop throughout the paragraph: from the general to the specific? From the specific to the general?

3. Which sentence tells the reader what the writer will focus on in the body of the essay?

INTRODUCTORY PARAGRAPHS

An essay is composed of an introduction, a body, and a conclusion. In the **introductory paragraph,** the author writes a statement to attract the reader's attention. This statement, known as "the hook," is the first of the paragraph's general statements, which introduce the general topic of the essay. There are many ways the writer can spark the reader's interest: with a question, a humorous remark, a shocking statement, a quotation, or an anecdote.

The flow of ideas in the paragraph goes from the general (large, broad ideas) to the specific (details, examples, particular cases). The most specific statement is the thesis statement, which is usually the last statement of the paragraph.

THESIS STATEMENT

The **thesis statement** communicates the main idea of the essay. It reflects the writer's narrow focus and point of view, attitude, or opinion, and it also forecasts which aspects of the subject the writer will discuss to support the thesis in the body of the essay. A good thesis statement should have all of the criteria mentioned above.

The thesis statement is not a statement of fact, nor is it a statement that simply announces the general topic of the essay.

Lies are distortions of the truth.	THIS IS NOT A THESIS STATEMENT. It states a fact. No point of view is given.
This essay is about the role of truth and lies in our life.	THIS IS NOT A THESIS STATEMENT. It only announces the topic.
Telling the truth in our life is important.	THIS IS NOT A THESIS STATEMENT. Although it gives us the writer's point of view, there is no focus here. Why exactly is telling the truth at all times "important"?
It is important for us to be honest with others because by being truthful, we stop living a lie in our own life, we show respect for others, and we create the conditions for meaningful relationships.	THIS IS A THESIS STATEMENT. It explains why the writer believes it is important for us to tell the truth. The three body paragraphs will deal with: 1. not living a lie in our own life 2. showing respect for others 3. creating the conditions for meaningful relationships

2 *Read the sentences from the introduction to an essay. Working with a partner, put the sentences in order. Using* **1** *for the first sentence and* **7** *for the last sentence (the thesis statement), write the numbers in the blanks.*

_____ We may say this because there are so many miraculous coincidences in our life that seem so unreal.

_____ That is why even my brothers, who grew up under the same roof as I, tell different stories about the same events that took place in our childhood.

_____ We often say that "truth is stranger than fiction."

_____ Another aspect of this may be that we can never completely trust the accuracy of anyone's story, given the fact that we all see the world through different eyes.

_____ In my opinion, thinking that truth is relative and that everyone has his or her own truth can be a very liberating force in our lives, allowing us to be more creative and spontaneous.

___6___ All this leads me to say that we have to accept the potential "lie" in the truth and, in so doing, disagree with Errol Morris who, in his essay "There is Such a Thing as Truth," argues that the truth is not relative.

_____ One day when I was visiting Norway, I wrote a postcard telling a friend how lonely I was and as I looked up, I saw my cousin miraculously sitting on the next bench in the park.

3 *Working in pairs, evaluate the statements and put checks (✓) next to the ones that are good thesis statements. Do not automatically think that the longer the statement, the better the thesis statement. For the statements you choose, discuss how you think the writer could develop each of them in the body of the essay.*

_____ **1.** The Old English word for "truth" was "trēowth."

_____ **2.** Learning to lie during childhood prepares us for our adult lives in higher education, the workplace, and society.

_____ **3.** Telling the truth all the time is a prudish concept that even the most orthodox believers cannot follow to the letter.

_____ **4.** Primatologists believe that deception is a trait associated with the development of higher intelligence.

_____ **5.** Without the truth, we would be insecure, unrefined, and uneducated fools.

_____ **6.** In this essay, the writer will discuss truth and lying.

_____ **7.** More than 70 percent of adults interviewed in 63 countries believe that liars avert people's gazes.

_____ **8.** A country that cannot confront the truth of its past can never move forward into the future.

4 *Using what you have learned about writing introductory paragraphs, write an introduction to an essay that responds to the question "Should we always tell the truth?" Refer to the work you did in Prepare to Write, page 38, and Write, pages 39–41, to write your first draft.*

◖ REVISE: Writing Introductory Hooks and General Statements

1 *Read the student's introduction to an essay. Then discuss the questions on the next page with a partner.*

> In "Looking for the Lie," Robin Marantz Henig expresses doubt about the possibility of living a healthy life in a world without lies. In "There is Such a Thing as Truth," Errol Morris emphasizes the importance of seeking out the truth. Apparently, these writers are on opposite ends of the spectrum. Morris seeks an absolute ideal while Henig is more flexible in her evaluation of human nature. However, Morris is looking at cases where ignoring untruths can have severe consequences, while Henig is primarily concerned with the smaller problems of everyday life. It would be difficult to apply Morris's ideal to everyday reality. We humans can't live by the truth at all times.

1. Does the writer spark the reader's interest at the very beginning?

2. Does the writer go from broad general statements to specific statements?

3. Does the writer have a thesis statement?

The writer of this introduction starts with specific statements, and goes from the specific statements right to the thesis statement, which is the last sentence of the paragraph. However, the writer does not do anything to spark the reader's interest. There is no "hook" and there are no general statements "flowing" from the hook that make the reader understand the subject's general importance and inspire the reader to continue reading.

For instance, at the beginning of Reading One, Robin Marantz Henig attracts the reader's attention by discussing all the different ways people believe they can detect liars. At the beginning of Reading Two, Errol Morris tells an interesting personal anecdote that involves the reader in the reading experience. In both cases, the reader is "hooked."

2 *Working with a partner, read the statements and write **YES** next to the ones that would be good "hooks" and would serve as inspiration for general statements and **NO** next to the ones that would not.*

_____ **a.** I'll never forget how terrible I felt in that moment of truth.

_____ **b.** All through history people have told lies.

_____ **c.** Did you ever think what life would be like if all our lies were broadcast on a huge video screen for everyone to see?

_____ **d.** Only 1 out of every 20 people has a natural ability to recognize liars.

_____ **e.** "A liar chatters with his fingertips, betrayal oozes out of him at every pore," said Freud.

3 *With your partner, start the student's introduction with one of the sentences from Exercise 2, and then write the general statements that would naturally connect with what the student has already written. Before you proceed, see what another student has done to improve the paragraph:*

> I'll never forget how terrible I felt in that moment of truth. When my friend asked me why the others didn't like her, I couldn't stop myself. I said, "You're too fat and you don't look good." I wish I had held my tongue. Whatever good I thought I was doing evaporated as my friend's face showed her pain. This experience had a great impact on me. Since then, I have been plagued by the idea that kindness is not always served by frankness. That is why this discussion about truth and lying, in response to the writing of Robin Marantz Henig and Errol Morris, interests me. In "Looking for the Lie," Robin Marantz Henig expresses doubt about the possibility of living a healthy life in a world without lies. In "There is Such a Thing as Truth," Errol Morris is determined to convince us to tell the truth. Apparently, these writers are on

opposite ends of the spectrum. Morris seeks an absolute ideal while Henig is more flexible in her evaluation of human nature. However, Morris is looking at cases where ignoring untruths can have severe consequences, while Henig is primarily concerned with the smaller problems of everyday life. It would be difficult to apply Morris's ideal to everyday reality. We humans can't live by telling the truth at all times.

Answer the questions. Compare your answers with a partner's.

1. What happened in the "moment of truth" mentioned in the hook?
2. How did it make the writer feel?
3. What is the link between these general statements and the specific opinions of Henig and Morris?
4. More specifically, how does the writer compare Henig and Morris?
5. What is the thesis statement?

Now write your introductory paragraph.

4 *Look at the draft of your introductory paragraph. Is it a good one? If not, decide what you can do to improve it.*

◀ **EDIT: Writing the Final Draft**

Write your final draft. Carefully edit it for grammatical and mechanical errors. Make sure you used some of the vocabulary and grammar from the unit. Use the checklist to help you write the final draft. Then neatly write or type your essay.

✓ FINAL DRAFT CHECKLIST

- ○ Does the introductory paragraph of your essay have a hook and go from general statements to specific statements, ending in a thesis statement?
- ○ Is it clear from the thesis statement what the focus will be in the body paragraphs?
- ○ Have you tried to use at least one double comparative to pinpoint the main issues of an argument?
- ○ Have you used new vocabulary and expressions (including negative and positive connotations) in the essay?

ALTERNATIVE WRITING TOPICS

Write an essay on one of the topics. Try to include vocabulary and grammar you have studied in the unit. In writing the essay, pay particular attention to:

- *making your introduction interesting and relevant to the topic*
- *expressing the main idea of the essay in a well-formulated thesis statement*

1. Should we always tell the truth? You may use the introductory paragraph you wrote in Exercise 4, page 41 and complete the essay here.

2. Should high school students be taught everything, whether good or bad, about their country's history? Or, is it better to conceal some aspects of the truth, such as the grave errors committed in the past, from young people? Can a country go forward if it does not teach its young citizens the truth about its past?

3. A whistleblower is an individual who tries to make the management of a company aware of a problem in its operation that can affect the health or safety of employees and the neighboring community. When management refuses to do anything, the individual "blows the whistle" and reveals the company's dangerous practices, often with great risk to his or her job and personal safety.

   The following films are all about this kind of situation: *Enron, The Smartest Guys in the Room* (a documentary); *Network; A Civil Action;* and *The Insider*. See one or more of these films. Then write a review, commenting on the effort to uncover the truth in business practices.

4. According to Machiavelli, author of *The Prince*, the rulers of a country (whether they be presidents, prime ministers, or princes) should be able to commit immoral acts if these acts help them to keep power because this stability will keep their country strong. Do you agree or disagree with this idea? As you develop your thesis, give examples from contemporary life.

RESEARCH TOPICS, see page 261.

UNIT

3

The Road to Success

① FOCUS ON THE TOPIC

A PREDICT

Do you think the photo is a good representation of the struggle for success? Why or why not? Share your thoughts with another student.

45

Look at the hope-scale. Where do you fall? Are you generally optimistic, pessimistic, or somewhere in-between? Complete the Self-Discovery Quiz with information about yourself. Then share what you have written with a partner.

SELF-DISCOVERY QUIZ

Achieving success has a lot to do with how you look at yourself.

1. Write down three things that you like about yourself.

_____

_____

_____

2. Write down a goal that you would like to achieve.

_____

3. What is your target date for achieving it?

_____

4. What obstacles or opposition to your goal might you encounter?

_____

5. What are some first steps you could take toward your goal?

_____

Katie from Reading One (page 48) took the Self-Discovery Quiz. Fill in the form with the correct word from the word box to see how she answered the questions.

back: support	**miss a beat:** hesitate and	**spare (something):** afford
come together: make sense	show surprise or shock	to give (time, money)
dim: gloomy, dark	**pace:** the speed of events	to others
discretion: good judgment	**reluctant:** unwilling	**take it out of me:** exhaust
		(me)

SELF-DISCOVERY QUIZ

Achieving success has a lot to do with how you look at yourself.

1. Write down three things that you like about yourself.

I know how to keep a secret; people can trust me. _____ is my middle name.

When I encounter difficulties or make a mistake, I never give up; I never _____ . I just keep going.

I am a generous person. I can always _____ a little money for people in need.

2. Write down a goal that you would like to achieve.

I would like to have all the different parts of my life _____ so I could feel like a whole person with no regrets. For this, I need to find some-one to _____ me in my dancing career: a helper and mentor.

3. What is your target date for achieving it?

I am _____ to set a date for success because I believe life should follow its own _____ , but I would like to join a major dance company in five years.

4. What obstacles or opposition to your goal might you encounter?

Sometimes I get discouraged at night. I sit alone in the _____ light of my room and worry. Depression can _____ , but I always remember my dreams.

5. What are some first steps you could take toward your goal?

I am going to New York to apply to dance school.

Ⓐ READING ONE: Gotta Dance

Before you read, discuss the questions with a partner.

Did you ever have a compulsion—something you felt you had to do, no matter what the obstacles or consequences? Did you act on your feelings? Were you glad you did?

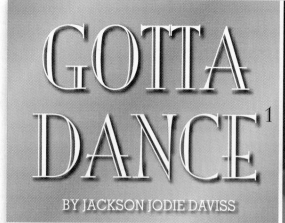

GOTTA DANCE[1]

BY JACKSON JODIE DAVISS

1   Maybe I shouldn't have mentioned it to anyone. Before I knew it, it was all through the family, and they'd all made it their business to challenge me. I wouldn't tell them my plan, other than to say I was leaving, but that was enough to set them off. Uncle Mike called from Oregon to say, "Katie, don't do it," and I wouldn't have hung up on him except that he added, "Haven't you caused enough disappointment?" That did it. Nine people had already told me no, and Uncle Mike lit the fire under me[2] when he made it ten. Nine-eight-seven-six-five-four-three-two-one. Kaboom.

2   On my way to the bus station, I stopped by the old house. I still had my key, and I knew no one was home. After ducking my head into each room, including my old one, just to be sure I was alone, I went into my brother's room and set my duffel bag and myself on his bed.

3   The blinds were shut so the room was **dim**, but I looked around at all the things I knew by heart and welcomed the softening effect of the low light. I sat there a very long time in the silence until I began to think I might never rise from that bed or come out of that gray light, so I pushed myself to my feet.

[1] **gotta dance:** slang expression for "I have got to dance," "I must dance"
[2] **lit the fire under me:** slang expression for "made me angry," "made me finally take action"

I eased off my sneakers and pushed the rug aside so I could have some polished floor, then I pulled the door shut.

4   Anyone passing in the hall outside might've heard a soft sound, a gentle sweeping sound, maybe a creak of the floor, but not much more as I danced a very soft shoe[3] in my stocking feet. Arms outstretched but loose and swaying, head laid back and to one side, like falling asleep, eyes very nearly closed in that room like twilight, I danced to the beat of my heart.

5   After a while, I straightened the rug, opened the blinds to the bright day, and walked out of what was now just another room without him in it. He was the only one I said good-bye to, and the only one I asked to come with me, if he could.

6   At the bus station, I asked the guy for a ticket to the nearest city of some size. Most of them are far apart in the Midwest, and I liked the idea of those long rides with time to think. I like buses—the long-haul kind, anyway—because they're so public that they're private. I also like the **pace**, easing you out of one place before easing you into[4] the next, no big jolts to your system.[5]

7   My bus had very few people in it and the long ride was uneventful, except when the little boy threw his hat out the window. The mother got upset, but the kid was happy. He clearly hated that hat; I'd seen him come close to launching it twice before he finally let fly. The thing sailed in a beautiful arc, then settled on a fence post, a ringer, just the way you never can do it when you try. The woman asked the driver if he'd mind going back for the hat. He said he'd mind. So the woman stayed upset and the kid stayed

happy. I liked her well enough, but the boy was maybe the most annoying kid I've come across, so I didn't offer him the money to buy a hat he and his mother could agree on. Money would have been no problem. Money has never been my problem.

8   There are some who say money is precisely my problem, in that I give it so little thought. I don't own much. I lose things all the time. I'm told I dress lousy. I'm told, too, that I have no appreciation of money because I've never had to do without it. That may be true. But even if it is, it's not all there is to say about a person.

9   There is one thing I do well, and money didn't buy it, couldn't have bought it for me. I am one fine dancer. I can dance like nobody you've ever seen. Heck, I can dance like everybody you've ever seen. I didn't take lessons, not the usual kind, because I'm a natural, but I've worn out a few sets of tapes and a VCR. I'd watch Gene Kelly and practice until I had his steps. Watch Fred Astaire, practice, get his steps. I practice all the time. Bill Robinson. Eleanor Powell. Donald O'Connor. Ginger Rogers. You know, movie dancers. I'm a movie dancer. I don't dance in the movies though. Never have. Who does, anymore? I dance where and when I can.

10   My many and vocal relatives don't think much, have never thought much, of my dancing—largely, I believe, because they are not dancers themselves. To be honest, they don't think much of anything I do, not since I left the path they'd set for me, and that's been most of my 23 years. These people, critical of achievement they don't understand, without praise for talents and dreams or the elegant risk, are terrified of

---

[3] **a soft shoe:** tap dance steps but without taps (metal caps) on the shoes; a silent dance
[4] **easing you out . . . easing you into:** taking you gently from one place to another
[5] **no big jolts to your system:** smoothly and carefully

(continued on next page)

being left behind but haven't the grace to come along in spirit.

11   Mutts and I talked a lot about that. He was a family exception, as I am, and he thought whatever I did was more than fine. He was my brother, and I **backed** everything he did, too. He played blues harmonica. He told bad jokes. We did have plans. His name was Ronald, but everyone's called him Mutts since he was a baby. No one remembers why. He never got his chance to fly, and I figure if I don't do this now, I maybe never will. I need to do it for both of us.

12   The bus depot was crowded and crummy, like most city depots seem to be. I stored my bag in a locker, bought a paper, and headed for where the bright lights would be. I carried my tap shoes and tape player.

13   When I reached the area I wanted it was still early, so I looked for a place to wait. I found a clean diner, with a big front window where I could read the paper and watch for the lines to form. I told the waitress I wanted a large cup of coffee before ordering. After half an hour or so, she brought another refill and asked if I was ready. She was kind and patient, and I wondered what she was doing in the job. It seems like nothing **takes it out of you** like waitress work. She was young; maybe that was it. I asked her what was good, and she recommended the baked chicken special and said it was what she had on her break. That's what I had, and she was right, but I only picked at[6] it. I wanted something for energy, but I didn't want to court a side-ache, so the only thing I really ate was the salad. She brought an extra dinner roll and stayed as pleasant the whole time I was there, which was the better part of two hours, so I put down a good tip when I left.

14   While I was in the diner, a truly gaunt[7] young man came in. He ordered only soup, but he ate it like he'd been hungry a long time. He asked politely for extra crackers, and the waitress gave them to him. When he left he was full of baked chicken special with an extra dinner roll. He wouldn't take a loan. Pride, maybe, or maybe he didn't believe I could **spare** it, and I didn't want to be sitting in a public place pushing the idea that I had plenty of money. Maybe I don't know the value of money, but I do know what **discretion** is worth. The guy was **reluctant** even to take the chicken dinner, but I convinced him that if he didn't eat it, nobody would. He reminded me of Mutts, except that Mutts had never been hungry like that.

15   When the lines were forming, I started on over. While I waited, I watched the people. There were some kids on the street, dressed a lot like me in my worn jeans, faded turtleneck, and jersey warm-up jacket. They were working the crowd like their hopes amounted to spare change.[8] The theater patrons waiting in line were dressed to the nines,[9] as they say. There is something that makes the well-dressed not look at the shabby. Maybe it's guilt. Maybe it's embarrassment because, relatively, they're overdressed. I don't know. I do know it makes it easy to study them in detail. Probably makes them easy marks[10] for pickpockets, too. The

---

[6] **picked at:** ate very little with no appetite
[7] **gaunt:** very thin
[8] **their hopes amounted to spare change:** extra coins; "their hopes were very small"
[9] **dressed to the nines:** dressed in expensive clothes
[10] **easy marks:** easy victims

smell of them was rich: warm wool, sweet spice and alcohol, peppermint and shoe polish. I thought I saw Mutts at the other edge of the crowd, just for a moment, but I remembered he couldn't be.

16   I was wearing my sneakers, carrying my taps. They're slickery[11] black shoes that answer me back. They're among the few things I've bought for myself, and I keep them shiny. I sat on the curb and changed my shoes. I tied the sneakers together and draped them over my shoulder.

17   I turned on my tape player, and the first of my favorite show tunes began as I got to my feet. I waited a few beats, but no one paid attention until I started to dance. My first taps rang off the concrete clear and clean, measured, a telegraphed message: Takka-takka-takka-tak! Takka-takka-takka-tak! Takka-takka-takka-tak-tak-tak! I paused; everyone turned.

18   I tapped an oh-so-easy, wait-a-minute time-step while I lifted the sneakers from around my neck. I gripped the laces in my right hand and gave the shoes a couple of overhead, bola-style swings, tossing them to land beside the tape player, neat as you please. I didn't **miss a beat**. The audience liked it. I knew they would. Then I let the rhythm take me, and I started to fly. Everything **came together**. I had no weight, no worries, just the sweet, solid beat. Feets, do your stuff.[12]

19   Didn't I dance. And wasn't I smooth. Quick taps and slow-rolling, jazz it, swing it, on the beat, off the beat, out of one tune right into the next and the next and I never took one break. It was a chill of a night, but didn't I sweat, didn't that jacket just have to come off. Didn't I feel the solid jar to the backbone from the heavy heel steps, and the pump of my heart on the beat on the beat.

20   Time passed. I danced. A sandy-haired man came out of the theater. He looked confused. He said, "Ladies and Gentlemen, curtain in five minutes." I'm sure that's what he said. Didn't I dance and didn't they all stay. The sandy-haired man, he was tall and slim and he looked like a dancer. Didn't he stay, too.

21   Every move I knew, I made, every step I learned, I took, until the tape had run out, until they set my rhythm with the clap of their hands, until the sweet sound of the overture drifted out, until I knew for certain they had held the curtain for want of an audience. Then I did my knock-down, drag-out, could-you-just-die, great big Broadway-baby finish.

22   Didn't they applaud, oh honey, didn't they yell, and didn't they throw money. I dug coins from my own pockets and dropped them, too, leaving it all for the street kids. Wasn't the slender man with the sandy hair saying, "See me after the show"? I'm almost sure that's what he said as I gripped my tape recorder, grabbed my sneakers, my jacket, and ran away, ran with a plan and a purpose, farther with each step from my beginnings and into the world, truly heading home.

23   The blood that drummed in my ears set the rhythm as I ran, ran easy, taps ringing off the pavement, on the beat, on the beat, on the beat. Everything was pounding, but I had to make the next bus, that I knew, catch that bus and get on to the next town, and the next, and the next, and the next. Funeral tomorrow, but Mutts will not be there, no, and neither will I. I'm on tour.

---

[11] **slickery:** patent leather, shiny and smooth
[12] **Feets, do your stuff:** Feet, start dancing.

"Gotta Dance" can be divided into three parts. Write a sentence that summarizes the main idea of each part of the story. Use your own words.

Part I: Saying Good-bye (paragraphs 1–5)

<u>After saying good-bye to her childhood home and the memory of her</u>

<u>brother, Katie decides to change her life.</u>

Part II: On the Road (paragraphs 6–14)

_____

_____

_____

Part III: Meeting the Challenge (paragraphs 15–23)

_____

_____

_____

◖ READ FOR DETAILS

Circle the correct answer to each question. Then compare your answers with another student's.

1. How would you describe the attitude of the majority of Katie's family?
   a. They were critical of Katie's desire to be a dancer.
   b. They encouraged her risk-taking.
   c. They were very supportive of all her plans.

2. Which statement is <u>not</u> true of Mutts's life and death?
   a. He loved playing the blues.
   b. He died before he could realize his dream.
   c. His sister was very upset at his funeral.

3. Which of the following did Katie do before setting out for the bus depot?
   a. She went straight to her brother's room after entering her old house.
   b. She danced a soft shoe in her brother's room to the beat of a jazz album.
   c. She danced with a lot of emotion in her brother's room knowing full well that no one else was in the house.

4. Which one of Katie's ideas must she re-evaluate as a result of her experiences?
   a. The pace of a long bus trip allows her time for reflection.
   b. Waiters and waitresses are generally impatient and unkind.
   c. Bus depots are usually dirty and packed with a lot of people.

5. What did Katie observe when she was in the bus?
   a. On his third attempt, the boy succeeded in throwing his hat out the window.
   b. The boy showed his perfect aim when his hat landed on a fence post.
   c. The bus driver responded to the mother with a great deal of compassion.

6. Why did Katie go to the diner?
   a. She needed to be in a quiet place to think more about her brother and what his life meant to her.
   b. She needed to wait for her audience to arrive and to mentally and physically prepare for her performance.
   c. She needed to sit down for a while to take care of a pain in her side that she got from dancing.

7. What thoughts did Katie have when she was watching the lines form in front of the theater?
   a. She considered how differences in dress can cause people to be uncomfortable with each other.
   b. She realized that one should dress up when going to the theater to show respect to the entertainers.
   c. She thought the street kids would be chased away by the police because they would be begging.

8. Which of the following is true about Katie's performance?
   a. The theatergoers liked it so much that they missed the first five minutes of the show they had been waiting in line to see.
   b. Katie was offered a job after she performed her dance so well in the street in front of the theater.
   c. Katie was satisfied with her performance.

◖ MAKE INFERENCES

*Based on what is implied in the story, discuss with your partner whether the statements are true or false, and write **T** (true) or **F** (false) on the short line. Then write a sentence explaining your decision. Include points in the story that support your inference.*

_____ 1. Katie was a very private person.

Support:

_____

_____ 2. Family was important to Katie.

Support:

_____

_____ 3. Dancing came easily to Katie.

Support:

_____

_____ **4.** Katie was ambitious.

Support:

_____

_____ **5.** Katie sympathized with children who rebel against their families.

Support:

_____

_____ **6.** Katie was careless with money.

Support:

_____

_____ **7.** To Katie, "heading home" meant fulfilling her dreams.

Support:

_____

◖ EXPRESS OPINIONS

Discuss the questions in a small group. Share your group's conclusions with the rest of the class.

1. If one of your relatives said to you, "You are a big disappointment to me," what would you say or do? Would you react the way Katie did? Why or why not?

2. Do you think rebelling against the family is part of growing up? Is it necessary or dangerous, or both?

3. How did Katie's feelings about her brother Mutts affect her decisions? Do you think it is good for siblings to have such a close relationship? Why or why not?

4. In the story, Katie left the money people gave her for the street kids who had been begging from the theatergoers. Do you do the same thing when strangers ask you for money? Why or why not?

Ⓑ READING TWO: Kids Learn Poise Through Dance

1 *Before reading the passage on the next page, answer the questions.*

What is poise? Why do you think dance can teach kids poise?

When you have finished, share your answers with a partner.

Kids Learn Poise Through Dance

CBS NEWS June 17, 2005

1   You might think that the only music kids today are dancing to is rap. But for *The Early Show's* Study Hall report, correspondent Melinda Murphy found that New York City's public schools are using classic dance tunes to teach kids manners and civility.[1]

2   The fact that a New York elementary school is located in one of the city's poorest neighborhoods doesn't mean that its fifth graders will lack poise or social graces. They are learning them on the dance floor. Dance instructor Daniel Ponickly notes, "They don't yet know how to be ladies and gentlemen. But I say to them, 'You are going to become ladies and gentlemen' and all of a sudden, when they come to class, their shirts are tucked in. They stand up straighter." Ponickly is one of more than 30 ballroom instructors teaching dances like the foxtrot and swing in New York City's inner city schools. "We're teaching them that they matter, and that they can show it," Ponickly says.

3   This program was started by Pierre Dulaine, a four-time British exhibition dance champion. Eleven years ago, Dulaine offered to teach ballroom in one school. Today, his instructors teach in more than 60 schools. Dulaine says, "It has developed into an arts and education program where the children learn about ballroom dancing, and dances from different countries. But most important, they learn teamwork, having to work with another human being. It's not easy for a young boy and girl, lady and gentleman, to work with each other." For Rosemary Tejada, the course had an added benefit. She says, "I've gotten to be better friends with a boy. I've known my partner since first grade, but we didn't really communicate a lot. But now, with ballroom dancing, we've communicated more." At the end of every course, all the schools compete in a series of competitions.

4   Tejada and her partner, Julian Perez, have made it to the semifinals. "At the competition, I'm really excited, but I'm also nervous," Tejada says. To compete, teams must be proficient in five dances: swing, rumba, foxtrot, tango, and merengue. But each couple also has a specialty, and Tejada's is swing. She says, "In swing, you really move a lot, and you feel in a happy mood. I get to express my feelings when I dance."

5   It is wonderful to see the students getting excited about something as old-fashioned as ballroom dance. Dulaine notes, "There is a camaraderie[2] that develops between them, and it's a camaraderie to excel." He adds, "Quite honestly, I'm not interested in whether they remember every single step. Learning to touch someone with respect is the key to all of ballroom dancing."

6   In this competition, Tejada and her teammates won a silver trophy. But Dulaine hopes that they've also gained an interest in a pastime that promotes grace, manners, and civility. He says, "All those children love to dance. They have their imagination, and this is what we need to nurture." If you'd like to learn more, there is a documentary movie about the program entitled "Mad Hot Ballroom."

[1] **civility:** politeness; appropriate behavior for social interactions
[2] **camaraderie:** a feeling of group loyalty and friendship

2 Circle the correct answer(s) to the questions below. There may be more than one correct answer. Compare your answers with a partner's.

1. What is true about this arts and education program?
   a. It began this year.
   b. It includes 11 schools.
   c. The teachers are experts.

2. Why must the students in the program dress correctly?
   a. to develop good manners
   b. to show respect for each other
   c. to pay attention in class

3. What is the significance of the international aspect of this program?
   a. Children learn about manners in other countries.
   b. Children learn dances from different countries.
   c. Children compete with dancers from other countries.

4. What does competing in a ballroom dance contest teach the 10- and 11-year-old children who represent their schools?
   a. to do the best they can
   b. to get along with children of the opposite sex
   c. to appreciate school spirit

C INTEGRATING READINGS ONE AND TWO

◖ **STEP 1: Organize**

Fill in the Venn diagram. Where the circles overlap, write the similar things Katie (Reading One) and Rosemary Tejada (Reading Two) learned or felt in their dance experiences. In Katie's circle, write what only Katie learned or felt from the experience and in Rosemary's circle, write what only Rosemary learned or felt. Share your answers with a partner.

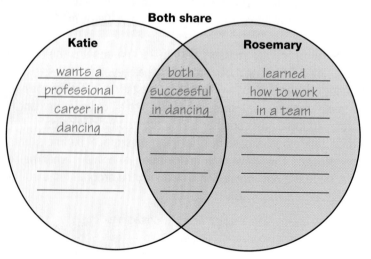

Both share

Katie
wants a
professional
career in
dancing

both
successful
in dancing

Rosemary
learned
how to work
in a team

Working with a partner, write a dialogue between Katie and Rosemary Tejada, in which they explain their feelings about dancing and what they learned from their experience. Use this sample beginning or create your own.

KATIE: I saw your school dance in the competition. You were great. I also love to dance for the public, but I do tap dancing, not ballroom dancing.

ROSEMARY: Do you dance with a partner? I would be scared to get up there alone.

(3) FOCUS ON WRITING

(A) VOCABULARY

◀ **REVIEW**

Read the possible thoughts of the sandy-haired man in "Gotta Dance." Match the underlined word(s) with a synonym from the word box below. Write the appropriate letter in the blank next to each number. Compare your answers with a partner's.

a. backed	**e.** miss a beat	**i.** proficient
b. civility	**f.** nurtured	**j.** reluctantly
c. comes together	**g.** pace	**k.** spare something
d. dim	**h.** poise	**l.** take it out of you

_____ 1. It may seem glamorous, but let me tell you, working in the theater can really <u>wear you out</u>. I've been a dancer, singer, ticket taker, scenery painter, and everything else you can think of. It's not an easy life and my sandy hair is turning gray.

_____ 2. Of course, show business can surprise you and then, one night, all of a sudden, it all <u>makes sense</u>.

_____ 3. I remember one night we were on tour in a shabby little theater in a small city in the Midwest. Despite the theater's lack of elegance, the people who were waiting outside in the <u>fading</u> light for the show to begin were all dressed to the nines.

_____ 4. They seemed to understand the meaning of <u>courtesy and good manners</u>.

_____ 5. But when we opened the doors, no one came in! No one! We couldn't understand it. All we could hear was music from the street. <u>With unwilling steps</u>, I went outside to announce the curtain and saw a young woman in jeans and tap shoes dancing for the crowd.

_____ 6. She didn't <u>hesitate for a minute</u> as she danced her heart out.

_____ 7. I couldn't <u>afford</u> the time, but I couldn't take my eyes off her. Neither could anyone else.

_____ 8. She had such <u>composure</u> and stage presence.

_____ 9. In addition, she was so <u>skilled</u> in her routine.

_____ 10. As she increased the <u>speed</u>, we all began clapping with her, marking the rhythms, showing our pleasure.

_____ 11. The joy we felt from her dancing <u>nourished</u> our imagination. For want of an audience, the company even agreed to hold the curtain.

_____ 12. I would've <u>helped</u> her to get a job dancing. I knew that right away. She was a natural! I guess she didn't hear me say, "Come see me after the show." I can still see her running off into the night and I wonder what happened to her.

◖ EXPAND

1 *Study the chart of collocations.*

COLLOCATIONS: NOUNS AND VERBS

People work hard to **achieve success** in the arts.

Collocations are combinations of words that are often used together. The noun "success" is frequently used with the verbs "achieve" or "attain."

Nouns	Verbs
degree, diploma	earn, obtain, receive
difficulties	encounter, face, run into
dream	realize, make (a dream) come true
effort	make
goal	achieve, attain, reach
mistake	make
obstacle	encounter, meet
opposition	encounter, face, confront
success	achieve, attain

2 Add pairs of nouns and verbs from Exercise 1 to the sentences to form collocations. There can be more than one correct answer. Compare your answers with a partner's.

1. Rosemary Tejada was able to _____ because she kept trying and never gave up even when she _____.

2. Without hard work, we cannot _____.

3. Teachers hope that the children will stay in school and _____ a high school diploma. They may even go on to _____ a college degree.

4. Persistence is one quality you need in order to _____ because the path is never smooth. Everyone _____.

3 Study the chart of hyphenated adjectives.

HYPHENATED ADJECTIVES

When we use a two-word or compound adjective, or a group of words before a noun, we use hyphens* to link them, and we also make some minor structural changes. Hyphenated adjectives can give texture, exuberance, and poetic feeling to a work of prose.

With descriptions
- a man with sandy hair (light brown or blond) = a sandy-haired man
- a table with three legs = a three-legged table

Measurements in time or space involving plurals
- a child who is two years old = a two-year-old child
- a house with three stories = a three-story house

---

* Many rules of hyphenation are complicated and may be unclear. If you are unsure, look up the word in a good dictionary.

---

4 Change the following expressions to hyphenated adjectives.

1. a boy with blue eyes   = _____
2. a hat with three corners = _____
3. a woman with thin lips   = _____
4. a girl with a broken heart = _____
5. a law that is ten years old = _____

5 *Look back at the story "Gotta Dance," and find two sentences that use a number of hyphenated adjectives in the climax of the story (the last six paragraphs). Then rewrite the expressions as hyphenated adjectives.*

    1. a dance step that tells the audience to wait a minute = _____

    _____

    2. an ending similar to what a performer in a Broadway musical would do = _____

    _____

    3. a finish that makes you want to die from happiness = _____

    _____

    4. a finish that knocks the audience out because it is so good = _____

    _____

◖ CREATE

Answer the questions about yourself and other people you know. Use the underlined expressions in your answer.

    1. When Katie's relatives criticized her, it <u>lit a fire under</u> her and she had to do something. What kinds of things make you angry?

    Answer: *When my brother talks back to my mother, it lights a fire under*

    me, and I end up yelling at him about his awful behavior.

    2. When Katie first started to work on her dance routine, it must have seemed like an impossible task, but after she practiced again and again, things started to <u>come together</u> and she did very well. How did you deal with a difficulty that you eventually conquered?

    Answer: _____

    _____

    _____

    3. Leaving home was not easy for Katie. Saying good-bye to her old room really <u>took it out of her</u>, and she felt drained of energy. What kind of physical or mental activity totally exhausts you?

    Answer: _____

    _____

    _____

4. Katie wanted to travel to a big city. She seemed to like the rapid, hectic <u>pace</u> of the city more than the tranquil rhythm of a small town. What do you prefer?

Answer: _____

_____

_____

5. For a long time, Katie was <u>reluctant</u> to start out on her own. But after her brother's death, she decided that she had to follow her dream. Can you think of anything that you were reluctant to do and then found the courage to do?

Answer: _____

_____

_____

6. The more Katie danced, the more she <u>nurtured her imagination</u> and became even more creative. What do you do that makes you become more and more creative?

Answer: _____

_____

_____

7. Katie seemed to have a lot of <u>poise</u> as she danced for her audience. What other activities in life can give us the confidence needed to participate in social situations?

Answer: _____

_____

_____

8. Katie's "<u>knock-down, drag-out, could-you-just-die, great big Broadway-baby finish</u>" left the audience speechless. Can you think of something that you or a friend or family member have done that impressed others a great deal?

Answer: _____

_____

_____

B GRAMMAR: Using Identifying and Nonidentifying Adjective Clauses

1 *Examine the sentences and discuss the questions on the next page with a partner.*
- People <u>who are unwilling to risk failure</u> are not capable of achieving big successes.
- The waitress stayed as pleasant the whole time I was there, <u>which was the better part of two hours</u>, so I put down a good tip when I left.

1. In the first sentence, which people are being discussed?

2. In the second sentence, how much time did Katie spend in the restaurant?

3. Which words come at the beginning of the underlined phrases?

4. Do you notice any difference in punctuation in the two sentences?

ADJECTIVE CLAUSES

Adjective clauses define, describe, or add information about nouns just as adjectives do. These clauses must have a subject and a verb, but they are fragments, not full sentences. The adjective clause can begin with the relative pronouns **who, whom, which, that,** and **whose,** or the relative adverbs **when** and **where.** **Who** is used for people, **which** is used for things, and **that** can be used for both people and things.

Identifying Adjective Clauses

Identifying adjective clauses give information that is essential to the meaning of the sentence.
- People **who are unwilling to risk failure** are not capable of achieving big successes.

If you take the adjective clause out of this sentence, the sentence itself no longer has any precise meaning. "People are not capable of achieving big successes" is vague and unclear because it implies that no one can ever succeed. The adjective clause is needed because it tells us specifically which people the statement is referring to. Identifying adjective clauses do not have any commas.

Nonidentifying Adjective Clauses

Nonidentifying adjective clauses have a different function in the sentence: They only provide extra or additional information. If nonidentifying adjective clauses are left out, the sentence still retains its basic meaning.
- The waitress stayed as pleasant the whole time I was there, **which was the better part of two hours,** so I put down a good tip when I left.

The significant clauses of this sentence are "The waitress stayed as pleasant the whole time I was there," and "so I put down a good tip when I left." The adjective clause is not essential to the meaning of the sentence. It provides only an additional piece of information about the time.

GRAMMAR TIP: In nonidentifying adjective clauses
- we do not use *that*
- we place commas at the beginning and end of the clause unless the clause comes at the end of a sentence.

2 *Underline the adjective clauses in the sentences. Decide whether they are identifying or nonidentifying, and write **I** or **N** on the line. Then add the appropriate punctuation. Note that there is at least one sentence here that could be both I and N.*

_____ 1. People who lack the courage to fail also lack what it takes to achieve big successes.

_____ 2. Attitudes that help you feel positive about yourself are the key to success.

_____ 3. Pierre Dulaine who is quoted in the article about kids and ballroom dancing is a British dance champion.

_____ 4. Children who practice ballroom dances with each other learn good teamwork.

_____ 5. A college speaker whose exact name I've now forgotten helped us to understand the power of positive thinking.

_____ 6. A modern idea which I do not share at all is that success can only be measured in financial terms.

_____ 7. The dance instructor patiently taught his students the steps which he had learned to do so naturally throughout the years.

_____ 8. Children who work so hard at learning the steps of the various ballroom dances all share the need to excel.

3 *Combine each pair of sentences into a single sentence, using relative pronouns and adjective clauses.*

1. Katie was a self-taught dancer. She considered herself a "natural."

   Katie, who considered herself a "natural," was a self-taught dancer.

2. A young man entered the restaurant hungry. He left it with a full belly.

   _____

3. Katie was off to find a new place in the world. Katie's brother had just died.

   _____

4. Katie was thinking about a mother. The mother's son had just thrown his hat out the window of the bus.

   _____

5. Katie waited two hours at a diner. At the diner she had an excellent view of the people lining up for the theater.

   _____

6. Tap dancing is an American dance form. It was popularized by Hollywood movies.

   _____

In this unit, you read the short story "Gotta Dance" and "Kids Learn Poise Through Dance," a passage that describes the advantages of teaching ballroom dancing to children.

You will **write an essay on the three main qualities that a person must have in order to be successful in life.***

◖ PREPARE TO WRITE: Freewriting

Success can be defined in many ways. Freewrite about a person who is successful in life. It can be a person you know or someone you have read about. Describe how this person's personality helped to overcome the obstacles on the road to success. What character traits were of value in this person's journey?

◖ WRITE: A Topic Sentence, Illustration, and Conclusion

1 *Working with a partner, read the paragraph and discuss the questions.*

> People who are unwilling to risk failure are not capable of achieving big successes. The careers of the inventor Thomas Edison and the comedian Charlie Chaplin serve as good examples. Without Thomas Edison, we might still be reading in the dark today. But did you know that Edison discovered the lightbulb after a thousand different attempts? When asked what he had learned from those one thousand mistakes, Edison responded that he had found one thousand ways in which a lightbulb could not be made. During his early days in London, people threw things at Charlie Chaplin to make him get off the stage. Would we be enjoying the starring film roles of this famous comedian today if he had taken those audiences' reactions to heart and stopped pursuing his dream to become an actor? Learning to cope with failure makes you strong enough to view every defeat as another step toward success.

1. What kind of information does the first sentence provide?

2. What do the next six sentences have to do with the first sentence?

3. Which sentence does the last sentence refer back to?

---

*For Alternative Writing Topics, see page 67. These topics can be used in place of the writing topic for this unit or as homework. The alternative topics relate to the theme of the unit, but may not target the same grammar or rhetorical structures taught in the unit.

Illustration, an essential ingredient of effective writing, is used to clarify or support the main idea that has been expressed in the **topic sentence** of a paragraph.

To illustrate an idea, a writer provides clear and concise examples, persuasive explanations, appropriate statistics, and relevant anecdotes (brief stories) that support the topic sentence.

In the example paragraph above, the writer provides statistics and anecdotes about the lives of Thomas Edison and Charlie Chaplin to show how both these famous people would not have become great successes if they had not risked failure. Thomas Edison's one thousand failed attempts before discovering the lightbulb and Charlie Chaplin's experiences of having things thrown at him when he first started to act are two examples that not only convince the reader of the logic of the topic sentence, but also prepare the reader for the **concluding sentence,** which reinforces the main idea of the paragraph.

2 *Work with a partner on developing an appropriate topic sentence for the fully developed paragraph below.*

Topic Sentence: _____

_____

Both Judy Garland and Marilyn Monroe were wonderful entertainers. Although they died in the 1960s, they are still remembered today for their genius as performers. Judy Garland was a fine actress and singer. There isn't a child who doesn't know her as Dorothy in the classic film *The Wizard of Oz.* Moreover, adults are still buying compact discs of her many record albums. Marilyn Monroe played comic and tragic roles in films and on the live stage. People today still watch videos of *Some Like It Hot, The Misfits,* and *Bus Stop,* her most famous films. Yet both these actresses tried to commit suicide many times. It is not clear if their actual deaths were the result of suicide attempts. What is clear, however, is that despite their great successes, they were not happy people.

3 *Develop the idea of the topic sentence below. Write a complete paragraph showing support with illustration and conclusion based on the information in Katie's story. Then, in a small group, compare your paragraphs.*

People who decide to follow their dreams sometimes have to be strong enough to go against the wishes of their family.

4 *Write an essay that discusses the three main qualities that a person needs to have in order to achieve success. Refer to the work you did in Prepare to Write on page 64 as you organize your thoughts. Pay careful attention to the main elements of a well-constructed paragraph—topic sentence, supporting details, and concluding sentence.*

Your well-organized essay will include an introduction culminating in a thesis statement, three body paragraphs (one for each quality) showing support with illustration, and a conclusion. The conclusion should refer back to the main idea contained in the thesis statement, but it must not repeat the idea in the exact words. The conclusion may also express a wish for the future. For more information on conclusions, see Unit 4.

Some Suggestions for Thesis Statements:

There are three main qualities necessary for success: _____, _____, and _____.

Of all the qualities needed for success, _____, _____, and _____ are the most important.

Success cannot be achieved without _____, _____, and _____.

◖ REVISE: Achieving Paragraph Unity

Well-written paragraphs have paragraph unity. There is unity in a paragraph if all sentences focus on the same topic that is introduced in the topic sentence. If other "topics" have been introduced, the paragraph does not have paragraph unity. One topic per paragraph is a good rule to follow: "unity" equals "one."

1 *Working with a partner, read the paragraph and answer the questions on the next page.*

> **(1)** Another trait that people need in order to achieve success is the ability to be passionately enthusiastic about the work they do. **(2)** Without passion, people won't have the drive or the joy necessary for creative thinking. **(3)** It is easy to see that the children in the ballroom dance program were passionate about their dancing and committed to upholding the reputation of their team and their school. **(4)** They also became friends, and their friendships lasted beyond the competition. **(5)** The students worked enthusiastically not because they were forced to, but because they loved what they were doing. **(6)** That quality is the key for many great innovators who made history, not because they were forced to do so, not even because they were thinking of financial rewards, but because they were passionately interested in their work.
> **(7)** Steve Jobs, for example, a founder of Apple Computer, was never sure he would succeed, and in fact, he failed several times. **(8)** Yet he never lost the enthusiasm for his ideas. **(9)** All successful people are passionate about what they are doing. **(10)** Intelligence is another essential ingredient you will find in all success stories.

1. According to the topic sentence, what is the subject of this paragraph?

2. Which sentences do not belong in this paragraph?

3. What is the best concluding sentence for this paragraph: 8 or 9 or 10?

2 *Look at the draft of your essay. Does each of your body paragraphs have paragraph unity? If not, decide what you can do to establish this unity.*

◀ EDIT: Writing the Final Draft

Write your final draft. Carefully edit it for grammatical and mechanical errors. Make sure you used some of the vocabulary and grammar from the unit. Use the checklist to help you write the final draft. Then neatly write or type your essay.

✓ FINAL DRAFT CHECKLIST

- ○ Is your essay divided into clear paragraphs with one main point in each paragraph?
- ○ Are the main points written in topic sentences?
- ○ Are all the main ideas well supported through proper illustration?
- ○ Are identifying and nonidentifying adjective clauses used to define, describe, or add information?
- ○ Have new vocabulary and expressions (including hyphenated adjectives) been used in the essay?

ALTERNATIVE WRITING TOPICS

Write an essay on one of the topics. Be sure to write an introduction with a thesis statement, use topic sentences in each of your body paragraphs, and end your essay with a conclusion. Use the vocabulary and grammar from the unit.

1. The CEO (chief executive officer) of a major company once said that the most successful person he knew was his gardener—a man loved by his family and respected by his friends, a man who worked hard and had a full life. Would you agree or disagree with this statement? Comment on the definition of success expressed here. Do you think the CEO would agree to change places with the gardener? Would you?

2. What do you think Katie's life will be like after the end of her story? Explain how certain aspects of her life and personality will influence her future.

3. Read the poem on the next page by Mary Oliver. Explain what you believe the poet is saying, and compare her "journey" with Katie's in "Gotta Dance."

The Journey

One day you finally knew
what you had to do, and began,
though the voices around you
kept shouting
their bad advice—
though the whole house
began to tremble
and you felt the old tug
at your ankles.
"Mend my life!"
each voice cried.
But you didn't stop.
You knew what you had to do,
though the wind pried
with its stiff fingers
at the very foundations—
though their melancholy
was terrible.

It was already late
enough, and a wild night,
and the road full of fallen
branches and stones.
But little by little,
as you left their voices behind,
the stars began to burn
through the sheets of clouds,
and there was a new voice,
which you slowly
recognized as your own,
that kept you company
as you strode deeper and deeper
into the world,
determined to do
the only thing you could do—
determined to save
the only life you could save.

Mary Oliver

RESEARCH TOPICS, see page 262.

Silent Spring

①FOCUS ON THE TOPIC

A ⃝ PREDICT

In the place you live now, what are some of the trends in the way people think about things like the environment, technology, fashion, music, politics, or other topics? Think about one trend in particular. Is this trend expressed in other countries? How do trends grow and develop? Why do people go along with them? Take five minutes to write down your thoughts about the questions.

Study the pictures below. Explain how the product in each picture represents a trend and what you think of each trend.

cell phone

_____

_____

_____

_____

_____

iPod®

_____

_____

_____

_____

YouTube®

_____

_____

_____

_____

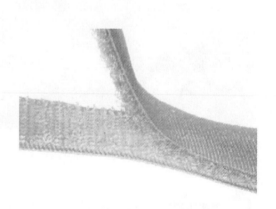

Velcro®

_____

_____

_____

_____

Read the definitions and choose the best words to complete the text.

abundance: a large quantity of something

blight: a plant disease; something that makes people unhappy or spoils their lives

counterparts: people or things that have the same job or purpose as people or things in another place

countless: too many to be counted

misfortune: very bad luck

prosperous: successful and having a lot of money

puzzled: confused about something you can't understand

specter: something that people are afraid of

stricken: very badly affected by trouble or illness

surroundings: natural and manmade things in the environment

Modern Trends: Environmental Protection

Are you ever _____ about why people believe what they believe
                    1.
and why they do what they do? In *The Tipping Point*, Malcolm Gladwell discusses

how ideas and trends spread, eventually changing _____ lives. For
                                                    2.
Gladwell, the "tipping point" is the moment when a long-accepted set of values

undergoes rapid change. In 1962, Rachel Carson's book *Silent Spring* brought

America to the tipping point: thanks to her work, the modern environmental

protection movement was born. Today, the movement she began has thousands of

_____ all over the world.
        3.

Insects and bacteria threatened to reduce the _____ of our food
                                                4.
supply. If a _____ spreads over a crop, the food decays and dies. In
            5.
order to be _____ and productive, American agriculture had to rely
            6.
on chemical pesticides used to kill the insects and bacteria that were destroying the

crops. But Rachel Carson realized that some chemicals were too dangerous to use on crops. She warned that using DDT* in farming raised the _____
7.
of a dying planet.

Because Rachel Carson had been a government scientist, her book *Silent Spring* created a great deal of discussion and controversy. Many people agreed that our natural _____ and our food supply must be saved from the
8.
dangers of industrialization. Carson was aware of the impact of her work, but she was _____ with cancer and died two years after her famous book was
9.
published. Despite her _____, she inspired millions to act to protect
10.
nature.

_____
*DDT: a pesticide that remains in the food chain and that is harmful to humans. Carson protested the large-scale, uncontrolled use of DDT, especially in crops.

2 FOCUS ON READING

A READING ONE: A Fable¹ for Tomorrow

Before you read, discuss the questions with a partner.

What are the sounds of spring where you live? What could cause these sounds to go "silent"?

Before Rachel Carson's book *Silent Spring* was published in 1962, not very many Americans worried about air and water pollution. Moreover, people were unaware of the long-term dangers of DDT. The book alerted millions to the dangers of DDT and inspired them to act to protect nature. This started the modern environmentalist movement, which seeks to protect the earth from the harmful effects of industrialization. "A Fable for Tomorrow" is the first chapter of *Silent Spring*.

_____
¹ fable: a short story, often about animals, that teaches a moral lesson

A Fable for Tomorrow
by Rachel Carson

1 There was once a town in the heart of America where all life seemed to live in harmony with its **surroundings**. The town lay in the midst of a checkerboard of **prosperous** farms, with fields of grain and hillsides of orchards where, in spring, white clouds of bloom drifted above the green fields. In autumn, oak and maple and birch trees set up a blaze of color that flamed and flickered across a backdrop of pines. Then foxes barked in the hills and deer silently crossed the fields, half hidden in the mists of the fall mornings.

2 Along the roads, laurel, viburnum and alder,[1] great ferns and wildflowers delighted the traveler's eye through much of the year. Even in winter the roadsides were places of beauty, where **countless** birds came to feed on the berries and on the seed heads of the dried weeds rising above the snow. The countryside was, in fact, famous for the **abundance** and variety of its bird life, and when the flood of migrants was pouring through in spring and fall, people traveled from great distances to observe them. Others came to fish the streams, which flowed clear and cold out of the hills and contained shady pools where trout lay. So it had been from the days many years ago when the first settlers raised their houses, sank their wells, and built their barns.

3 Then a strange **blight** crept over the area and everything began to change. Some evil spell[2] had settled on the community: mysterious maladies swept the flocks of chickens; the cattle and sheep sickened and died. Everywhere was a shadow of death. The farmers spoke of much illness among their families. In the town the doctors had become more and more **puzzled** by new kinds of sickness appearing among their patients. There had been several sudden and unexplained deaths, not only among adults but even among children, who would be **stricken** suddenly while at play and die within a few hours.

4 There was a strange stillness. The birds, for example—where had they gone? Many people spoke of them, puzzled and disturbed. The feeding stations in the backyards were deserted. The few birds seen anywhere were moribund;[3] they trembled violently and could

---

[1] **laurel, viburnum and alder:** types of plants
[2] **evil spell:** in old superstitions, an act of harmful magic.
(The witch cast an evil spell on the prince, turning him into a frog.)
[3] **moribund:** dying

(continued on next page)

not fly. It was a spring without voices. On the mornings that had once throbbed with the dawn chorus of robins, catbirds, doves, jays, wrens, and scores of other bird voices there was now no sound; only silence lay over the fields and woods and marsh.

5   On the farms the hens brooded, but no chicks hatched.[4] The farmers complained that they were unable to raise any pigs—the litters were small and the young survived only a few days. The apple trees were coming into bloom, but no bees droned among the blossoms, so there was no pollination and there would be no fruit.

6   The roadsides, once so attractive, were now lined with browned and withered vegetation as though swept by fire. These, too, were silent, deserted by all living things. Even the streams were now lifeless. Anglers[5] no longer visited them, for all the fish had died.

7   In the gutters[6] under the eaves and between the shingles of the roofs, a white granular powder still showed a few patches; some weeks before it had fallen like snow upon the roofs and the lawns, the fields and the streams.

8   No witchcraft, no enemy action had silenced the rebirth of new life in this stricken world. The people had done it themselves.

9   This town does not actually exist, but it might easily have a thousand **counterparts** in America or elsewhere in the world. I know of no community that has experienced all the **misfortunes** I describe. Yet every one of these disasters has actually happened somewhere, and many real communities have already suffered a substantial number of them. A grim **specter** has crept upon us almost unnoticed, and this imagined tragedy may easily become a stark reality we all shall know.

---

[4] **brooded, but no chicks hatched:** the hens sat on their eggs, but no new chicks were born
[5] **anglers:** fishermen
[6] **gutters:** drain pipes for rainwater; usually found on the roofs of houses

◖ READ FOR MAIN IDEAS

1 *Summarize the main points of the fable.*

1. The way the town was before:

_____

_____

_____

2. The way it is now:

_____

_____

_____

3. Rachel Carson's predictions for the future:

_____

_____

_____

2 *In one sentence, summarize the lesson you think this fable teaches. Share your sentence with a partner.*

_____

◖ READ FOR DETAILS

"A Fable for Tomorrow" illustrates the idea that DDT could have many disastrous, long-term consequences for the environment. What are the negative effects of DDT that Rachel Carson foresaw? Write your answers below.

Cause: The use of DDT

Effects: _____

_____

_____

_____

_____

_____

◖ MAKE INFERENCES

Discuss the questions with a partner. There can be more than one correct answer for each question.

1. Rachel Carson uses a symbol, a spring that is "silent." What is she trying to communicate with the use of the word *silent*?

2. When Rachel Carson says "The people had done it themselves," what does she mean? Explain.

3. How could you summarize Rachel Carson's view of the relationship between humans and nature?

Discuss the questions in a small group. Share your group's conclusions with the rest of the class.

1. What was your opinion of DDT after reading "A Fable for Tomorrow"? Do you think Rachel Carson was objective in her treatment of the problem of DDT? Did she present both sides of the story? Why or why not?

2. Why did Rachel Carson start her book with a fable?

3. Who was the intended audience for this fable?

4. What do you think the response of people in the chemical industry would be to this fable?

B READING TWO: The Story of Silent Spring

Before reading the essay, discuss the question with a partner.

How do you think people responded to *Silent Spring* when it first appeared?

FROM A BOOK TO A MOVEMENT
THE STORY OF *SILENT SPRING*

1   Developed in 1939, DDT was the most powerful pesticide the world had ever known. It was used throughout the 1940s and 1950s to clear regions of mosquitos carrying malaria. Its inventor was awarded the Nobel Prize. When DDT became available for purely commercial use and was sprayed over crops, only a few people, like Rachel Carson, felt that there was some danger. When she finally published her book, *Silent Spring*, her fears were heard loud and clear. The impact of *Silent Spring* was great; with this book, Rachel Carson laid the foundation for the modern environmental protection movement.

2   Carson did not originally intend to write a book about the harmful effects of DDT. Her interest in the subject was sparked by a letter from old friends telling about the damage that aerial spraying had done to the ecological system[1] on their land. Although Rachel Carson was a best-selling author, no magazine would agree to her idea for an article investigating the negative effects of DDT. She decided to go ahead and deal with the issue in a book, *Silent Spring*, which took her four years to complete. It described how DDT entered the food chain and accumulated in the fatty tissues of animals, including human beings, and caused cancer and genetic damage. The book's most famous chapter, "A Fable for Tomorrow," depicted a nameless American town where all life—from fish to birds to apple blossoms to children—had been "silenced" by the insidious[2] effects of DDT.

"The Story of *Silent Spring*" is adapted from a Natural Resources Defense Council Publication.

[1] **ecological system:** a system of plants, animals, and people that depend on each other and their environment
[2] **insidious:** gradually and secretly causing serious harm

3   First serialized in *The New Yorker* mag azine in June 1962, the book alarmed readers across the country and, not surprisingly, brought howls of anger from the chemical industry. "If man were to faithfully follow the teachings of Miss Carson," complained an executive of the American Cyanamid Company, "we would return to the Dark Ages,[3] and the insects and diseases would once again inherit the earth." Some of the attacks were more personal, questioning Carson's integrity and even her sanity.

4   Her careful preparation, however, had paid off. Foreseeing the reaction of the chemical industry, she had written *Silent Spring* like a lawyer's brief, with no fewer than 55 pages of notes and a list of experts who had read and approved the manuscript. Many well-known and respected scientists rose to her defense, and when President John F. Kennedy ordered the President's Science Advisory Committee to examine the issues the book raised, its report supported both *Silent Spring* and its author. As a result, DDT came under much closer government supervision and was eventually banned.

5   Conservation had never attracted much public interest before Rachel Carson's book, but the dangers she analyzed were too frightening to ignore.

For the first time, the need to regulate industry[4] in order to protect the environment became widely accepted, and environmentalism was born. Carson was well aware of the implications of her book. Appearing on a CBS documentary about her work shortly before her death from breast cancer in 1964, she remarked:

> The public must decide whether it wishes to continue on the present road, and it can only do so when in full possession of the facts. We still talk in terms of conquest. We haven't become mature enough to think of ourselves as only a tiny part of a vast and incredible universe. Man's attitude toward nature is today critically important simply because we have now acquired a fateful power to alter[5] and destroy nature. But man is part of nature, and his war against nature is inevitably a war against himself.

6   One of the landmark books[6] of the twentieth century, *Silent Spring* still speaks to us today, many years after its publication. Equally inspiring is the example of Rachel Carson herself. Against overwhelming difficulties and hardship, despite her own shyness and reserve, and motivated only by her love of nature, she rose like a gladiator in its defense.

---

[3] **Dark Ages:** a time in western Europe (about A.D. 400–1000) when Roman civilization had been destroyed and with it almost all learning and trade

[4] **regulate industry:** limit the activities of business in the public interest through laws passed by the government

[5] **alter:** change

[6] **landmark book:** a book that changes history

Working with a partner, answer the questions based on Reading Two.

1. According to Rachel Carson, why is DDT so dangerous?

   _____

   _____

2. What did Carson do to prepare for the criticism that her book would receive?

   _____

   _____

3. According to Carson, how should people think of themselves in relation to nature?

_____

_____

_____

4. How does the reading describe Carson as a person?

_____

_____

_____

5. At first, no magazine would agree to publish an article on DDT. Why do you think magazine editors were so reluctant?

_____

_____

_____

6. "If man were to faithfully follow the teachings of Miss Carson, we would return to the Dark Ages, and the insects and diseases would once again inherit the earth." What did the executive of the American Cyanamid Company mean here?

_____

_____

_____

C INTEGRATE READINGS ONE AND TWO

◀ **STEP 1: Organize**

A movement for major change in society can take place:

a. when a person with the right qualifications comes forward;

b. when that person is able to explain a complex situation in simple and moving terms.

Under the headings, show how Rachel Carson embodied the requirements.

The Right Qualifications (Reading Two)	A Clear Explanation (Reading One)
was a best-selling author	using vivid images in her writing
_____	_____
_____	_____
_____	_____

◀ **STEP 2: Synthesize**

Work with a partner. Refer to the notes you took in Step 1 to write this interview: A journalist is interviewing Rachel Carson. The journalist wants to know how she was able to spark such an important movement of environmental protection.

JOURNALIST: Ms. Carson, I'm honored to be able to talk to you about the environmental protection movement that your work started. How do you explain why so many important people listened to your warnings?

RACHEL CARSON: _____

_____

_____

③ FOCUS ON WRITING

A VOCABULARY

◀ **REVIEW**

Read the selection below. Fill in each blank with the word from the box that matches the definition under the blank. Not all the words are used.

abundance	~~damage~~	insidious	puzzled
alter	depicted	misfortune	stricken
countless	harmful	prosperous	surroundings

The struggle to save the food supply from _____*damage*_____ did not end
                                                    1. (harm)

with *Silent Spring*. The need to maintain a _____ agricultural
                                               2. (successful)

economy has led to many difficulties. For example, in order to increase the protein

in cattle feed, people began to _____ the diet of cows. Cows do not
                                  3. (change)

eat meat in their natural _____, but farm industries in many
                           4. (environment)

countries began feeding cows the ground-up parts of dead sheep. Many scientists

believe that some cows' nervous systems were _____ by a sheep
                                               5. (attacked)

disease called scrapie. According to them, this _____ process, begun
                                                  6. (gradual and harmful)

Silent Spring   **79**

by humans for greater profits, led to outbreaks of "mad cow disease" in several countries of Europe and Asia. This was a _____ for the beef industry.
7. (disaster)

Farmers also often feed large amounts of antibiotics and hormones to their animals to make them stronger. These large doses accumulate in animal organs and are eaten by humans. This is _____ to us all because human diseases
8. (damaging)
are becoming less responsive to antibiotics, and the hormones are not good for children.

Recently, food manufacturers in the United States have developed a new method of irradiating food to kill bacteria. Many people want to ban irradiated food because they are not sure such food is safe. The dangers to the food supply

_____ by the environmental movement have led many people to buy
9. (described)
only natural products from organic farms, which do not use chemical pesticides. But organic foods are expensive and hard to find. People in many countries are

_____ about how to carry on the legacy of being responsible for the
10. (unsure)
environment, which is the message of *Silent Spring*.

◖ EXPAND

1 *Study the charts of prefixes, suffixes, and example words.*

PREFIX	MEANING	EXAMPLE
mis-	bad or badly	misfortune (bad luck, or what happens as a result of bad luck)
un- im- in- dis- non-	not	unclear (not clear) impossible (not possible) incredible (not believable) disrespectful (not respectful) nontoxic (not poisonous)
re-	again	rebirth (born again)
fore-	ahead	foresee (to see the future)

SUFFIX	MEANING	EXAMPLE
–cide	killing	pesticide (killing bugs)
–craft	art or skill	witchcraft (the art of being a witch)
–ful	full of	powerful (full of power)
–less	without	nameless (without a name)
–ship	the state of or condition of	friendship (the state of being a friend)

2 *Complete the sentences by adding the correct prefix or suffix to the root word. Use the correct form of the word.*

1. In *Silent Spring*, Rachel Carson (*un-/fore-*told) _____foretold_____ a grim future where nature's abundance had been destroyed.

2. However, she wanted to prove that it was not (*im-/fore-*possible) _____ to change the way people treated the environment.

3. If people would agree to eliminate DDT, the destruction of nature and the (life-*ful/-less*) _____ future she foresaw could be avoided.

4. Rachel Carson made a good case for the (harm-*ful/-less*) _____ nature of certain pesticides.

5. Banning DDT created economic (hard-*ship/-craft*) _____ for chemical companies.

3 *Read the quotations from "A Fable for Tomorrow." Circle the correct word to complete the summary that follows each quotation.*

1. "The countryside was . . . famous for the abundance and variety of its bird life, and when the flood of migrants was pouring through in spring and fall, people traveled from great distances to observe them."

   _____ birds came through the district.

   a. harmful   **b.** countless   **c.** uninteresting

2. "In autumn, oak and maple and birch trees set up a blaze of color that flamed and flickered across a backdrop of pines."

In autumn, the trees were very _____.

   a. colorful   **b.** incredible   **c.** powerful

3. "Deer silently crossed the fields, half hidden in the mists of the fall mornings."

The deer were almost _____.

   a. invisible   **b.** colorless   **c.** misplaced

4. "The roadsides, once so attractive, were now lined with browned and withered vegetation as though swept by fire."

The roadsides are now very _____.

   a. refreshed   **b.** disorganized   **c.** unattractive

Everything looks washed out and _____.

   d. cheerful   **e.** colorless   **f.** nonstop

5. "Everywhere was a shadow of death."

We could see death coming. It was a death _____.

   a. foreseen   **b.** unforeseen   **c.** reborn

◖ CREATE

On a separate piece of paper, write a paragraph describing the change inspired by one of the trends in popular culture you discussed on page 69 or another trend of your choice. Discuss the causes and results of this change. Use at least eight words from the list below.

abundance	countless	insidious	specter
alter	damage	misfortune	surroundings
blight	depict	prosperous	
counterpart	hardship	puzzled	

B **GRAMMAR: Adverb Clauses and Discourse Connectors Expressing Cause and Effect**

1 *Examine the sentences and the underlined phrases. Then discuss the questions on the next page with a partner.*

- <u>Because it was a very powerful pesticide</u>, DDT cleared regions of malaria throughout the 1940s and 1950s.
- Rachel Carson's *Silent Spring* made people aware of the dangerous effects of DDT; <u>consequently, DDT came under closer government supervision and was eventually banned</u>.
- Every detail in *Silent Spring* has <u>such good documentation that not one factual error has ever been found in the book</u>.

1. In the first sentence, what word suggests that a reason is going to be given?

2. In the second sentence, what word suggests that a result is going to be given?

3. In the third sentence, what words suggest that a reason and a result are going to be given?

ADVERB CLAUSES AND DISCOURSE CONNECTORS EXPRESSING CAUSE AND EFFECT

Adverb clauses and **discourse connectors** can be used to link ideas and to express cause and effect. In compound sentences these **cause-and-effect structures** reveal the connection between the reason for an event or a situation (the *cause*) and the influence this event or situation has on people, places, or things (the *result*, or the *effect*).

CAUSE: Stating a reason with adverb clauses that begin with *because* and *since*

- *Because / Since* **it was a very powerful pesticide,** DDT cleared regions of malaria throughout the 1940s and 1950s.
- DDT cleared regions of malaria throughout the 1940s and 1950s *because / since* **it was a very powerful pesticide.**

PUNCTUATION TIP: When the adverb clause beginning with *because* or *since* comes at the beginning of a sentence, a comma separates the clause from the result.

EFFECT: Stating a result with the discourse connectors *consequently, thus, therefore,* and *so*

- Rachel Carson's *Silent Spring* made people aware of the dangerous effects of DDT; *consequently / thus / therefore,* **DDT came under much closer government supervision and was eventually banned.**
- Rachel Carson's *Silent Spring* made people aware of the dangerous effects of DDT, *so* **DDT came under much closer government supervision and was eventually banned.**

PUNCTUATION TIP: When using discourse connectors, you may write one sentence and join the other as above with a semicolon (*consequently / thus / therefore*) or a comma (*so*). If you decide to separate the two sentences with a period, the discourse connectors are capitalized and followed by a comma.

DEGREE OF EFFECT: *such* **and** *so . . . that*

Compound sentences using the pattern "*such* (+ noun) or *so* (+ adjective or adverb) . . . *that* . . ." dramatically describe the great degree to which the cause has had an effect (*that* + the explanation) on the situation.

- Every detail in *Silent Spring* has **such** good **documentation that** not one factual error has ever been found in the book.
- Every detail in *Silent Spring* is **so well documented that** not one factual error has ever been found in the book.

2 Combine the pairs of sentences to show cause and effect. Write two sentences for each item, one using **because / since** and the other using **consequently / therefore / thus / so.**

1. Rachel Carson spent her childhood on a Pennsylvania farm. She developed a love of nature at a young age.

   _____

   _____

   _____

   _____

2. Rachel Carson was a wonderful writer. Her books about nature were a blend of scientific as well as beautiful poetic prose.

   _____

   _____

   _____

   _____

3. Rachel Carson was very respected in scientific circles. She had the opportunity to speak out on various issues that were important to her.

   _____

   _____

   _____

   _____

4. The content of *Silent Spring* presented a threat to the manufacturers of chemical pesticides. *Silent Spring* disturbed the business world immediately.

   _____

   _____

   _____

   _____

5. The angry protests of the big chemical companies were not heeded. The government listened to the message of *Silent Spring*, and the modern environmental protection movement was born.

   _____

   _____

   _____

   _____

3 *Combine the pairs of sentences with* **such / so . . . that** *patterns.*

1. Rachel Carson was brought up with a great love of nature.

   It was not surprising that she changed her major from writing to zoology in her third year of college.

   _____

   _____

   _____

2. She became very interested in the sea when she spent a summer at Woods Hole, Massachusetts, in her early twenties.

   The first three books she wrote were about the sea environment.

   _____

   _____

   _____

3. By 1952 Rachel Carson was enjoying a great deal of success as a writer.

   She was able to retire from the U.S. Fish and Wildlife Service to write full-time.

   _____

   _____

   _____

4. Magazine publishers were very afraid to lose their advertisers.

   They refused to publish Rachel Carson's articles about the dangers of DDT.

   _____

   _____

   _____

5. Rachel Carson was very upset about how DDT was being used without regard for the consequences.

   She decided to write her own book on the topic.

   _____

   _____

   _____

4 *Working with a partner, complete the paragraphs by filling in the blanks with the cause-and-effect structure (because, since, consequently, therefore, thus, so, such, so ... that) that is missing.*

Silent Spring made _____ an impact in America at the time it
                1.

was published _____ people's general thinking about nature changed
           2.

dramatically from that point on. _____ the book made people see
               3.

that whatever they did to nature they were also doing to themselves, their blind

faith in science and industry was shaken. _____, our modern era of
                4.

environmental awareness was launched. In the years immediately following the

book's publication, people became _____ interested in their
               5.

connections with the natural world _____ TV shows such as Marlin
               6.

Perkins's *Wild Kingdom* became very popular in the early 1960s. By 1970, the

United States had celebrated its first Earth Day.

Within the first year of *Silent Spring*'s publication, over 40 state laws were

proposed to regulate pesticide use _____ government scientists had
               7.

backed Rachel Carson fully after their researchers supported all her claims. The

pressure of the legislation passed was _____ great
             8.

_____ many national laws
        9.

were created afterwards to protect the

environment: The National

Environment Protection Act (1969), the

Clean Air Act (1970), the Clean Water

Act (1972), and the Endangered Species

Act (1973) are just a few of them.

In this unit, you read the introduction to Rachel Carson's book, *Silent Spring*, and an essay entitled "From a Book to a Movement: The Story of *Silent Spring*."

You will **write a short cause-and-effect essay based on the work of Rachel Carson.** You will write about what made Rachel Carson write *Silent Spring* (causes) and what the results of the publication of her book were (effects).*

PREPARE TO WRITE: Listing

Write notes about the causes and effects of Rachel Carson's movement to ban DDT.

Causes   **Effects**

_____   _____

_____   _____

_____   _____

_____   _____

WRITE: A Cause-and-Effect Essay

A cause-and-effect essay most often focuses on either the causes or the effects of an event or a situation. This focus is reflected in the thesis statement. In the essay entitled "The Story of Silent Spring," we can see that the writer introduces both causes and effects; however, the focus of the essay is clear from the thesis statement in the introductory paragraph.

1 *Working with a partner, reread the introductory paragraph in Reading Two and discuss the questions on the next page.*

Developed in 1939, DDT was the most powerful pesticide the world had ever known. It was used throughout the 1940s and 1950s to clear regions of mosquitos carrying malaria. Its inventor was awarded the Nobel Prize. When DDT became available for purely commercial use and was sprayed over crops and populated areas, only a few people, like Rachel Carson, felt that there was some danger. When she finally published her book, *Silent Spring,* her fears were heard loud and clear. The impact of *Silent Spring* was great; with this book, Rachel Carson laid the foundation for the modern environmental protection movement.

*For Alternative Writing Topics, see page 91. These topics can be used in place of the writing topic for this unit or as homework. The alternative topics relate to the theme of the unit, but may not target the same grammar or rhetorical structures taught in the unit.

1. What are the general statements in this introduction?

2. Underline the more specific statements.

3. Circle the thesis statement. What is the focus of the thesis: causes or effects?

2 *Make a decision on the focus of your essay, causes or effects, and write the thesis statement you need:* _____

_____

_____

PARAGRAPH ORGANIZATION

Paragraphs about causes or effects must follow a logical pattern of organization. Some common ways of organizing cause-and-effect paragraphs are:

- *Immediate versus long-term:* If you are discussing what caused Rachel Carson to write *Silent Spring*, you may want to begin with the immediate cause—the letter that she received from friends about ecological damage caused by aerial spraying. Or you may want to discuss the author's general concern about making changes that can damage the natural environment, and her lifelong preoccupation with nature.

- *A coherent order of importance:* You may want to begin with the least important effects of an event and work up to the most important. Or you may find that you need to begin with the historical background of a situation and then go on to the present-day situation. The choice will be determined by the nature of the material, but you must give a logical order to your essay. Much of the model essay (Reading Two), for example, follows chronological order.

- *Order of familiarity or interest:* You may want to work from what your readers know or would be most interested in, to what is new and different from what they expect.

- *Causal chain:* Another type of cause-and-effect essay is the causal chain. As in "A Fable for Tomorrow," one effect can become the cause of another effect, which, in turn, can become the cause of another effect.

---

3 Writing Strategy: *Based upon what you have just read in Paragraph Organization, explain what your **writing strategy** will be in the essay that you are going to write. Will your method of organization be based on the "immediate versus long-term," "a coherent order of importance," "order of familiarity or interest," or a "causal chain"?*

_____

4 *Using what you have learned about writing cause-and-effect essays, write an essay focused on the causes or the effects of the publication of Silent Spring. Refer to the work you did in Prepare to Write and Write, pages 87–88, as you organize your notes into logical patterns.*

A strong conclusion will keep your ideas in the reader's mind and may even change his or her mind about the topic. A conclusion can also give an emotional view of what remains to be done.

Read the conclusion. Is it effective? Why or why not? Share your thoughts with a partner.

> Today's problem of global warming again brings challenges for all the friends of the earth. Is there reason to despair? Absolutely not! We should always keep in mind the example of Rachel Carson and *Silent Spring*. Only then will we realize that science and popular opinion can indeed make a difference. Through Carson's work and her careful reasoning, the environmental protection movement was born. Never before had scientists and ordinary people been able to join together in one movement to defend our planet. This legacy of working together to save our environment gives us hope for tomorrow.

One way to emphasize important ideas is to use sentences with inverted word order.* In sentences beginning with negative or restrictive words such as ***never, rarely,*** or ***only,*** the verb is placed before the subject. Because this structure is used to highlight an especially strong point, it should not be overused.

Normal Word Order

We will realize only then that science and popular opinion can indeed make a difference.

Inverted Word Order

Only then will we realize that science and popular opinion can indeed make a difference.

Work with a partner. Make the sentences more emphatic.

1. Scientists and ordinary people had never been able to join together in one

   movement before. _____

   _____

2. I realized what a great leader Carson was only when I read her book. _____

   _____

---

*Note that when inverted word order is used, auxiliary verb forms are needed, as in "question formats":

	Normal Word Order		**Inverted Word Order**
(Present Tense)	I <u>realize</u> only when . . .	→	Only when . . . <u>do I realize</u>
	He/she <u>realizes</u> only when . . .	→	Only when . . . <u>does he/she realize</u>
(Past Tense)	I <u>realized</u> only when . . .	→	Only when . . . <u>did I realize</u>
(Future Tense)	I <u>will realize</u> only when . . .	→	Only when . . . <u>will I realize</u>

3. A book rarely causes such controversy.

_____

4. We should never turn our backs on the natural environment.

_____

5. A national movement was started only after Rachel Carson had done her work.

_____

6. People rarely want to accept "inconvenient truths" about the environment because these truths force them to consider sacrificing aspects of their "convenient" lifestyle.

_____

Look back at your conclusion and see if you can strengthen some points by using negative inversions.

◖**EDIT: Writing the Final Draft**

Write your final draft. Carefully edit it for grammatical and mechanical errors. Make sure you used some of the vocabulary and grammar from the unit. Use the checklist to help you write the final draft. Then neatly write or type your essay.

> ✓ **FINAL DRAFT CHECKLIST**
>
> ○ Does your thesis statement prepare the reader adequately for the focus of the essay, the causes or the effects?
> ○ Does the thesis statement give the reader a clear idea of the topics that will be discussed in the body paragraphs in support of the thesis?
> ○ Do the details in the body paragraphs provide unified support of the topic sentence of each body paragraph?
> ○ Are the adverb clauses and discourse connectors expressing cause and effect used correctly in the essay?
> ○ Have you tried to use inverted word order to emphasize an important point in at least one sentence in your conclusion?
> ○ Have new vocabulary and expressions been used in the essay?

ALTERNATIVE WRITING TOPICS

Write an essay on one of the topics. Use the vocabulary, grammar, and style structures from the unit.

1. What do you think of some of the issues that environmental activists raise? Do you support any of their campaigns to save endangered species, to oppose the wearing of fur, to save the rain forests, or protect against global warming? Write an essay about an environmental issue. Why has this issue gained widespread attention? How has the attention changed the way people think and / or behave? Explain.

2. What is your first reaction when you look at nature? When you see a waterfall, do you see the beauty of the light sparkling on the waters, or do you see the threat of roaring waters pounding on the rocks below? In general, do you see the beauty or the danger of nature? What causes this reaction in you? What effect does it have on your choice of a place to live?

3. "The obligation to endure gives us the right to know." It is with these words that Rachel Carson ends the second chapter of *Silent Spring*. Explain what you think this quote means and whether or not you agree with it. How do these words relate to Rachel Carson's motivation to write *Silent Spring*?

4. A scientist usually works for the government, a business, or a university. What do you think the responsibility of the scientist is when he or she is asked to work on projects that may be dangerous for humans, such as biological or chemical warfare or nuclear weapons?

5. The introduction to the current edition of *Silent Spring* was written by Al Gore, the former vice president and producer of the documentary *An Inconvenient Truth*. In it, he writes that *Silent Spring* "changed the course of human history." Can you think of other landmark books in the history of civilization for which the same comment would apply? Choose a book that you believe fits this description, and show how it changed the course of human history.

RESEARCH TOPICS, see page 263.

5
What Is Lost in Translation?

1 FOCUS ON THE TOPIC

A PREDICT

Look at the title of this unit and the photo. What are the advantages of living in a multicultural society? What could be "lost in translation" for these young people? Take five minutes to write down your thoughts about the questions.

SHARE INFORMATION

1 *Work in a small group. For each of the behaviors, discuss the questions.*

Is the behavior acceptable? In what circumstances? What reaction do you get if you go against the social rules concerning this behavior?

Behaviors

1. Kissing in public

2. Commenting on people's choice of clothing

3. Touching people you are talking to

4. Criticizing people directly and strongly

5. Two women walking arm in arm

6. Eating as you walk down the street

2 *Discuss your responses. Are there regional, class, gender, or age variations to these situations in your culture? Have you had any experiences of these behaviors in other cultures that you can share with your group?*

C **BACKGROUND AND VOCABULARY**

1 *Read the passage about Eva Hoffman and Elizabeth Wong, the writers of the two texts you are going to read. See if you can understand the boldfaced vocabulary according to the contexts in which it appears.*

Being a teenager is difficult under any conditions. Even in the most normal circumstances, the teenage years are often a **(1) chaotic** period for both children and parents alike. Parents are afraid of losing their authority. How much should they **(2) scold** their children? When is **(3) restraint** of any kind advisable? That is, under what circumstances should they loosen or **(4) tighten the reins?** How often should they be **(5) demonstrative** about their love for their children in order to give them the confidence they need to fight life's battles? This kind of normal conflict is all the more dramatic when an immigrant family is **(6) beleaguered** by the tragic memory of its recent past.

Such was the case for Eva Hoffman. Born in Poland in 1945 to Jewish parents who were Holocaust survivors, she left her homeland at age thirteen with her parents and sister to start a new life in Canada. In her autobiography, *Lost in Translation,* she writes about the **(7) grief** they all felt about leaving their old life. This new existence threatened to unravel the **(8) fabric** of their family life. As she **(9) gives vent to** the feelings that she suffered from during this transition, Ms. Hoffman takes us on the journey from Old World Kracow to New World Vancouver; this journey prepared her for her studies at Harvard University, for her literary career at the *New York Times*, and for her work as a well-known author. In her objective and **(10) stoical** tone, Eva Hoffman writes the story of all immigrants. She describes how her Polish identity was transformed into a new Canadian identity as she experienced the physically and emotionally exhausting process of learning to communicate in English. As the title of her book indicates, during this period Eva Hoffman was "lost in translation." In their attempts to "translate" their personalities from one language and culture to another, don't all immigrants find themselves both linguistically and culturally "lost in translation"?

Although Elizabeth Wong, who was born in Los Angeles, California, in 1958, was not an immigrant herself, she too may have understood Eva Hoffman's feeling of being "lost in translation" as a young girl. In "The Struggle to Be an All-American Girl," she writes how she was torn between two cultures and how she continually resisted her Chinese mother's **(11) nagging** attempts to get her to learn Chinese and be aware of her cultural background. She did everything in her power to **(12) dissuade** her mother from continuing such efforts. Ms. Wong is an award-winning playwright, a teacher of playwriting at several universities, and a writer for television.

These stories show how difficult it is to create an identity in a changing world. Eva Hoffman and Elizabeth Wong give us insight into the difficulties faced by people who must adapt to a new life.

2 *Refer to the reading passage and match the words and phrases on the left with the definitions on the right.*

_____ 1. chaotic	**a.** expresses
_____ 2. scold	**b.** sadness
_____ 3. restraint	**c.** annoying
_____ 4. tighten the reins	**d.** be stricter
_____ 5. demonstrative	**e.** advise against
_____ 6. beleaguered	**f.** confusing
_____ 7. grief	**g.** criticize angrily
_____ 8. fabric	**h.** unemotional
_____ 9. gives vent to	**i.** structure
_____ 10. stoical	**j.** pressured
_____ 11. nagging	**k.** showing emotion (emotional)
_____ 12. dissuade	**l.** control

Before you read, discuss the information and question with a partner.

The first reading in this section portrays the difficulties of a Polish-Canadian family. This memoir is told from the point of view of Eva, a 13-year-old girl from Poland. Along with her mother, father, and sister, Alinka, she becomes an immigrant to Canada after World War II. The second reading is about a Chinese-American family. This story is told from the point of view of 10-year-old Elizabeth. She and her brother were born in the United States. Do you think these families will have many things in common, or do you think they will be very different?

Lost in Translation

BY EVA HOFFMAN

1 "In Poland, I would have known how to bring you up, I would have known what to do," my mother says wistfully,[1] but here, she has lost her sureness, her authority. She doesn't know how hard to **scold** Alinka when she comes home at late hours; she can only worry over her daughter's vague evening activities. She has always been gentle with us, and she doesn't want, doesn't know how, to **tighten the reins**. But familial bonds seem so dangerously loose here!

2 Truth to tell, I don't want the **fabric** of loyalty and affection, and even obligation, to unravel either. I don't want my parents to lose us, I don't want to betray our common life. I want to defend our dignity because it is so fragile, so **beleaguered**. There is only the tiny cluster, the four of us, to know, to preserve whatever fund of human experience we may represent. And so I feel a kind of ferociousness about protecting it. I don't want us to turn into perpetually cheerful sub-urbanites, with hygienic smiles and equally hygienic feelings. I want to keep even our sadness, the great sadness from which our parents have come.

3 I abjure my sister[2] to treat my parents well; I don't want her to challenge our mother's authority, because it is so easily challenged. It is they who seem more defenseless to me than Alinka, and I want her to protect them. Alinka fights me like a forest animal in danger of being trapped; she too wants to roam throughout the thickets and meadows. She too wants to be free.

4 My mother says I'm becoming "English." This hurts me, because I know she means I'm becoming cold. I'm no colder than I've ever been, but I'm learning to be less **demonstrative**. I learn this from a teacher who, after contemplating the gesticulations[3] with which I help myself describe the digestive

---

[1] **wistfully:** sadly
[2] **I abjure my sister:** I have made my sister promise
[3] **gesticulations:** movements with the arms and hands, usually while speaking

system of a frog, tells me to "sit on my hands and then try talking." I learn my new reserve from people who take a step back when we talk, because I am standing too close, crowding them. Cultural distances are different, I later learn in a sociology class, but I know it already. I learn **restraint** from Penny, who looks offended when I shake her by the arm in excitement, as if my gesture had been one of aggression instead of friendliness. I learn it from a girl who pulls away when I hook my arm through hers as we walk down the street—this movement of friendly intimacy is an embarrassment to her.

5 I learn also that certain kinds of truth are impolite. One shouldn't criticize the person one is with, at least not directly. You shouldn't say, "You are wrong about that"—although you may say, "On the other hand, there is that to consider." You shouldn't say, "This doesn't look good on you"—though you may say, "I like you better in that other outfit." I learn to tone down my sharpness, to do a more careful conversational minuet[4].

6 Perhaps my mother is right after all; perhaps I'm becoming colder. After a while, emotion follows action, response grows warmer or cooler according to gesture. I'm more careful about what I say, how loud I laugh, whether I **give vent to grief**. The storminess of emotion prevailing in our family is in excess of the normal here, and the unwritten rules for the normal have their osmotic effect.[5]

---

[4] **minuet:** a slow graceful dance of the 17th and 18th century
[5] **osmotic effect:** an effect of being gradually absorbed

THE STRUGGLE TO BE AN
All-American Girl

by Elizabeth Wong

1 It's still there, the Chinese school on Yale Street where my brother and I used to go. Despite the new coat of paint and the high wire fence, the school I knew ten years ago remains remarkably, **stoically**, the same.

2 Every day at 5 P.M., instead of playing with our fourth- and fifth-grade friends or sneaking out to the empty lot to hunt ghosts and animal bones, my brother and I had to go to Chinese school. No amount of kicking, screaming, or pleading could **dissuade** my mother, who was solidly determined to have us learn the language of our heritage. Forcibly, she walked us the seven long, hilly blocks from our home to school, depositing our defiant tearful faces before the stern principal. My only memory of him is that he swayed on his heels like a palm tree and he always

(continued on next page)

clasped his impatient, twitching hands behind his back. I recognized him as a repressed maniacal child killer, and that if we ever saw his hands, we'd be in big trouble.

3   We all sat in little chairs in an empty auditorium. The room smelled like Chinese medicine, an imported faraway mustiness,[1] like ancient mothballs[2] or dirty closets. I hated that smell. I favored crisp new scents like the soft French perfume that my American teacher wore in public school. There was a stage far to the right, flanked by an American flag and the flag of the Nationalist Republic of China, which was also red, white, and blue but not as pretty.

4   Although the emphasis at school was mainly language—speaking, reading, and writing—the lessons always began with exercises in politeness. With the entrance of the teacher, the best student would tap a bell and everyone would get up, kowtow,[3] and chant "Sing san ho," the phonetic for "How are you, teacher?"

5   Being ten years old, I had better things to learn than ideographs[4] copied painstakingly in lines that ran right to left from the tip of a *moc but*, a real ink pen that had to be held in an awkward way if blotches were to be avoided. After all, I could do the multiplication tables, name the satellites of Mars, and write reports on *Little Women* and *Black Beauty*. Nancy Drew, my favorite heroine, never spoke Chinese.

6   The language was a source of embarrassment. More times than not, I had tried to dissociate myself from the **nagging** loud voice that followed me wherever I wandered in the nearby American supermarket outside Chinatown. The voice belonged to my grandmother, a fragile woman in her seventies who could outshout the best of the street vendors. Her humor was raunchy,[5] her Chinese rhythmless, patternless. It was quick, it was loud, it was unbeautiful. It was not like the quiet, lilting romance of French or the gentle refinement of the American South. Chinese sounded pedestrian. Public.

7   In Chinatown, the comings and goings of hundreds of Chinese on their daily tasks sounded **chaotic** and frenzied. I did not want to be thought of as mad, as talking gibberish. When I spoke English, people nodded at me, smiled sweetly, said encouraging words. Even the people in my culture would cluck[6] and say that I would do well in life. "My, doesn't she move her lips fast," they would say, meaning that I'd be able to keep up with the world outside Chinatown.

8   My brother was even more fanatical than I about speaking English. He was especially hard on my mother, criticizing her, often cruelly, for her pidgin speech[7] —smatterings of Chinese scattered like chop suey in her conversation. "It's not 'What it is,' Mom," he'd say in exasperation. "It's 'What is it, what is it, what is it.'" Sometimes Mom might leave out an occasional "the" or "a," or perhaps a verb of being. He would stop her in

---

[1] **mustiness:** moldy dampness, a smell of decay
[2] **mothballs:** made of a strong-smelling substance; used to keep moths away from clothes
[3] **kowtow:** to bow with respect
[4] **ideograph:** a written sign, for example in Chinese, that represents an idea or thing rather than a sound
[5] **raunchy:** obscene
[6] **cluck:** a clicking sound with the tongue showing concern or interest
[7] **pidgin speech:** simplified, uneducated speech

mid-sentence: "Say it again, Mom. Say it right." When he tripped over his own tongue, he'd blame it on her: "See, Mom, it's all your fault. You set a bad example."

9   What infuriated my mother most was when my brother cornered her on her consonants, especially "r." My father had played a cruel joke on Mom by assigning her an American name that her tongue wouldn't allow her to say. No matter how hard she tried, "Ruth" always ended up "Luth" or "Roof."

10   After two years of writing with a *moc but* and reciting words with multiples of meanings, I was finally granted a cultural divorce. I was permitted to stop Chinese school.

11   I thought of myself as multicultural. I preferred tacos to egg rolls; I enjoyed Cinco de Mayo more than Chinese New Year.

12   At last, I was one of you; I wasn't one of them.

13   Sadly, I still am.

◀ **READ FOR MAIN IDEAS**

Work in pairs. Read the statements in the chart about the cultural values expressed in the stories that you have just read. Write down each author's opinion based on your understanding of the reading.

STATEMENTS	HOFFMAN	WONG
1. Parents have more difficulty adapting to a new culture than their children do.		
2. When people move to another culture, their new language becomes more important to them than their native language.		
3. Parents lose authority over their children when the family moves to another culture.		
4. Families may have trouble maintaining closeness when they must adapt to a new culture.		
5. People who move to a new culture worry about betraying or forgetting their old cultural traditions.		

1 *Compare and contrast the cultural customs of Poland and Canada as Eva describes them in* Lost in Translation. *Try to find at least five examples.*

POLISH WAYS	CANADIAN WAYS
1. In Poland, Eva was comfortable showing her feelings openly.	1. Eva felt Canadians were more reserved about their feelings.
2.	2.
3.	3.
4.	4.
5.	5.

2 *Compare and contrast Elizabeth's attitude toward Chinese things and her attitude toward American things when she was young, as told in "The Struggle to Be an All-American Girl." Try to find at least five examples.*

ELIZABETH'S ATTITUDE TOWARD CHINESE THINGS	ELIZABETH'S ATTITUDE TOWARD AMERICAN THINGS
1. Chinese smells were musty, like old mothballs or dirty closets.	1. American smells seemed new and crisp, like her teacher's perfume.
2.	2.
3.	3.
4.	4.
5.	5.

◖ MAKE INFERENCES

1 *Based on what is implied in the readings, discuss with your partner who might have made the statements. In the blank space, write **Ev** (Eva), **El** (Elizabeth), **B** (Both girls), or **N** (Neither of them).*

_____ **1.** "My mother has no idea what I'm going through."

_____ **2.** "I am hurt by my mother's criticism of me."

_____ **3.** "I miss the old country."

_____ **4.** "I just want to fit in and stop thinking about the past."

_____ **5.** "I feel comfortable in two cultures."

_____ **6.** "Sometimes I want to express myself in one language and sometimes in another."

_____ **7.** "Now that I am older, I regret losing so much of the past."

_____ **8.** "When people just look at me, they don't really know who I am."

2 *Answer the questions based on your understanding of the readings. Then compare your answers with a partner's.*

1. " 'In Poland, I would have known how to bring you up, I would have known what to do,' my mother says wistfully, but here, she has lost her sureness, her authority."

Why do you think Eva's mother has lost her authority?

_____

_____

_____

_____

2. "I don't want us to turn into perpetually cheerful suburbanites, with hygienic smiles and equally hygienic feelings."

Explain the meaning of this statement.

_____

_____

_____

_____

3. At the end of the story "The Struggle to Be an All-American Girl," Elizabeth Wong writes, "At last, I was one of you; I wasn't one of them. Sadly, I still am."

What do you think she means?

_____

_____

_____

_____

◖ EXPRESS OPINIONS

Discuss the questions in a small group. Share your group's conclusions with the rest of the class.

1. Eva Hoffman writes about being "lost in translation" culturally and linguistically as she adapts to life in a new country. Is it possible for individuals who grow up in the same country in which they were born to be "lost in translation" for other reasons? Why or why not?

2. Elizabeth Wong says that she was granted "a cultural divorce." Do you think that a cultural divorce is possible? Is it necessary? Does the need for a "cultural divorce" change with age?

3. Eva Hoffman finds that gestures generate emotions, that "emotion follows action, response grows warmer or cooler according to gesture." Do you agree? Why or why not?

B ❱ READING TWO: In One School, Many Sagas

1 *Before reading the article on the next page, write a short answer to the question.*

A **saga** is a story. Judging from this title, what do you expect Reading Two to be about?

In One School, Many Sagas

By Alan Riding
(from the *New York Times*)

1   Sabine Contrepois well remembers the day two years ago when she explained to her high school class how the Vietnam War eventually spilled into Cambodia. Suddenly, Meak, an Asian girl in the front row, burst into tears. "I asked her what was wrong," Mrs. Contrepois recalled. "She said her father was shot the day the Khmer Rouge took power in Cambodia in 1975. She and her mother spent years in concentration camps before they escaped through Thailand. There was absolute silence in the classroom."

2   The incident set the teacher thinking. A traditional role of French schools is to prepare children of immigrants to become French citizens. Yet Meak's reaction made Mrs. Contrepois realize that she knew nothing of the background of the young people of different races whom she faced every day. Clearly, some students' parents came to France simply to find work. Others came fleeing wars and dictatorships. Yet Mrs. Contrepois, who comes from an immigrant family herself, also wondered whether the teenagers themselves knew why they were in France. Did they know their own family history?

3   A year ago, seeking answers, she gave the 120 students in her six classes a research project titled: "In what way has your family been touched by history?" If they did not know, she told them, they should ask their parents and grandparents. The result is *History, My History*, a document in which 41 students, mostly in their late teens, describe the tumultuous[1] paths—wars in Armenia, Spain, Algeria, Vietnam, and the former Yugoslavia; repression in Poland, Portugal, and Cameroon—that brought their families here.

4   Mrs. Contrepois sees the problem through the prism of her students[2] at Frédéric Mistral High School in this town south of Paris. Her job is to teach youths who are considered by the school system to be slow learners. Many are immigrant children who have trouble finding jobs after school.

5   To Mrs. Contrepois, the youths' main liability[3] is not a lack of ability, but confusion about their identity. "It's easier for them to accept being French if they can also come to terms with their roots,"[4] she said. "This project tried to do that. It made them communicate with their parents. In many cases, they discovered things that made them proud. And I think it taught them tolerance toward each other."

6   Yassine, a 19-year-old born in France of Algerian parents, said he discovered that his grandfather had been tortured and killed by French troops during Algeria's war of independence. "I didn't know anything about this," he said. "We never spoke about Algeria at home. I had never dared ask before."

7   Stephanie, also 19, said she learned that her grandfather was shot by invading German troops in Poland in 1939. "My father came here illegally in 1946, but this topic was taboo[5] at home," she said. "He died two years ago, and my mother told me the story.

---

[1] **tumultuous:** full of activity, confusion, or violence
[2] **through the prism of her students:** through the eyes of her students
[3] **liability:** disadvantage
[4] **come to terms with their roots:** understand and accept their past
[5] **taboo:** forbidden

(continued on next page)

When she saw the final project, she cried. She was very proud."

8 To insure the authenticity[6] of the stories, Mrs. Contrepois asked her "student authors," as she now calls them, to provide documentation. Sevana, 16, found newspaper photos of the Turkish atrocities[7] against Armenians in 1915, when her great-grandparents were killed. Slawomir, whose father, a Pole, sought asylum[8] in France in 1981, offered a photograph of her grandmother with Lech Walesa.[9]

9 This month, the work was awarded the "Memories of Immigration" prize by the Foundation for Republican Integration, headed by Kofi Yamgnane, a former Minister for Integration who was born in Togo.

10 Mrs. Contrepois was well equipped to oversee the project. The 36-year-old teacher was born in a run-down Paris hotel shortly after her Spanish-born father and Algerian-born mother arrived here fleeing the Algerian War. "They were penniless immigrants, and they knew all about discrimination," she said. While her family eventually found a place in French society, she knows that it is more difficult for immigrants today. But at least with this group of young people, she has made an impact. "She has changed our lives," Yassine said, speaking for the "student authors" at a recent ceremony here attended by Mr. Yamgnane and the town mayor, Gabriel Bourdin.

11 *History, My History* will soon be published as a book here, and the students have made another plan—they want to visit New York. Their prize brought them $5,000, but they must raise $39,000 more. "We want to compare our experiences with those of young Americans like us, how they study, what their culture is," Yassine said. "The only New York I've seen is on television."

---

[6] **authenticity:** truthfulness
[7] **atrocity:** an act of great evil, especially cruelty
[8] **asylum:** refuge, shelter
[9] **Lech Walesa:** leader of a workers' movement in Poland who became the head of state after Poland gained its independence from the former Soviet Union

2 *Based on what you have read in "In One School, Many Sagas," answer the questions about the text. When you are finished, compare your answers with a partner's.*

1. Why did Sabine Contrepois decide to do the *History, My History* project with her students?

   _____

   _____

2. What, according to Mrs. Contrepois, was the main "liability" of her students at Frédéric Mistral High School? How did French administrators view these students?

   _____

   _____

3. To assure the authenticity of the students' stories, what did Mrs. Contrepois require?

_____

_____

4. Why did Mrs. Contrepois identify with her students?

_____

_____

3 _Read the three quotes from Reading Two and write short answers to the questions. Compare your answers in a small group._

    1. Sabine Contrepois: "It's easier for them to accept being French if they can also come to terms with their roots."

    What does this statement mean? Do you agree with Mrs. Contrepois?

_____

_____

    2. Yassine: "I didn't know anything about this. We never spoke about Algeria at home. I had never dared ask before."

    Why do you think Yassine never asked his family any questions?

_____

_____

    3. Stephanie: "When [my mother] saw the final project, she cried."

    Why do you think Stephanie's project made her mother cry?

_____

_____

C INTEGRATE READINGS ONE AND TWO

◖ STEP 1: Organize

Work with a partner. Consider the people whose names appear in the grid on the next page in relation to the categories in the column on the left. Place an **X** in the boxes where the category relates directly to the person's story.

	Eva	Alinka	Eva's Mother	Elizabeth	Elizabeth's Mother	Stephanie	Yassine	Meak	Mrs. Contrepois
Immigrants									
Children of immigrants									
Pride in the past									
Secrets									
Embarrassment									
Identity conflicts									

◀ **STEP 2: Synthesize**

Read the introduction to an essay. Add a few body paragraphs to it based on the work you did in Step 1.

The immigrant experience affects many people's lives today either directly or indirectly. Whether an individual is an immigrant, or the child or grandchild of an immigrant, he or she encounters problems in life that those from non-immigrant families cannot even imagine. That is why reading three passages about the immigrant experience, an excerpt from Eva Hoffman's book, *Lost in Translation*, Elizabeth Wong's narrative of her childhood—"The Struggle to Be an All-American Girl," and Alan Riding's account of French teenagers' quest to learn about their past, "In One School, Many Sagas"—is so useful. These texts explain people's different immigrant backgrounds and show us how pride in the past, secrets, embarrassment, and identity conflicts play a role in their lives.

Work with a partner. Based on the information in the grid in Organize, write a few paragraphs that compare and contrast the immigrant backgrounds of three or more of these characters (at least one from each reading): Eva, Alinka, Eva's mother, Elizabeth, Elizabeth's mother, Stephanie, Yassine, Meak, or Mrs. Contrepois. Show how pride in the past, secrets, embarrassment, and identity conflicts play a role in their lives.

3 FOCUS ON WRITING

A VOCABULARY

◀ REVIEW

Read the thoughts that may have gone through the mind of Alinka, Eva's younger sister. Complete the thoughts with words and phrases from the box—they are synonyms for the items in parentheses.

asylum	come to terms with their roots	grief
atrocities	dissuade	stoical
beleaguered	fabric	tighten the reins
chaotic	giving vent to	tumultuous

These have been difficult years for my parents. The

_____ of their emotional lives has been made ever so fragile
1. (structure)

because of their own suffering and their firsthand knowledge of the terrible

_____ suffered by so many of their loved ones during World
2. (torment)

War II. My parents wanted to make a new life for us in Canada.

Although they had hoped that their new home in Canada would provide an

_____ for them from their tragic past, my parents' sense of
3. (safe place)

sorrow still dominates them. Despite their _____
4. (self-controlled)

appearance, their every gesture is still _____ by their
5. (troubled)

memories of their _____ past.
6. (violent)

You may think that as the youngest family member of our cluster of four, I

have been untouched by all this. Yet it was not until we moved to Canada that I

realized how very trapped I had been by my parents' _____. I
7. (sadness)

had never realized how simple life could be. None of my Canadian friends seem to

have a history or to be troubled by the need to _____. Their
8. (understand their family history)

perpetually happy faces, which my sister sarcastically describes as reflecting not only

"hygienic smiles," but also "hygienic feelings," are a welcome relief to me.

While my sister may laugh at my friends and their parents because of their superficiality, I disagree. She cannot _____ me from thinking
9. (discourage)
that they are better off than we are. I want more than anything else to blend in with this Disneyland mentality, with this fairy tale of a life where "everyone lives happily ever after."

So, if I am putting a lot of makeup on my face and behaving in ways that make my mother think of the loose girls in our Polish town, be happy for me! As I take advantage of my mother, who has decided not to _____
10. (impose restraints)
because she is afraid of losing me, I am doing two things at once. I am rebelling as only teenagers know how to rebel, and, in so doing, I am "painting" a new life for myself. Through my actions, not only am I _____ my
11. (expressing)
frustrations and liberating myself from the storminess of my family's

_____ inner life, but I am also creating a new identity for
12. (confused)
myself. I am becoming free!

◖ EXPAND

The suffixes **-ness, -ty, -ity,** and **-ment** mean "the state, quality, or condition of being." When you add -ness, -ty, and -ity to certain adjectives and -ment to certain verbs, you create nouns that relate to the state, quality, or condition of being a particular way. For adjectives of two syllables or more that end with a y, the y changes to i when -ness is added. Other spelling changes may be needed; check your dictionary.

Examples
quiet (adjective)
quietness (noun = "the state, quality, or condition of being quiet")

happy (adjective)
happiness (noun = "the state, quality, or condition of being happy")

cruel (adjective)
cruelty (noun = "the state, quality, or condition of being cruel")

authentic (adjective)
authenticity (noun = "the state, quality, or condition of being authentic")

move (verb)
movement (noun = "the state, quality, or condition of moving/being moved")

Work with a partner. Read the sentences and identify the noun that can be created from the underlined words. Then write a sentence using the noun, without changing the meaning of the original sentence. Other words will have to be changed.

1. Elizabeth likes the <u>refined</u> manner in which Southerners speak English.

   Noun: _refinement_

   Sentence: _Elizabeth likes the refinement of Southerners' speech._

2. Penny does not understand that Eva is being <u>friendly</u> when she shakes her arm in excitement.

   Noun: _____

   Sentence: _____

3. Eva learns that hooking her arm through Penny's as they walk down the street together <u>embarrasses</u> Penny.

   Noun: _____

   Sentence: _____

4. Eva does not want her father, mother, and sister to stop being <u>loyal</u> to one another.

   Noun: _____

   Sentence: _____

5. Many French immigrant children are surprised to learn that their ancestors were the unfortunate victims of <u>atrocious</u> crimes.

   Noun: _____

   Sentence: _____

6. The Hoffman family's <u>stormy</u> emotional state is far from normal in Canada.

   Noun: _____

   Sentence: _____

7. Eva is <u>ferocious</u> about protecting her family's common bond.

   Noun: _____

   Sentence: _____

◖ CREATE

Working with a partner, complete an imaginary dialogue between Elizabeth Wong and her mother. Elizabeth is young and does not want to go to Chinese school. Her mother is upset and tries to persuade her daughter to respect traditional culture. The daughter wants to be more American than Chinese. In your dialogue, use at least eight words or phrases from the box on the next page.

chaotic	friendliness	restraint
~~come to terms with your roots~~	give vent to	scold
demonstrative	loyalty	stoical
dissuade	~~nagging~~	storminess
embarrassment	refinement	tighten the reins

ELIZABETH: Why are you always *nagging* me about going to Chinese school? I hate it there.

MOTHER: It's important for you to learn to speak Chinese and to *come to terms with your roots.*

ELIZABETH: _____

_____

MOTHER: _____

_____

ELIZABETH: _____

_____

MOTHER: _____

_____

ELIZABETH: _____

_____

MOTHER: _____

_____

B GRAMMAR: Adverb Clauses of Comparison and Contrast

1 *Examine the sentence from "Lost in Translation" and discuss the questions with a partner.*

"You shouldn't say, 'You are wrong about that,' although you may say, 'On the other hand, there is that to consider.'"

1. Is this one sentence or two?

2. Which part of the sentence contains words that are polite to say in Canadian culture?

3. What is the difference between the two parts of the sentence?

4. What is a synonym for *although* in this sentence?

ADVERB CLAUSES

Adverb clauses can be used to combine two ideas into one sentence. They can be used in the first or second part of the sentence. They provide variety for the sentence and smooth transitions from one idea to another in your paragraphs. The following adverbials used to introduce adverb clauses will be particularly helpful in comparison and contrast essays. Look at the examples carefully to see where commas are needed.

Comparison or Similarity	Examples
just as	**Just as** Eva is struggling to be accepted in Canada, Elizabeth is struggling to be accepted in the United States.
in the same way that	**In the same way that** many immigrants have chosen to come to North America, many are choosing France as their new home.

Contrast or Difference	
whereas	**Whereas France has an official ministry to help with assimilation of immigrants,** the United States does not have such an institution.
while	Mrs. Contrepois felt that children need to know their roots, **while their parents felt the past was too painful.**
despite the fact that	**Despite the fact that Americans have tolerated the use of many immigrant languages,** they remain profoundly attached to the English language.
although	**Although Americans have tolerated the use of many immigrant languages,** they remain profoundly attached to the English language.
while	**While Americans have tolerated the use of many immigrant languages,** they remain profoundly attached to the English language.

GRAMMAR TIP: As you can see, *while* can be used in two distinct ways: either as a synonym for *whereas* or as a synonym for *despite the fact that* and *although*. Sentences with *despite the fact that* and *although* often include an unexpected idea or a contradiction. In these sentences, the subject of both clauses is usually the same.

2 *For each of the topics, write one or two sentences of comparison and contrast. Use the cues given and* **although, despite the fact that, in the same way that, just as, whereas,** *or* **while.**

   1. Telling the truth

   Poles / Canadians

   While Poles may prefer to be honest and direct when giving criticism, Canadians may choose to be more diplomatic and keep their opinions to themselves.

2. **Cultural identity**

   Elizabeth / Eva

   _____

   _____

   _____

3. **Respecting one's parents**

   Elizabeth's brother / Alinka (Eva's sister)

   _____

   _____

   _____

4. **Showing intimacy**

   Eva / Penny (Eva's friend)

   _____

   _____

   _____

5. **Obedience**

   American children / Chinese children

   _____

   _____

   _____

6. **American ways / Canadian ways**

   Elizabeth / Eva's mother

   _____

   _____

   _____

7. **Independence**

   Elizabeth / Eva

   _____

   _____

   _____

8. Personal stories

Lost in Translation / History, My History

_____

_____

_____

C WRITING

In this unit, you read from *Lost in Translation* and "The Struggle to Be an All-American Girl," two texts that reflect their authors' efforts to come to terms with their roots.

You will **write a point-by-point comparison and contrast essay about Eva and Elizabeth.***

◀ **PREPARE TO WRITE:** Identifying Similarities, Differences, and Common Categories

Step One: Fill in the Venn diagram. In the part on the left, write notes about Eva that are true only of Eva. In the part on the right, write notes about Elizabeth that are true only of Elizabeth. In the middle, write notes about what the two of them share.

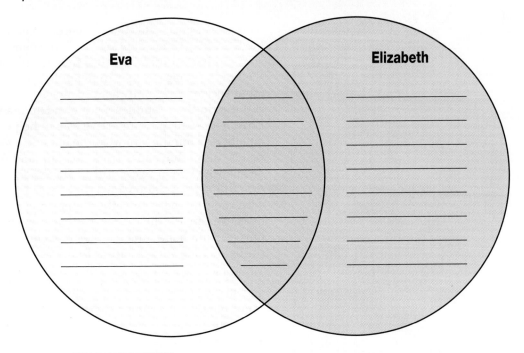

---

*For Alternative Writing Topics, see page 122. These topics can be used in place of the writing topic for this unit or as homework. The alternative topics relate to the theme of the unit, but may not target the same grammar or rhetorical structures taught in the unit.

What Is Lost in Translation? **113**

Step Two: Look at the Venn diagram. From the similarities and differences that you have noted, identify the categories to which they belong. Place the various ideas under their respective categories, then fill in the Similarities and Differences in the chart. Two possible categories have been given to you. You should be able to identify one or two more.

CATEGORIES	SIMILARITIES	DIFFERENCES
Family Life		
Cultural Identity		

◖ **WRITE: A Comparison and Contrast Essay**

1 *Working with a partner, read the essay and discuss the questions on the next page.*

A Comparison of Eva and Elizabeth

INTRODUCTORY PARAGRAPH	Whoever once said that the children of immigrants have an easy time adapting to life in their new country was surely mistaken. Because they usually learn to speak the new language sooner than adults, immigrant children often become the family spokesperson. As the oldest children in their families, both Eva Hoffman and Elizabeth Wong play an active role in helping their family members communicate with the outside world. As a result, they often suffer from the pain and frustration that people who live in two cultures can experience. By examining the relationships that these two girls have with their mothers and other important people in their lives, we can see that although Eva and Elizabeth may have certain hopes and feelings in common, they are at the same time very different from one another.
BODY PARAGRAPH 1	Like Eva, Elizabeth wants to be accepted by her peers, and she is embarrassed when she is made to feel different from them. In the same way that Eva becomes self-conscious about expressing her feelings, Elizabeth is ashamed as she wanders through the American supermarket and hears her grandmother calling after her

in Chinese. Elizabeth also hates it when her mother speaks English. But on the surface at least, she does not seem to be as bothered by this as her younger brother. This brings us to another common area of concern. Eva and Elizabeth are both unhappy about the ways in which their brother and sister treat their mother. Just as Eva is angered when her sister, Alinka, challenges her mother's authority, Elizabeth views her brother's constant criticisms of her mother's English as fanatical and cruel. Both Eva and Elizabeth are more outwardly protective of their mothers' feelings than their brother and sister are.

BODY
PARAGRAPH 2

Although Eva and Elizabeth share similar attitudes, they also differ from each other in many respects. Unlike Eva, Elizabeth does not feel that her identity is bound to her family's cultural heritage and history. Whereas Eva embraces her Polish heritage, Elizabeth flees her Chinese background. While Eva wants to hold on to the memory of the family's sad past, Elizabeth is happy when her mother grants her a "cultural divorce" and says she no longer has to attend the Chinese school. In contrast to Elizabeth, Eva is flexible: She is willing to compromise and best of both cultures. Wh bicultural, Elizabet everything America American girl." How Nancy Drew, her fav Of course, all this ca and the different circ thirteen years old, wh In addition, whereas Elizabeth was born an ... the United States. Such basic differences in their lives leave a wide gap between them.

CONCLUSION

Eva and Elizabeth have made different adjustments to their cross-cultural experiences. When children like Eva immigrate, they understand the sacrifices their parents have made in order to provide them with a better life because they themselves have participated in the immigration process. However, children like Elizabeth often don't understand the sacrifices their parents have made for them until they become adults. And when they finally do, can it sometimes be too late?

1. Which words and phrases does the writer use to point out similarities and differences?

2. In the body of the essay, can you readily identify the paragraph that deals with the similarities and the paragraph that deals with the differences? Explain how the writer makes this easy for the reader.

3. What does the writer do to connect the two body paragraphs?

4. Are the similarities between the two characters more important than the differences, or are the differences more important than the similarities? Explain.

PURPOSE OF COMPARISON AND CONTRAST ESSAYS

When you write a comparison and contrast essay, the purpose is not just to point out similarities and differences or advantages and disadvantages. The purpose is—as with all essays—to persuade and explain a point of view. The emphasis should be on either the similarities or the differences, and details should be included according to which emphasis is chosen.

The thesis statement of the essay you have just read, the last sentence of the introductory paragraph, tells the reader something about the emphasis that will be developed in the body of the essay. "By examining the relationships that these two girls have with their mothers and other important people in their lives, we can see that although Eva and Elizabeth may have certain hopes and feelings in common, they are at the same time very different from one another." We know by the last sentence of the body of the essay that the differences outweigh the similarities: "Such basic differences in their lives leave a wide gap between them." This point of view is reinforced in the conclusion of the essay.

PATTERNS OF ORGANIZATION

There are two ways to organize a comparison and contrast essay: through block organization or point-by-point organization.

Block Organization	**Point-by-Point Organization**
• Similarities: *Both subjects are discussed (similarities of Eva and Elizabeth).* • Differences: *Both subjects are discussed (differences of Eva and Elizabeth).* OR - All about Eva - All about Elizabeth - Summary of similarities and differences	• Subject One: *Similarities and differences are discussed.* • Subject Two: *Similarities and differences are discussed.* • Subject Three: *Similarities and differences are discussed.*

Block Organization

In a **block organization** essay, the writer discusses each part of the comparison in clearly distinct parts (or blocks) of the essay. For example, the writer could first refer only to Eva and then only to Elizabeth, or, as in the essay "A Comparison of Eva and Elizabeth," the writer could first discuss the similarities between the two girls and then the differences between them.

The paragraph dealing with similarities contains many words and expressions that point out likenesses: *like, in the same way that, just as, both,* and so on. Similarly, the paragraph revealing the differences contains words and expressions that show differences: *unlike, whereas, while, in contrast to,* and so on.

In order to connect one block of the essay with the other, the writer uses a transitional sentence that prepares us for the change in emphasis of the next block: "Although Eva and Elizabeth share similar attitudes, they also differ from each other in many respects."

Point-by-Point Organization

In **point-by-point organization,** the writer organizes the development of ideas according to "points," or categories, which are common to both subjects. In each paragraph of the body, a different point is discussed. For example, a comparison of Eva and Elizabeth might (after the introductory paragraph) begin with a paragraph exploring the differences in their *backgrounds.* A second paragraph might discuss the similarities and differences in their *family life,* and so on. It is usually better to limit the categories to three or four. A point-by-point organization is usually chosen when there are many complex aspects to a comparison; a block organization is more suitable for a simpler subject.

The following is an example of a point-by-point body paragraph:

Eva and Elizabeth's contrasting backgrounds help us to reflect on the differences between them. As a teenager who directly experienced the tragic history of her family's past, Eva cannot ignore the fact that she is in the middle of two cultures. She holds on to her Polish values while adapting to newly-learned Canadian values. Whereas Eva dips willingly into two cultures and sees herself becoming bicultural, Elizabeth resents her mother's insistence that she learn about her Chinese heritage. Elizabeth was born in America; her mother's native country is not hers. She does not feel bicultural because she is not an immigrant. She adores the sights and sounds of everything American and wants only to fit in and be an "all-American girl." While Elizabeth feels trapped studying about a past she has never known and is too young to appreciate, Eva is mature enough to realize that she must embrace a double identity because of her immigrant status. These basic differences in their situations therefore leave a wide gap between them.

ORGANIZING INFORMATION THROUGH OUTLINES

Whether you choose block or point-by-point organization for your comparison and contrast essay, preparing an **outline** can help you to organize your main ideas, topic sentences, and supporting details. After you prepare an outline, you know exactly what you want to write and how you want to write it.

Once you know the topics you wish to include in your essay, you will be ready to write the thesis statement. The thesis statement should tell the reader the main idea and announce the topics that will be explored in the body paragraphs. The thesis statement cannot simply state the similarities and differences; it must take a position on the comparison. Are the differences more important than the similarities, or are the similarities more important than the differences?

2 *Working with a partner, read the thesis statements. Give the main idea that is to be emphasized (that is, more similar than different or more different than similar) and write down the "keywords" (topics and possible focal points) of the supporting body paragraphs.*

a. It is easy to overlook the differences in family relationships and childrearing attitudes between Asian and North American parents because of their similar educational aspirations for their children.

Main Idea: Differences are more important than similarities.

Supporting Body Paragraph Topics

    Similarities: aspirations

    Differences: family relationships and childrearing attitudes

b. Most people believe that Dominicans and Puerto Ricans have a lot in common because of their Caribbean island heritage; however, they do not know that the Dominicans' love of the *bachata* and the Puerto Ricans' love of *salsa* create a great cultural divide between the two groups on the dance floor.

Main Idea: _____

Supporting Body Paragraph Topics

    Similarities: _____

    Differences: _____

c. To fully understand the differences between American and Samoan teenagers' relationships with their parents, you need to look at the differences in the parents' methods of discipline, the amount of time they usually spend with their children, and their expectations for help from their children in their daily lives.

Main Idea: _____

Supporting Body Paragraph Topics

    Similarities: _____

    Differences: _____

d. By examining the two men's tumultuous family lives and their love of their respective cultures, we can see that although Sergio and Ernest are from different countries, they have many points in common.

Main Idea: _____

Supporting Body Paragraph Topics

    Similarities: _____

    Differences: _____

e. Despite the different modes of transportation used by immigrants today and immigrants who came to America one hundred years ago, immigrants from all over the world still come to America for the same reasons: to escape political oppression and to seek better job opportunities.

Main Idea: _____

Supporting Body Paragraph Topics

    Similarities: _____

    Differences: _____

3 *Write the thesis statement for the essay on Eva and Elizabeth. Then compare your thesis statement with a partner's.*

Thesis Statement:

_____

_____

_____

4 *Work with a partner and prepare an outline that will help you to organize your main ideas, topic sentences, and supporting details. Use the following framework as a guide.*

> **Outline: A Comparison of Eva and Elizabeth**
> (Point-by-Point Organization)
>
>   **I. Introduction**
>
>   Thesis Statement: _____
>
>   _____
>
>   _____
>
>   **II. Topic Sentence of Body Paragraph 1:** _____
>
>   _____
>
>   **1.** Eva: _____
>
>   _____
>
>   **2.** Elizabeth: _____
>
>   _____
>
>   **III. Topic Sentence of Body Paragraph 2:** _____
>
>   _____
>
>   **1.** Eva: _____
>
>   _____

2. Elizabeth: _____

_____

IV. Topic Sentence of Body Paragraph 3: _____

_____

1. Eva: _____

_____

2. Elizabeth: _____

_____

V. Conclusion: _____

_____

_____

_____

5 *Using what you have learned about organizing a point-by-point comparison and contrast essay, write a comparison and contrast essay about Eva and Elizabeth. Refer to the work you did in Prepare to Write, pages 113–114, and Write, pages 114–120, to write your first draft.*

◖ **REVISE: Combining Sentences for Variety**

The writer of the body paragraph below on cultural heritage in a point-by-point comparison and contrast essay has written correct sentences. However, the writing style needs more polish:

- Some sentence patterns are unnecessarily repeated.
- Some sentences conceptually related to each other should be combined either by means of a coordinating conjunction (*and, but*), a cause-and-effect structure (*because, since, however, nevertheless, therefore, consequently*), or a comparison and contrast structure (*both, like, unlike, just as, in the same way that, although, despite the fact that, while, whereas*).

With such revisions, the paragraph should be in good form.

Working with a partner, revise the paragraph. There is more than one correct answer here. After you have finished, check the answer key for suggested answers.

Sergio and Ernest are both loyal to their cultural heritage. Sergio was eight years old when he came to the United States. Ernest was eight years old. Sergio was born in Brazil. Ernest was born in Rwanda. America was a beacon of hope for both their families. They came to America for different reasons. Sergio left Brazil with his parents in search of a better future. Ernest came with his parents to escape the atrocities of the civil war in Rwanda. Their transition to American life was smooth. They both made American friends quickly and had no trouble adapting to American life. They were both able to respond to the challenges of the American dream. They now have successful careers. They have been in America for a long time. They have never forgotten their origins. Sergio goes back to Brazil for Carnival every February. Ernest does volunteer work throughout the year on the Rwandan Relief Fund. Both Sergio and Ernest are successful Americans who maintain close ties with the countries of their birth.

◀ **EDIT: Writing the Final Draft**

Write your final draft. Carefully edit it for grammatical and mechanical errors. Make sure you used some of the vocabulary and grammar from the unit. Use the checklist to help you write the final draft. Then neatly write or type your essay.

✓ FINAL DRAFT CHECKLIST

- ○ Does your essay have an introduction, a body, and a conclusion?
- ○ Does the essay follow the point-by-point organizational pattern for comparison and contrast essays?
- ○ Does the thesis statement prepare the reader for the topics of the body paragraphs?
- ○ Does each body paragraph begin with an appropriate topic sentence and include sufficient support?
- ○ Are the adverbials and other comparison and contrast words and phrases in the essay used correctly?
- ○ Does the writing have good sentence variety?
- ○ Have new vocabulary and expressions been used in the essay?

ALTERNATIVE WRITING TOPICS

Write an essay on one of the topics. In order to organize your ideas effectively, write a clear thesis statement and create an outline based on it. Follow the outline as you write the essay. Use vocabulary, grammar, and points of style that you studied in the unit.

1. Have you ever had a friend whose culture, background, talents, or qualities were different from yours? Consider how your similarities and differences contributed to your friendship. Did your friendship grow because you were similar or because you were different?

2. When immigrants arrive in a new country, should they assimilate into the new culture or try to preserve their old culture? In what ways do you think people need to assimilate? What kinds of things do people usually want to preserve from their old culture? What is the risk to the nation if assimilation is too extreme? What is the risk if immigrants do not assimilate?

3. What is the meaning of the following extract? In what ways might Luc Sante have felt "other"? How has your own identity been formed? Have you ever had the experience of being "other"?

> "Ethnically, I am about as homogeneous as it is possible to be: Aside from one great-grandmother who came from Luxembourg, my gene pool derives entirely from an area smaller than the five boroughs of New York City. I was born in the same town [Verviers, Belgium] as every one of my Sante forebears at least as far back as the mid-sixteenth century, which is as far back as the records go. Having been transplanted from my native soil [to live in the United States], and having had to construct an identity in response to a double set of demands, one from my background and one from my environment, I have become permanently 'other.'"
>
> —Luc Sante, "Living in Tongues"
> (from the *New York Times Magazine*)

4. You are Mrs. Contrepois. Write to thirteen-year-old Eva or ten-year-old Elizabeth telling them why they should do what your students did in France. Explain to them how you believe such a project would help them.

5. You are Eva or Elizabeth answering a letter from Mrs. Contrepois. Explain why you agree or disagree with Mrs. Contrepois. If you are Eva, do you think reading your story to your class in Canada would help your classmates to understand you, or would it just make you seem too different from the others? If you are Elizabeth, do you think writing your family's story would help you to understand your mother's motivation to bring you closer to your cultural heritage, or would it make you want to keep your distance from it?

RESEARCH TOPICS, see page 264.

UNIT
6

The Landscape of Faith

FOCUS ON THE TOPIC

A PREDICT

Look at the title of the unit and the photo above. In spite of different practices, why do you think religion is such an important part of life all over the world? Write down your ideas, and share them with the class.

123

Interview a partner using this questionnaire about religion. You will need to summarize in a few sentences your partner's answer to the last question. After you have finished, show your summary to your partner to check the content. Then discuss your answers in a small group.

RELIGION IN YOUR LIFE

	YES	NO
1. Were you brought up in a particular religion?	☐	☐
2. Do you still feel a part of that religion today?	☐	☐
3. Do you participate in a religion today?	☐	☐
4. Do you follow all the customs, rules, and traditions of this religion?	☐	☐
5. Is religion an important part of your family's life?	☐	☐

Explain. _____

_____

_____

C BACKGROUND AND VOCABULARY

Work in pairs. Read the information below and match each underlined word with a synonym from the list. Write the word next to the correct synonym.

In this chapter, there is an interview with one of the most well-known Buddhists in the world, the Dalai Lama, the religious leader of the Tibetan Buddhist community.

The Buddhist religion is based on the teachings of Siddhartha Gautama, a Hindu prince who lived about 2,500 years ago in India. (This was about the same time Confucius was teaching in China.) Siddhartha became the Buddha, or "Enlightened One," after a personal journey away from the worldly, <u>temporal</u> concerns of a rich man toward a spiritual awakening. He spent the rest of his life teaching people. Buddhist teachings have <u>propagated</u> all over Asia, and today there are more than 290 million <u>practitioners</u>. Buddhism is divided into many different schools and sects, but all Buddhists share certain basic principles that they believe are <u>relevant</u> to living a good life.

For Buddhists, all life is suffering. This suffering is caused by selfish efforts and desires. A soul goes through many lives, many cycles of <u>reincarnation</u>, because there is always something more to learn: how to turn away from the <u>shortsighted</u> focus on the self in order to pay more attention to long-term spiritual values. Nirvana, the end of rebirth and suffering, the release into the highest stage of happiness, is achieved only by learning to give up self-interest. Buddhists are taught to speak kindly, to do no harm, and to avoid killing, stealing, lying, drinking alcohol, and committing sexual offenses. Some religions <u>predict</u> the end of the world, but Buddhism sees no end and no beginning, no creation and no Higher Being.

Tibetan Buddhism suffered greatly in the last generation. In the 1950s the Chinese Communist government <u>mobilized</u> the army and invaded Tibet. The spiritual and cultural basis of the religion was almost destroyed. In 1959 the Dalai Lama, the <u>designated</u> head of the religion there, had to <u>cease</u> his activities and leave the country with 70,000 of his followers; he now lives in <u>exile</u>. It is difficult to <u>speculate</u> about what the future may bring for Tibetan Buddhism.

a. chosen ___designated___

b. followers _____

c. foretell _____

d. interested only in the moment

_____

e. living in a foreign land

_____

f. material, worldly _____

g. rebirth after death

_____

h. prepared for war

_____

i. related _____

j. spread _____

k. stop _____

l. theorize _____

②FOCUS ON READING

Ⓐ READING ONE: Peace Prevails

Before you read the interview with the Dalai Lama, answer the question in a written paragraph. Then discuss your answer with a partner.

Do you think the world will be better or worse 100 years from now?

PEACE PREVAILS

By Claudia Dreifus

(from the *New York Times Magazine*)

1   In the Buddhist tradition, the future counts for little. Nonetheless, when Tenzin Gyatso, fourteenth Dalai Lama and the spiritual and **temporal** leader of Tibet in **exile**, was asked to **speculate** on the landscape of faith a century from now, he gave it his best try. He was interviewed in Bloomington, Indiana, on a brilliant summer morning, after having laid the cornerstone[1] for a new Buddhist temple.

2   **Question:** In the next hundred years, thanks to organ transplants and genetic therapies, people may be able to live much longer lives. If you had the chance to do that, would you take it?

3   **Dalai Lama:** The mere living is not so important. The important thing is usefulness. So if I could get another hundred years more and be useful, then . . . good. Otherwise, you just create more problems for others. And then, from the Buddhist viewpoint, isn't it better to have another young body [through **reincarnation**]? There's a Buddhist story about an old monk who was dying and everyone was very sad. He said, "Don't be sad. Right now, I have an old, decaying body. But very soon . . . I will get a fresh young body."

4   **Q:** Three years ago, you **predicted** that the next hundred years would be a century of peace, hope, and justice. Since then, there have been massacres in Rwanda and Burundi, and the Chinese have kidnapped the young boy you **designated** to be the Panchen Lama.[2] Are you still optimistic about the future?

5   **DL:** Oh, yes. Of course. A handful of **shortsighted** people have always existed. But overall, their day is over because the public's attitude toward war and violence has become much healthier than at any time in history. People used to be much more jingoistic[3] and nationalistic compared with the way they are now.

---

[1] **cornerstone:** a foundation, a stone laid at a formal ceremony
[2] **Panchen Lama:** chief spiritual adviser to the Dalai Lama
[3] **jingoistic:** believing strongly that your own country is better than others

6   Recently I was talking with the English Queen Mother. She was 96, and I asked her, "What changes have you seen in your lifetime?"[4] She answered, "When I was young, we had not much concern about the outside world. Now people have a great concern about what is happening all over the world." This is a very positive change.

7   So I believe that due to [the revolution in] information, generally speaking, any leader, if he tried to **mobilize** the whole nation for war, would find it impossible. In previous times, it was quite possible. Well, small-scale wars, perhaps they can still do. But large-scale wars, I think, are not likely. I do believe that in the next century we have to seriously think about putting a complete stop to the arms trade.

8   **Q:** Buddhism has become quite popular in the West. Could you see a future American president who is a practicing Buddhist?

9   **DL:** No, I think someone in the Judeo-Christian tradition would be better. I prefer that people in Western countries follow their own traditions. I have no desire to **propagate** [my religious beliefs].

10   **Q:** A hundred years in the future, what will be the role of women in religion?

11   **DL:** I think improved. Because the women want it.

12   **Q:** Can you see a situation where there might be a woman as Pope, a woman as Archbishop of Canterbury, a woman as Dalai Lama?

13   **DL:** In the Buddhist world, there's not much of a problem. Some of the Lamas of high reincarnation are women.

14   **Q:** Is it possible that you, the 14th Dalai Lama, might be the last Dalai Lama?

15   **DL:** It is possible. Not as a result of external force, though. If the majority of the Tibetan people feel that the Dalai Lama institution is no longer **relevant**, then the institution will automatically **cease**. Now, if that happens while I'm alive or just after my death, then I am obviously the last Dalai Lama. But if my death comes in the next one or two years, then most probably the Tibetan people will want to have another incarnation. Of that I'm quite certain. Of course, there is the possibility that Tibetans become insignificant in our land and all decisions are made by the Chinese. It is possible and very sad.

16   **Q:** Are you concerned that you might have a violent death?

17   **DL:** It is possible, I don't know. Airplanes trouble me. Dying in the ocean. And ending up in the stomach of a shark.

18   **Q:** One hundred years from now, what would you like to be remembered for?

19   **DL:** As a Buddhist **practitioner**, I have no interest in that. So long as I am alive, my time and my life must be utilized properly. Then after my death, I don't care how people remember me.

20   **Q:** Is it true that you like to go shopping when you travel?

21   **DL:** I like it. I'm a human being. I think human beings have a lot of curiosity. I go to Los Angeles; sometimes I shop for myself. Shoes . . . small electronic equipment . . . cat food. I go to shopping malls just like they were museums.

---

[4] The Queen Mother was born on August 5, 1900, and died on March 29, 2002.

(continued on next page)

22   **Q:** Many people get a sense of God by observing nature. What will religions be like in a hundred years if there is little nature left on earth?

23   **DL:** The world itself is nature. The sun, the moon, they are nature. Even if there were no more animals, nature would still be here. For those religions that believe in a creator, they would have to find reasons to explain why our beautiful blue planet became a desert.

24   If you ask me whether it's good or bad, of course it's bad. But in the Buddhist tradition, something like that would not change our attitude. We believe the whole world will come and disappear, come and disappear—so eventually the world becomes desert and even the ocean dries up. But then again, another new world is reborn. It's endless.

◖ READ FOR MAIN IDEAS

Under each of the questions about the main themes of the reading, write a few sentences summarizing the Dalai Lama's point of view.

1. What does the Dalai Lama say about his philosophy of death?

_____

_____

_____

_____

2. What does the Dalai Lama say about his attitude toward war?

_____

_____

_____

_____

3. What does he say about the role of the Dalai Lama in the future?

_____

_____

_____

_____

4. What does he say about the future of the earth?

_____

_____

_____

_____

◖ READ FOR DETAILS

Read the sentences below and cross out those that are not part of the Dalai Lama's predictions. Then decide which major theme of the reading each remaining sentence supports. Write the number of the sentence on the blank next to the appropriate main idea.

Predictions

1. The Chinese government may go further in opposing the Tibetan people's religion.

2. Buddhists will be converting thousands of Americans to their religion.

3. Improvements in information technology will continue to create concern for people in other countries.

4. World wars will be less likely than in the twentieth century.

5. Nature may go through a cycle where much is destroyed.

6. Tibetans will be true to their religion unless external force obliges them to change.

7. Nationalism will decrease as different peoples draw closer together.

8. The Dalai Lama will not worry about how people will remember him 100 years from now.

9. Buddhists will have to accept the idea of a creator.

10. Old bodies should be discarded.

Main Ideas / Themes

_____ **a.** The Role of the Dalai Lama in the Future

_____ **b.** The Dalai Lama's Attitude toward War

_____ **c.** The Dalai Lama's Philosophy of Death

_____ **d.** The Future of the Earth

◖ MAKE INFERENCES

1 *Based on what you read in the interview, imagine what the Dalai Lama would say if he were asked the questions below. Write short answers and explain your conclusions, referring to specific parts of the interview. Then compare your answers with those of another student.*

The Dalai Lama

1. **Question:** Should the Tibetans mobilize against the Chinese?

   Answer: The Dalai Lama would probably say no because he speaks out against war and violence in paragraph 5 of the interview.

2. **Question:** Should religious people refuse to go to the movies?

   Answer: _____

   _____

3. **Question:** Should society invest a great deal of money in keeping very old and ill people alive as long as possible?

   Answer: _____

   _____

4. **Question:** Should society be concerned about endangered species?

   Answer: _____

   _____

2 *Now invent two questions of your own for the Dalai Lama and ask a classmate to answer them.*

1. **Question:** _____

   Answer: _____

   _____

2. **Question:** _____

   Answer: _____

   _____

◖ EXPRESS OPINIONS

Discuss the questions in a small group. Share your group's conclusions with the rest of the class.

1. The Dalai Lama feels that nationalism is bad. Do you agree or disagree?

2. The Dalai Lama wants to be useful in his old age. Are older people entitled to special respect or privileges because of their age? Do older people have a responsibility to help the younger generation?

3. Do you think it is possible to change a society by using peaceful, nonviolent methods?

B READING TWO: Religion

1 *Below is an excerpt from an essay that offers a general definition of the word* **religion.** *Although there can be diverse views on this subject, the passage tries to make broad generalizations applicable to many religions and different periods of history. Before you read the passage, answer the question. Write a short definition and discuss it with a partner.*

How would you define the word *religion*?

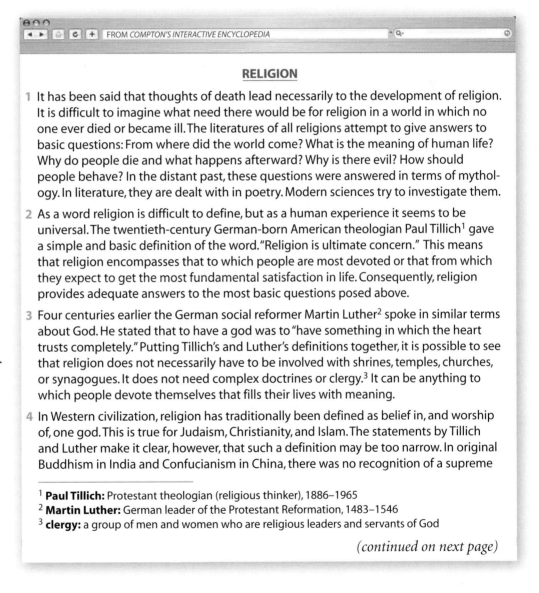

FROM *COMPTON'S INTERACTIVE ENCYCLOPEDIA*

RELIGION

1 It has been said that thoughts of death lead necessarily to the development of religion. It is difficult to imagine what need there would be for religion in a world in which no one ever died or became ill. The literatures of all religions attempt to give answers to basic questions: From where did the world come? What is the meaning of human life? Why do people die and what happens afterward? Why is there evil? How should people behave? In the distant past, these questions were answered in terms of mythology. In literature, they are dealt with in poetry. Modern sciences try to investigate them.

2 As a word religion is difficult to define, but as a human experience it seems to be universal. The twentieth-century German-born American theologian Paul Tillich[1] gave a simple and basic definition of the word. "Religion is ultimate concern." This means that religion encompasses that to which people are most devoted or that from which they expect to get the most fundamental satisfaction in life. Consequently, religion provides adequate answers to the most basic questions posed above.

3 Four centuries earlier the German social reformer Martin Luther[2] spoke in similar terms about God. He stated that to have a god was to "have something in which the heart trusts completely." Putting Tillich's and Luther's definitions together, it is possible to see that religion does not necessarily have to be involved with shrines, temples, churches, or synagogues. It does not need complex doctrines or clergy.[3] It can be anything to which people devote themselves that fills their lives with meaning.

4 In Western civilization, religion has traditionally been defined as belief in, and worship of, one god. This is true for Judaism, Christianity, and Islam. The statements by Tillich and Luther make it clear, however, that such a definition may be too narrow. In original Buddhism in India and Confucianism in China, there was no recognition of a supreme

---

[1] **Paul Tillich:** Protestant theologian (religious thinker), 1886–1965
[2] **Martin Luther:** German leader of the Protestant Reformation, 1483–1546
[3] **clergy:** a group of men and women who are religious leaders and servants of God

(continued on next page)

being. Both of these philosophies were basically concerned with patterns of human behavior.

5 Regardless of definition, all religions (as the word is normally used) have certain elements in common: rituals to perform, prayers to recite, places to frequent or avoid, holy days to keep, means by which to predict the future, a body of literature to read and study, truths to affirm, charismatic[4] leaders to follow, and ordinances[5] to obey. Many have buildings set aside for worship, and there are activities such as prayer, sacrifice, contemplation, and perhaps magic.

6 Closely associated with these elements is personal conduct. Although it is possible to separate ritual observances from moral conduct, worship has normally implied a type of relationship with a god from which certain behavior patterns are expected to follow. A notable exception in history is the official state religion of ancient Rome, which was kept separate from personal commitment and morality.

---

[4] **charismatic:** embodying a personal magic of leadership, creating great loyalty and enthusiasm among followers
[5] **ordinances:** orders or regulations to follow

2 *Paraphrase the quotes from the text. Compare your sentences with a partner's.*

1. "In the distant past, these questions were answered in terms of mythology. In literature, they are dealt with in poetry. Modern sciences try to investigate them." (paragraph 1)

_____

_____

_____

2. "Putting Tillich's and Luther's definitions together, it is possible to see that religion does not necessarily have to be involved with shrines, temples, churches, or synagogues. It does not need complex doctrines or clergy. It can be anything to which people devote themselves that fills their lives with meaning." (paragraph 3)

_____

_____

_____

3. "Although it is possible to separate ritual observances from moral conduct, worship has normally implied a type of relationship with a god from which certain behavior patterns are expected to follow." (paragraph 6)

_____

_____

_____

STEP 1: Organize

In Reading Two, the author lists five basic questions that the literatures of all religions attempt to answer. Write the letter of the correct statement by the Dalai Lama in Reading One in the blank after each question. Consider the full context in which his statements were made.

Questions (R.2)

1. Where does the world come from? _____

2. What is the meaning of human life? _____

3. Why do people die and what happens afterward? _____

4. Why is there evil? _____

5. How should people behave? _____

Statements (R.1)

a. "The public's attitude toward war and violence has become much healthier than at any other time in history."

b. "Even if there were no more animals, nature would still be here."

c. "The whole world will come and disappear. . . . But then again, another new world is reborn. It's endless."

d. "So long as I am alive, my time and my life must be utilized properly. Then after my death, I don't care how people remember me."

e. "Any leader, if he tried to mobilize the nation for war, would find it impossible [today]. In previous times, it was quite possible."

f. "The mere living is not so important. The important thing is usefulness."

g. "People used to be much more jingoistic and nationalistic compared with the way they are now."

h. "I do believe that in the next century we have to seriously think about putting a complete stop to the arms trade."

i. "Don't be sad. Right now, I have an old decaying body. But very soon . . . I will get a fresh young body."

◀ STEP 2: Synthesize

Based on your work in Step 1, write how you think the Dalai Lama would respond to the questions. Discuss with a partner what answers you would expect to find in Buddhist literature. Then write your answers in the spaces provided.

1. Where did the world come from?

   _____

   _____

   _____

2. What is the meaning of human life?

   _____

   _____

   _____

3. Why do people die, and what happens afterward?

   _____

   _____

   _____

4. Why is there evil?

   _____

   _____

   _____

5. How should people behave?

   _____

   _____

   _____

③ FOCUS ON WRITING

A VOCABULARY

◀ REVIEW

Fill in the crossword puzzle with words from the readings.

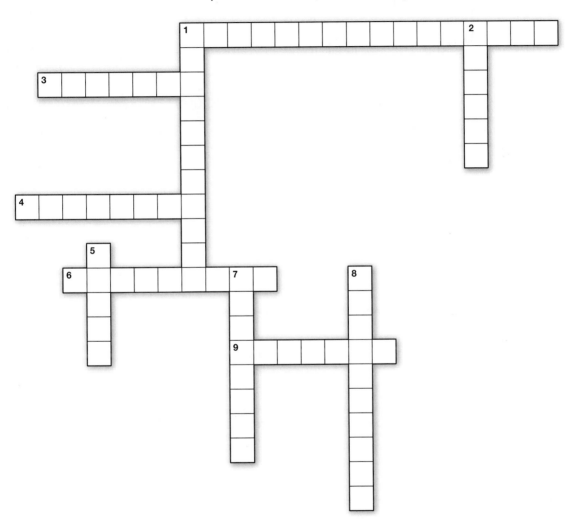

Across

1. lack of long-range thinking
3. significant
4. appropriate, pertinent
6. appoint
9. foretell

Down

1. theory
2. restricted
5. stop
7. worldly
8. believing in a religion

1 *The words below are all related to religion. Working in a small group, put them in the correct categories in the chart. Add any other words you can think of to these categories.*

bishop	Confucianism	monk	rabbi	temple
Buddhism	contemplation	mosque	rituals	theologian
Christianity	Hinduism	ordinances	sacrifice	worship
church	Islam	prayer	shrine	
clergy	Judaism	priest	synagogue	

NAMES OF RELIGIONS	PLACES OF WORSHIP	RELIGIOUS LEADERS	RELIGIOUS PRACTICES

2 *Analogies compare relationships between things that are alike in some ways. The analogy* **Buddhism : temple :: Judaism : synagogue** *is expressed in English as follows:* **"Buddhism is to a temple as Judaism is to a synagogue."** *In other words,* **"Buddhism is practiced in a temple just as Judaism is practiced in a synagogue."** *Complete these analogies. Circle the correct answer from the choices given.*

1. **church : Christianity :: ? : Islam**

   A church is to Christianity as a _____ is to Islam.
   a. church   **b.** mosque   **c.** synagogue

2. **? : temple :: priest : church**

   A(n) _____ is to a temple as a priest is to a church.
   a. pope   **b.** imam   **c.** monk

3. **Islam : Turkey :: ? : China**

   Islam is to Turkey as _____ is to China.
   a. Confucianism   **b.** Christianity   **c.** Judaism

4. **politician : political scientists :: clergy : ?**

   Politicians are to political scientists as clergy are to _____.

   a. theologians   **b.** practitioners   **c.** worshipers

5. **Roman Catholicism : France :: ? : the United States**

   Roman Catholicism is to France as _____ is to the United States.

   a. Protestantism   **b.** Catholicism   **c.** Christianity

6. **imam : Islam :: ? : Protestantism**

   An imam is to Islam as a _____ is to Protestantism.

   a. rabbi   **b.** priest   **c.** minister

7. **perform : rituals :: recite : ?**

   Perform is to rituals as recite is to _____.

   a. ordinances   **b.** prayers   **c.** practitioners

8. **laws : customs :: ? : rituals**

   Laws are to customs as _____ are to rituals.

   a. prayers   **b.** ordinances   **c.** theologians

9. **Mecca : ? :: Vatican City : Roman Catholicism**

   Mecca is to _____ as Vatican City is to Roman Catholicism.

   a. Judaism   **b.** Buddhism   **c.** Islam

◖ **CREATE**

In order to learn more about one of the religions mentioned in this unit (Buddhism, Christianity, Confucianism, Hinduism, Islam, or Judaism), interview a knowledgeable person. On a separate piece of paper, write down the questions that you would ask this expert, using at least six vocabulary words studied in this unit.

Example

Thank you for coming to our school. We are very interested in finding out more about _____ . Where do people of your religion go to worship?

Ⓑ GRAMMAR: Definitions with Definite / Indefinite Articles and Count / Non-Count Nouns

1 *Examine the sentences. Pay special attention to the underlined words. Discuss the questions on the next page with a partner.*

Islam is <u>a religion</u>.
Islam is <u>the religion</u> practiced by all believers in the Koran.

Islam and Hinduism are <u>religions</u>.
Islam and Hinduism are <u>the religions</u> practiced by the majority of people on the Indian subcontinent.

Honesty is a virtue.
The honesty of the man is his greatest virtue.

1. Which sentence means that Islam is one of many religions?

2. How do the meanings of the nouns change when *a* and *the* are used in the above sentences?

DEFINITE AND INDEFINITE ARTICLES

For Singular Count Nouns

Whether an article is needed before a singular noun depends on if the noun is a count noun or not. All singular count nouns must be preceded by either an **indefinite article** [*a(n)*] or a **definite article** [*the*]. You choose *a(n)* or *the* depending on the situation.

If you are describing "one of many," use the indefinite article *a(n)*.	Islam is **a religion.**
If you are describing "the specific one," use the definite article *the.* Imagine that the definite article, unlike the indefinite article, creates a limit and refers precisely to "a specific one."	Islam is **the religion** practiced by all believers in the Koran.

For Plural Count Nouns

The same concepts apply to count nouns in the plural. When it is obvious that the plural count noun does not represent all the nouns in a group, no article comes before it.

In the example sentence, we know that Islam and Hinduism are only two of many religions.	Islam and Hinduism are **religions.**
When information given in the sentence limits the plural count noun to a specific category, the definite article *the* is used.	Islam and Hinduism are **the religions** practiced by the majority of the people on the Indian subcontinent.

For Non-Count Nouns

Non-count nouns are always singular because they cannot be counted. ***Honesty, knowledge, wisdom, ignorance, information, evidence, research,*** and ***advice*** are examples of non-count nouns. No article comes before them when a specific reference is not being made. But when it is obvious that a specific reference is being made, the definite article is used.

In the example sentence "the man's honesty," and not just "honesty" in general, is the subject.	***The*** **honesty** of the man is his greatest virtue.

2 Work with a partner. Decide whether the singular nouns in the items below are count or non-count nouns. Circle your choice. Then write two sentences using each noun. For count nouns, show how both the definite and indefinite articles can be used. For non-count nouns, show how the indefinite article is omitted and the definite article can be used.

1. **purity**   Count / (Non-Count)

   Purity is a state sought by many religious people.

   The purity of his intentions was admired by all his friends.

2. **church**   (Count) / Non-Count

   The people saw a church in the distance.

   The church that they saw was the one that had just been built.

3. **belief**   Count / Non-Count

   _____

   _____

4. **spirituality**   Count / Non-Count

   _____

   _____

5. **ceremony**   Count / Non-Count

   _____

   _____

3 Work with a partner. In the text below about the Religious Society of Friends, a Protestant religion, add a definite or an indefinite article in the spaces provided if an article is necessary. If no article is necessary, put an **X** in the space.

_____ Religious Society of Friends, commonly referred to as
    1.

_____ Quakers, was founded in Northwest England in 1652 after
    2.

George Fox received _____ vision from God at a place called Pendle
                          3.

Hill. _____* vision helped Fox to realize that _____
         4.   **5.**

spiritual presence of God was _____ source of all religious truth.
                                    6.

Such _____ realization became the basis for _____
         7.   **8.**

_____

* Wherever a definite article is possible, you may also consider using demonstrative adjectives (*this, that, these, those*) if the noun to which they refer has been mentioned—as this one is—in a preceding sentence.

Quaker doctrine of the inner light. The Quakers believe that _____
9.

spirit of God enters _____ consciousness of both men and women
10.

equally and that it is evidenced in human beings' most honorable behavior.

The Quakers believe in _____ equality and in
11.

_____ pacifism, which involves an opposition to war and service in
12.

an army. Their insistence on _____ equality of all human beings has
13.

been demonstrated in their refusal to show any signs of respect such as removing

one's hat to _____ person regarded as _____ social
14.   15.

superior. It has also been evident in _____ leadership roles that
16.

Quaker women Susan B. Anthony and Lucretia Mott assumed in

_____ struggle for women's rights in _____ United
17.   18.

States.

Because of their beliefs, the Quakers faced many conflicts with the political

and religious authorities in England, and they were often persecuted as a result.

_____ founding in 1681 of _____ colony of
19.   20.

Pennsylvania by William Penn, _____ Quaker, provided
21.

_____ haven for many Quakers and exiles of other persecuted
22.

religious groups. Some Quakers also settled in Rhode Island, Massachusetts, and the

South. They were not welcome in the South because of their opposition to

_____ slavery. Nevertheless, despite their pacifist views, they played
23.

_____ major role during the American Civil War (1861–1865) by
24.

helping _____ African-American slaves make their way to
25.

_____ safety of the North.
26.

In this unit, you read an interview that Claudia Dreifus held with the Dalai Lama about his Buddhist beliefs, and you read a definition of the word "religion" from *Compton's Interactive Encyclopedia.*

You will **write a definition essay about a religion or philosophy.** You will explain its most important beliefs and practices.*

◀ PREPARE TO WRITE: Looped Freewriting

Looping is a prewriting technique that is particularly useful either for generating ideas when you already know what your topic is or for narrowing down your topic. To do looped freewriting, first freewrite on your topic. Then pick an interesting idea from your freewriting, and use this idea as the topic for a new freewriting. Repeat this procedure as many times as you need or want to.

1 *Think of a religion or philosophy. What are the defining beliefs in this religion or philosophy? What are its most important rituals, sacred objects, practices, and holidays? How does it manifest itself in the daily lives of those who follow it? How does it affect the goals and aspirations of its followers? What in particular do you find interesting about it? Freewrite about your topic, keeping the questions in mind.*

2 *Read your freewriting. Highlight the main ideas. Choose one highlighted idea and use this idea as a topic for a new freewriting. Take a few minutes to discuss this topic with another student. Then freewrite about the new topic. Repeat the procedure as long as you find it useful. Alternatively, return to your original freewriting, and choose another of your highlighted ideas to freewrite about.*

◀ WRITE: A Definition Essay

WHAT IS A DEFINITION ESSAY?

When writing a **definition essay,** the writer enters the world of classification. Through classification, we analyze a subject by dividing it into categories. First we find what the categories have in common—the "common characteristics"—then we seek to determine how the categories can be distinguished from one another.

This is precisely what a definition is: the process of putting nouns in categories or "classes." In a definition, we show how the item or concept to be defined is part of a broader category and how it is different from the other members of this category. This box gives examples.

---

*For Alternative Writing Topics, see page 146. These topics can be used in place of the writing topic for this unit or as homework. The alternative topics relate to the theme of the unit, but may not target the same grammar or rhetorical structures taught in the unit.

CLASSIFICATION

Member / Smaller Class	Larger Class	Specific Details
1. a rabbi	a religious leader	Judaism
2. an imam	a religious leader	Islam
3. rabbis and imams	religious leaders	

DEFINITIONS

1. A rabbi is a religious leader in the Jewish community.
2. An imam is a religious leader in the Islamic community.
3. Rabbis and imams are religious leaders.

RESEARCH AND PREPARATION

The author of the definition essay "Religion" went through a similar process of analysis throughout the research stage. After studying "all religions" and analyzing their "common characteristics" and differences, as in the classification box above, the writer was then ready to write an essay defining "religion."

ESSAY STRUCTURE

As is evident in Reading Two, the definition essay goes from the realm of the "indefinite" (a religion is . . . /religions are . . .) to the realm of the "definite" (the Muslim religion, unlike the Buddhist religion, is . . .). The writer first tells us what "all religions" have in common ("all religions attempt to give answers to basic questions"). Then, after interpreting the quotes by Paul Tillich and Martin Luther, the writer shows that the Western belief in one God is not shared by followers of the Eastern religions. The writer then refers to other "elements in common: rituals to perform, prayers to recite, holy days to keep." It is apparent from the way this brief excerpt unfolds that in the rest of the essay the writer will continue to show a pattern of common characteristics and specific differences.

In a definition essay, as in all other kinds of essays, the writer introduces examples, shows similarities and differences, uses quotations, and so on, in order to make sure the information is communicated as effectively as possible. The writer provides a thesis statement ("As a word religion is difficult to define, but as a human experience it seems to be universal."). The writer also permits his point of view to surface. For example, at the beginning of the essay "Religion," the statement "It is difficult to imagine what need there would be for religion in a world in which no one ever died or became ill" immediately familiarizes the reader with the writer's point of view. Thus, despite the difficult task of objective analysis that the writer must go through when preparing a definition essay, one thing is certain: The writer's point of view remains very important.

1 *Reread Reading Two and discuss the questions with a partner.*

    1. In the first paragraph, how does the writer "unify" all the religions in the world?

    2. In the second and third paragraphs, what does the writer do to come closer to a definition of the word *religion*?

    3. What kind of comparison do you find in the fourth paragraph?

    4. How is the fifth paragraph similar to the first paragraph?

2 *Practice creating definitions with a partner. Look at each word in the Member / Smaller Class column. Determine its larger class and give specific details if possible. Then write its definition in the space provided below. Use a dictionary if necessary.*

Member / Smaller Class	Larger Class	Specific Details
1. synagogue	a house of worship	Judaism
2. prayer		
3. sin		
4. prophet		
5. ritual		

Definitions

    1. synagogue: A synagogue is a house of worship where Judaism is practiced.

    2. prayer: _____

    3. sin: _____

    4. prophet: _____

    5. ritual: _____

3 *Now that you have carefully considered the main elements of a definition essay, write an essay that defines a religion or philosophy. Explain its most important beliefs and practices in a five-paragraph essay. Include an introductory paragraph, three body paragraphs, and a concluding paragraph. Plan your first draft by completing the outline below and on the next page.*

I. Introductory Paragraph

You may want to explain what the word "religion" or "philosophy" means to you and why you have chosen to write about a particular religion or philosophy.

Thesis Statement (in relation to the religion's or philosophy's beliefs and practices that you will describe)

_____

_____

II. Body Paragraphs

Topic Sentence:

_____

Supporting Details:

_____

_____

_____

Topic Sentence:

_____

Supporting Details:

_____

_____

_____

Topic Sentence:

_____

Supporting Details:

_____

_____

_____

III. Concluding Paragraph

_____

_____

_____

_____

4 *Use your outline and your notes from Prepare to Write, page 141, and Write, pages 141–145, to write your first draft.*

◀ **REVISE:** Providing Sufficient Supporting Details

The supporting details in your body paragraphs should give the reader complete information about the points you are making. Without the necessary examples, explanations, facts or reasons, the supporting details are not effective and the essay is weak.

1 *Read the body paragraph from an essay on Islam. Below are supporting details that should be integrated with the paragraph to make it a fuller and more complete paragraph. Read the supporting details and decide where they should be placed.*

(1) Islam's rituals and practices in daily life and at the mosque always make the individual feel that he or she is a part of a greater whole. (2) The call to prayer is the first thing that comes to mind. (3) This aspect of the lives of observant Muslims is indeed an affirmation of their devotion to their religion. (4) The gatherings with family and friends that take place throughout Ramadan are also noteworthy. (5) These intimate moments spent together make the sacrifices of the day seem worthwhile. (6) In addition, because all believers follow the same dietary laws each day, each one of them feels that he or she is a member of a larger group. (7) In practicing Islam, therefore, the individual is never alone because followers have the pleasure of belonging to a community of individuals with shared beliefs and values.

Working with a partner, place the appropriate numbers in the blanks:

Between sentences _____ and _____:
Muslims, for example, do not drink alcoholic beverages and do not eat pork.

Between sentences _____ and _____:
Five times a day the melodious sounds of the muezzin's voice call the faithful to prayer.

Between sentences _____ and _____:
After fasting from sunrise to sunset every day during Ramadan, observers enjoy having a dinner with loved ones in the evening.

2 *Look at the first draft of your essay. Are your supporting details effective? Do they include some reasons, facts, examples, and explanations that make your ideas clear?*

◀ **EDIT: Writing the Final Draft**

Write your final draft. Carefully edit it for grammatical and mechanical errors. Make sure you used some of the vocabulary and grammar from the unit. Use the checklist to help you write the final draft. Then neatly write or type your essay.

✔ **FINAL DRAFT CHECKLIST**

○ Does your essay have an effective introduction, three body paragraphs, and a conclusion?

○ Does the introduction clearly state what is going to be defined?

○ Does the thesis statement clearly announce the point of view?

○ Does each paragraph include sufficient support?

○ Does the concluding paragraph leave the reader with something to think about?

○ Is the essay edited for the use of definite and indefinite articles with count and non-count nouns?

ALTERNATIVE WRITING TOPICS

Write an essay on one of the topics. Remember to provide a thesis statement and sufficient explanations, examples, and support to develop your definition or essay. Use the vocabulary you have studied in the unit.

1. Many religions preach "love your fellow human beings." But what exactly is love? Write an essay that gives your definition of love.

2. George Bernard Shaw* wrote, "There is only one religion, though there are a hundred versions of it." Do you agree or disagree? Explain your answer.

3. How has religion influenced and affected your life? Write an essay defining the positive and/or negative effects of religion on various aspects of your life.

4. Would you marry someone of a different faith? Why or why not? What difficulties would you have to overcome, and what would be the positive or negative results?

5. Can a person be "religious" without following a formal religion? Answer the question with reference to the poem by Emily Dickinson** on the next page.

---

* *George Bernard Shaw* (1856–1950), Irish-born British playwright and author

** *Emily Dickinson* (1830–1886), American poet

Some keep the Sabbath going to church;
I keep it staying at home,
With a bobolink[1] for a chorister,[2]
And an orchard for a dome.

Some keep the Sabbath in surplice;[3]
I just wear my wings,
And instead of tolling the bell for church,
Our little sexton[4] sings.

God preaches,—a noted clergyman,—
And the sermon is never long;
So instead of getting to heaven at last,
I'm going all along.

                                        Emily Dickinson

[1] **bobolink:** an American songbird
[2] **chorister:** a singer in a church choir
[3] **surplice:** a loose, white robe worn by members of the clergy
[4] **sexton:** a church officer or employee who takes care of church property and, in some churches, rings the bell for services

RESEARCH TOPICS, see page 265.

UNIT
7
In Business, Size Matters

"WE'D LIKE to GET AWAY FROM IT ALL, BUT STAY WITHIN WALKING DISTANCE to A STARBUCKS."

SCHWADRon

①FOCUS ON THE TOPIC

A PREDICT

Discuss the humor of the cartoon with another student. What do you hope to find when you travel? Do you like the comfort of familiar surroundings or do you enjoy experiencing new things? Are there other stores besides Starbucks that you can now find all over the world? Why do people like to go to these stores?

149

Answer the marketing questionnaire. Share your responses in a small group.

MARKETING QUESTIONNAIRE: A Focus Group on Retail Sales

1. Do you go to chain stores like Printemps, Starbucks, Barnes and Noble, Takashimaya? About how many times a month? Which ones do you like best? What influences you? Price, selection, cleanliness, quality, style? Explain your answer.

_____
_____
_____

2. Have you been to multinational fast food stores in other countries? Are they always exactly the same or have you noticed some differences between countries?

_____
_____
_____

3. Multinational chain stores have caused controversy because some people believe that these stores promote the "globalization of culture" (the sameness or the Americanization of culture) all over the world. What do you think about this issue?

_____
_____
_____

4. Do you like to buy clothes or accessories with designer labels such as Armani and Coach? Why or why not?

_____
_____
_____

5. Do you prefer to shop for groceries in big megastores and supermarkets or do you like small neighborhood stores? Explain. Do you think that big stores can ever promote social responsibility to the community?

_____
_____
_____

Thank you for your input! Pick up your $5 coupon when you submit your answers.

C BACKGROUND AND VOCABULARY

Read the advice to future business owners below and on the next page. Try to understand from the context the meanings of the boldfaced words. Then look for their synonyms in the word box and write the correct forms on the lines following each piece of advice.

NOUNS	ADJECTIVES	VERBS	PHRASAL EXPRESSIONS
generosity	attentive (to)	~~be successful~~	get money with difficulty
hardship	uninteresting	fail	try to avoid
salary		go beyond, exceed	
		imagine, see in the future	
		keep	
		pressure those in power for support	

Advice on Starting a Business

- It's not easy to succeed in business. According to the U.S. Department of Commerce, out of every 10 small businesses that opened last year, only seven **prospered.** Only two will remain after five years.

  were successful

- How can you get ahead of the competition? First, you need to develop a business plan and clearly **envisage** how you will make money, what your expenses will be, and what will make your business unique or superior.

  _____

- After you develop a strong, thought-out plan, it's time to deal with the financial **burden** of starting a business. Best advice: use your own savings, or ask for a loan from the bank.

  _____

- It's better to **scrape together** your last cent than to borrow from family or friends. Even if you are able to pay them back, it won't be for years, and this can create conflict.

  _____

- If possible, take a partner. Many people find that a partner helps them **retain** their enthusiasm in difficult times and reminds them of what is important. No one can do everything.

- Location, location, location! Choose your community carefully and, once you are there, **steer clear** *of* any disputes dividing the people of the community. of

---

- Don't undercharge, but be flexible about pricing. You need to receive appropriate **compensation** for your work in order to make your business pay.

- Do workers expect health insurance, paid holidays, other benefits? A certain amount of **benevolence** in an employer helps to maintain staff loyalty and efficiency.

- Don't fail to ask for business benefits! **Lobby** for tax credits and zoning privileges with the local government.

- Be sure to maintain a positive image of your company. Mindless, **insipid** advertising can make clients turn away.

- Be **mindful** *of* the need to keep clear records and save important papers. Hire an accountant to help with contracts and taxes.

- Remember that running a business takes long hours, a willingness to learn, and lots of luck. Even the most enthusiastic business plans can **flop**.

- However, the rewards of success—being your own boss, **surpassing** your own expectations, feeling a sense of accomplishment—are more than worth the risks.

Before you read, discuss the question with a partner.

Is a CEO with a humanitarian vision more or less likely to succeed in business?

HOWARD SCHULTZ'S FORMULA FOR STARBUCKS

The Economist, Feb. 25, 2006

1 **STARBUCKS** knows it cannot ignore its critics. Anti-globalization protesters have occasionally trashed[1] its coffee shops. Posh[2] neighborhoods in San Francisco and London have resisted the opening of new branches, and the company is a favorite target of Internet critics. Mr. Schultz is watchful, but relaxed: "We have to be extremely **mindful** of the public's view of things….Thus far, we've done a pretty good job."

2 The reason, argues Mr. Schultz, is that the company has **retained** a "passion" for coffee and a "sense of humanity." Starbucks buys expensive beans and pays the owners—whether they are in Guatemala or Ethiopia—an average of 23% above the market price. A similar **benevolence** applies to company employees. Where other corporations try to eliminate the burden of employee benefits, Starbucks gives all employees working at least 20 hours a week a package that includes stock options ("Bean Stock") and comprehensive health insurance. For Mr. Schultz, raised in a Brooklyn housing project[3], this health insurance—which now costs the company more than coffee–is a moral obligation. At the age of seven, he came home to find his father, a truck driver, in a plaster cast, having slipped and broken an ankle. No insurance, no **compensation**, and then no job.

3 Hence what amounts to a personal crusade. Most of America's corporate chiefs **steer clear of** the sensitive topic of health care reform. Not Mr. Schultz. He makes speeches, **lobbies** politicians, and has even hosted a commercial-free hour of television, arguing for the reform

---

[1] **trashed:** completely destroyed
[2] **posh:** elegant, expensive (e.g., rich people live in "posh" neighborhoods)
[3] **housing project:** an apartment development subsidized by the government for low income families

(continued on next page)

of a system that he thinks is both socially unjust and a **burden** on corporate America. Meanwhile, the company pays its workers' premiums[4], even as each year they rise by double-digit percentages. The goal has always been "to build the sort of company that my father was never able to work for." By this he means a company that "remains small even as it gets big," treating its workers as individuals. Starbucks is not alone in its emphasis on "social responsibility," but the other firms Mr. Schultz cites off the top of his head—Timberland, Patagonia, Whole Foods—are much smaller than Starbucks, which has 100,000 employees and 35 million customers.

Why Size Matters

4   Indeed, size has been an issue from the beginning. Starbucks, named after the first mate in Herman Melville's *Moby Dick*,[5] was created in 1971 in Seattle's Pike Place market by two hippyish[6] coffee enthusiasts. Mr. Schultz, whose first "decent cup of coffee" was in 1979, joined the company in 1982 and then left it in 1985 after the founding trio, preferring to stay small, took fright at his vision of the future. Inspired by a visit to Milan in 1983, he had **envisaged** a chain of coffee bars where customers would chat over their expressos and capuccinos. Mr. Schultz set up a company he called "Il Giornale," which grew to a modest three coffee bars. Somehow **scraping together** $3.8 million dollars, he bought Starbucks from its founders in 1987.

5   Reality long ago **surpassed** the dream. Since Starbucks went public in 1992, its stock has soared by some 6,400%. The company is now in 37 different countries. China, which has over 200 stores, will be the biggest market after America, and Russia, Brazil, and India are all in line to be colonized over the next three years. The long-term goal is to double the number of American outlets to 15,000—not least by opening coffee shops along highways—and to have an equal number abroad.

6   No doubt the coffee snobs will blanch at[7] the prospect. Yet they miss three points. The first is that, thanks to Starbucks, today's Americans are no longer condemned to drink the **insipid**, over-percolated brew that their parents endured. The second, less recognized, is that because Starbucks has created a mass taste for good coffee, small, family-owned coffee houses have also **prospered**.

7   The most important point, however, is that Mr. Schultz's Starbucks cultivates a relation-ship with its customers. Its stores sell carefully selected (no hiphop, but plenty of world music and jazz) CD-compilations. Later this year, the store will promote a new film and take a share of the profits. There are plans to promote books. Customers can even pay with their Starbucks "Duetto" Visa card.

8   Apart from some health scare that would bracket coffee with nicotine, there is no obvious reason why Starbucks should fail, however ambitious its plans and however misconceived the occasional project (a magazine called "Joe" **flopped** after three issues, and the Mazagran soft drink, developed with Pepsi, was also a failure). Mr. Schultz says, "I think we have the license from our customers to do more." The key is that each Starbucks coffee house should remain "a third place," between home and work, fulfilling the same role as those Italian coffee houses that so inspired him 23 years ago.

---

[4] **premiums:** money amounts paid to maintain insurance policies
[5] *Moby Dick:* one of the most famous American novels, written by Herman Melville (1819–1891)
[6] **hippyish:** representative of the "hippy" generation of the 1960s; inclined to be unconventional
[7] **blanch at:** suddenly become "pale" because you are shocked

Answer each of the questions in one or two sentences. Share your answers with a partner.

1. How did the family background and experiences of CEO Howard Schultz influence his company's policies?

   _____

   _____

   _____

   _____

2. What are two ways that Howard Schultz puts "social responsibility" into practice?

   _____

   _____

   _____

   _____

3. How does size influence Starbuck's success?

   _____

   _____

   _____

   _____

4. What is the "coffee culture" of Starbucks?

   _____

   _____

   _____

   _____

All the statements below are false. Correct them in the space provided. Then compare answers with a partner.

1. Howard Schultz was the founder of Starbucks.

   Howard Shultz joined the company in 1982, 11 years after it was founded.

2. Since he joined the company, Schultz has been its unquestioned leader.

   _____

3. Most corporate leaders speak out on the topic of health care reform.

   _____

4. All workers in Starbucks stores get health insurance from the company.

   _____

5. Giving employees health benefits does not cost Schultz very much.

   _____

6. Starbucks pays $23 more than the market price for coffee beans.

   _____

7. The biggest market for Starbucks is China.

   _____

8. There are now 15,000 Starbucks outlets in the United States.

   _____

9. The name Starbucks comes from the name of one of the founders of the company.

   _____

10. Starbucks is the only U.S. corporation that emphasizes social responsibility.

    _____

◖ MAKE INFERENCES

*Read the statements. Mark them **T** (true) or **F** (false) based on information in the reading. Then write a sentence explaining your decision. Include points in the article that support your inference. Share your answers in a small group.*

Shultz believes that:

_____ 1. the company has not been responsive enough to public opinion.

   Support: _____

_____ 2. nothing is more important than maximizing profits.

Support: _____

_____ 3. most large corporations do not respect their employees enough.

Support: _____

_____ 4. you can maintain a feeling for the individual in a large company.

Support: _____

_____ 5. Starbucks is following an American tradition of quality coffee.

Support: _____

_____ 6. his customers want the coffee culture of Starbucks to be more like home.

Support: _____

◖ EXPRESS OPINIONS

Discuss the questions in a small group. Share your group's conclusions with the rest of the class.

1. Would you like to work for a company like Starbucks? How important would its social policies be in influencing your decision? What other factors would influence your decision?

2. How do Starbucks' social policies affect the atmosphere Schultz is trying to create in the stores? What kinds of movies and books do you think Schultz will sell in his stores?

3. Do you think businesses have a responsibility to their employees? Do employees have a responsibility to the company? How much responsibility?

B READING TWO: Swiping at Industry

1 _Discuss the question with a partner._

When you shop in a store or go to a restaurant, do you ever think about the employees and how well they are treated by the management?

Wal-Mart, the world's largest retailer, the second largest corporation, and America's largest private employer, has some 2,700 stores in 14 foreign countries. Founded in 1962 by Sam Walton, the son of a farmer, it is now run by his oldest son. All Sam Walton's children are billionaires, members of one of the world's richest families.

SWIPING AT INDUSTRY

Floyd Norris (*New York Times*, Sunday, August 20, 2006)

1 Wal-Mart is under attack for paying too little, providing benefits that are too small, and even exploiting illegal immigrants. Laws have been written with Wal-Mart in mind and more are being proposed. The company may not appreciate the honor, but its place in the political debate reflects its revolutionary effect on the American economy. Put simply, the big winners as the economy changes have often been scary to many, particularly to those with a stake in the old economic order being torn asunder. "Twice as many Americans shop in Wal-Mart over the course of a year as voted in the last Presidential election," said H. Lee Scott, Jr. the company's chief executive. Wal-Mart's success reflects its ability to charge less for a wide variety of goods. That arguably has reduced inflation and made the economy more efficient. It has introduced innovations in managing inventory and shipping goods.

2 But Wal-Mart's success has brought pain to others. The company has been blamed for destroying downtown as shoppers desert local merchants for the big-box store. Local newspapers lost some of their best advertisers. That may not influence news coverage, said Alex Jones, director of the Shorenstein Center on the Press, Politics, and Public Policy at Harvard, but "I don't think you will see many editorials blasting[1] the government for taking on[2] Wal-Mart." The company's ability to negotiate good deals from suppliers, some of which would probably go out of business if Wal-Mart walked away, has also created anxiety and resentment, both among the suppliers and among merchants who complain that Wal-Mart gets better deals.

3 It has infuriated unions by opposing the organization of its employees—even to the point of closing a Canadian store whose workers voted for a union. (The company said the closure was not related to that vote.) In some locations, unions have been forced to agree to reductions in wages and benefits at other stores because they must lower costs to compete with the giant.[3]

4 Opponents say some Wal-Mart employees are paid wages so low that they can still qualify for government Medicaid health insurance and call that a government subsidy[4] for a company that is forcing down pay for workers at other companies.

5 But the fact that Wal-Mart has more shoppers than any politician has voters shows that many of those workers—and many people higher on the income scale—find its prices irresistible. That group no doubt includes some of the company's critics.

6 Wal-Mart has been on the defensive in some legislative chambers. Maryland adopted legislation intended to force the company to spend more on health insurance, but that was struck down[5] by a federal judge. Chicago passed legislation to force the company to raise its wages.

7 Wal-Mart is one of the most successful companies in the world, but last week it reported a decline in quarterly profits for the first time in a decade, partly because of problems with its international business and partly because competitors are getting better.

---

[1] **blast:** criticize strongly

[2] **take on:** to fight against something

[3] In the United States, many supermarket employees belong to unions that negotiate collectively with employers for higher wages and better working conditions. Wal-Mart's competitors often have to cut wages in order to compete.

[4] **subsidy:** money that is paid by a government or organization to make prices lower

[5] **strike down** [a law]: a court decides not to allow it

2 *Complete the following sentences based on your understanding of the reading. When you have finished, compare your answers with a partner.*

1. Wal-Mart has been criticized for _____
   _____.

2. Wal-Mart has been able to achieve marketing success because _____
   _____.

3. Local newspapers do not support Wal-Mart because _____
   _____.

4. According to Wal-Mart's opponents, _____
   _____.

5. Wal-Mart may have to reconsider some of its policies because _____
   _____.

C INTEGRATE READINGS ONE AND TWO

◖ STEP 1: Organize

Work with a partner. Go back to the reading selections and fill in the chart with notes giving relevant facts for all the categories.

	STARBUCKS	WAL-MART
Company innovations and demand for the product		
Criticism of the company		
Response to the community and employees		
Financial success and size		

Work with a partner. You are a financial investment counselor. Your client is interested in investing in either Starbucks or Wal-Mart and has asked you for advice. Decide which company would be a better investment. Using the notes you have put together in Step 1, write a report explaining your decision.

You can start your report this way:

Dear Client,

You have expressed an interest in investing in one of two companies: either Starbucks or Wal-Mart. Please find below a report explaining why we feel _____ would be a better addition to your investment portfolio.

There are several reasons why we feel that _____ would be the better choice.

_____

_____

Although _____ is also an interesting company, we did not recommend it for the following reasons.

_____

_____

We hope that this analysis will be helpful to you in making your decision. Please feel free to consult with us at any time. When you have made your decision, we will be glad to help with your investment needs.

Sincerely,

Chandler and Smith
Investment Counselors

3 FOCUS ON WRITING

A VOCABULARY

REVIEW

Fill in the blanks with words from the box.

blasted	envisaged	prospering	steer clear
burden	lobbied	retain	subsidies
compensation	~~mindful~~	scraped together	take on

Corporate Responsibility: The Fall of Enron

How many business students still believe that "morality has nothing to do with business"? The story of Enron's fall from the seventh largest U.S. corporation to the largest corporate bankruptcy in U.S. history should make future MBAs more

_____mindful_____ of their responsibilities to the community.
1.

Enron, a Texas energy corporation, overstated its profits, hid its

_____ of debt, and became the symbol of a corporate culture of
2.

greed and corruption. One method Enron used was to make it seem that the

company was _____ by moving their losses to fake companies, which
3.

did not appear on the Enron accounts. The company was determined to

_____ its reputation on Wall Street (and a high price for its stock) at
4.

any cost.

One of Enron's worst schemes _____ aggressively using "mark-
5.

to-market" techniques. If the company made a deal that promised to earn $10

million in ten years, the executives would mark the money as profit already made.

These supposed and often imaginary profits were used as _____ to
6.

top executives in the form of huge bonuses.

Most shocking was the fact that Enron traders dared to _____
7.
the state of California. They created the California energy crisis to drive up the

price of energy, cutting off 30% to 50% of the state's power plants, and costing

California more than $6 billion in overcharges. Many people blame the California

crisis on the fact that the government in Washington took away the strict

regulations that used to control energy companies. Enron vigorously

_____ lawmakers for that deregulation.
8.

In the company's last year, Enron's executives were selling off their stock as fast

as they could to make sure that their personal finances would _____
9.
of the collapse. CEO Jeff Skilling made $200 million selling his stock, while at the

same time encouraging employees and workers not to sell. In its last days, the

corporate heads of the company _____ the last money they could
10.
find by stealing the pension fund of their employees. A lineman in Oregon, who

had been an Enron employee all his working life, thought he had an Enron

retirement fund worth $248,000 as _____ for his loyal service. After
11.
the collapse, it was worth about $1,200.

Twenty thousand workers lost their jobs, their pensions, and their savings.

When an employee, Sherrin Watkins, alerted the government, the press

_____ the company and the courts sent Jeff Skilling to prison.
12.

◖ EXPAND

1 *Read the sentences from the readings in this unit. Pay attention to the underlined expressions. Discuss with a partner what the sentences mean.*

1. "Most of America's corporate chiefs <u>steer clear</u> of the sensitive topic of health care reform." (Reading One)

2. "Starbucks is not alone in its emphasis on "social responsibility," but the other firms Mr. Schultz cites <u>off the top of his head</u>—Timberland, Patagonia, Whole Foods—are much smaller than Starbucks. . . ." (Reading One)

3. "Somehow <u>scraping together</u> $3.8 million dollars, he bought Starbucks from its founders in 1987." (Reading One)

4. "I don't think you will see many editorials blasting the government for <u>taking on</u> Wal-Mart." (Reading Two).

5. "Maryland adopted legislation intended to force the company to spend more on health insurance, but that was <u>struck down</u> by a federal judge." (Reading Two)

2 *Read the sentences using the expressions underlined in Exercise 1 and related expressions. Discuss their meanings with a partner.*

1. **steer clear / steering committee / steer**

   a. Our company should STEER CLEAR of all wrongdoing.
   b. The STEERING COMMITTEE of our firm has decided to hire four more office employees.
   c. If we are not careful, he will STEER this company in the wrong direction with those dangerous policies.

2. **off the top of his head / top an offer / top-down / top-drawer**

   a. The company director was able to tell us their profit statistics right OFF THE TOP OF HIS HEAD.
   b. We can TOP THAT OFFER by $500 a share.
   c. This was a TOP-DOWN company, where ordinary workers had no say in policy decisions.
   d. The law firm deals only with TOP-DRAWER clients, and provides specialized advice for their lifestyle.

3. **scrape together / scrape / scrape the bottom of the barrel / scrape the surface**

   a. We'll have to SCRAPE TOGETHER every last dime we own to make the debt payments.
   b. This employee is a troublemaker and gets into too many SCRAPES with other employees.
   c. You're SCRAPING THE BOTTOM OF THE BARREL when you bring up such a ridiculous argument.
   d. Your report barely SCRAPED THE SURFACE of the many issues involved in this sale.

4. **take on / take care of / take over**

   a. We shouldn't TAKE ON such a large and powerful opponent.
   b. The client is missing a delivery. Please TAKE CARE OF this problem as soon as possible.
   c. The Midtown Bank TOOK OVER Cedars Trust in 2007.

5. **strike down / strike out on one's own / on strike**

   a. The judge decided to STRIKE DOWN the city law against globalization protestors because it went against the Constitution's guarantee of free speech.
   b. I didn't want to work for someone else any more, so I decided to STRIKE OUT ON MY OWN.
   c. When union workers are not satisfied with their working conditions, they can go out ON STRIKE.

3 On a separate piece of paper, explain the meaning of the expression. Compare your answers with a partner's. Look up the expressions in the dictionary to confirm your definitions.

1. steer clear
2. steering committee
3. steer
4. off the top of his head
5. top an offer
6. top-down
7. top-drawer
8. scrape together
9. scrape

10. scrape the bottom of the barrel
11. scrape the surface
12. take on
13. take care
14. take over
15. strike down
16. strike out on one's own
17. on strike

CREATE

Howard Schultz of Starbucks and Rob Walton, the Chairman of the Board of Wal-Mart, have come to the campus for a discussion about business. Write the script for this interview. Use at least eight of the expressions listed below.

benevolent	lobby	steer
blasted	mindful	steer clear of
burden	prosper	surpass
compensation	retain	take care of
envisage	scrape the bottom of the barrel	take on
flop	scrape together	

INTERVIEWER: Thank you both for coming here today to speak to our students. Mr. Schultz, you are the leader of a megacompany with 100,000 employees and more than 35 million customers. Yet you say that your company has to be MINDFUL of its customers and "think small." What do you mean?

SCHULTZ: _____

_____

INTERVIEWER: What about you, Mr. Walton? You are the CEO of Wal-Mart, the world's largest retailer. How does size matter for your company?

WALTON: _____

_____

INTERVIEWER: Mr. Schultz, you are known as a generally BENEVOLENT employer. Can you explain to us about "socially responsible business"?

SCHULTZ: _____

_____

B GRAMMAR: Specific Uses of Infinitives and Gerunds

1 *Examine the underlined words in the sentences and discuss the questions with a partner.*
- Wal-Mart has the ability <u>to charge</u> less for a wide variety of goods.
- Wal-Mart is committed to <u>introducing</u> innovations in inventory management.

1. What form is underlined in the first sentence?

2. What form is underlined in the second sentence?

3. Why are these forms used?

THE INFINITIVE

The **infinitive** (**to + verb;** *to play, to watch*) is commonly used:

1. When it answers the questions "Why?" or "For what purpose?"
   - Schultz bought Starbucks **to get** Americans used to good coffee.

2. In certain verb + infinitive + object patterns
   - Employees sometimes **try to force** Wal-Mart to accept a union.

3. After many adjectives
   - A socially responsible company is more **willing to spend** money for employees' health benefits.

4. After certain expressions

   Many expressions are followed by the infinitive when "*to do* what?" is the answer that the infinitive gives the reader or the listener. In the sentence "He had the opportunity to work in another country," the infinitive *to work* tells us "what" he had "the opportunity *to do*." Here is a list of expressions that follow this pattern:

be ready	**have a tendency**
be required	**have the time**
have the ability / have an inability	**have the will**
have the courage	**it is difficult**
have the opportunity	**it is easy**
have the option	**it is economical**
have the right	**it is practical**

The **gerund** (a verb form ending in *-ing* used as a noun; *playing, watching*) is commonly used:

1. After such verbs as *avoid, consider, enjoy, favor, include, involve, spend*

   - Wal-Mart should *consider* **changing** its salary scale if it wants to receive less criticism about its policies.

   - Starbucks now *spends* a lot of time **promoting** films and books.

2. After all prepositions (for example, ***about, from, in, to, with***)

   - The CEO was concerned *about* **making** a profit.

3. After certain expressions

   Many expressions are followed by the gerund because they end with prepositions (for example, "have a commitment *to going*," "be concerned *about going*," "be interested *in going*"). The rule regarding the use of gerunds after all prepositions is simple to apply if you remember that the preposition is "a part of" the expression. Thus, in the sentence at the beginning of this section, "He was committed to *going* back to school," the gerund (*going*) is used because the *to* is part of the expression.

   Because it is difficult to remember which expressions end in prepositions, familiarize yourself with the most common expressions that are followed by the gerund. Here is a list:

be accustomed to	**have (no) difficulty (in)***
be committed to / have a commitment to	**have (no) experience (in)***
be concerned about	**have (no) luck (in)***
be dedicated to	**have (no) trouble (in)***
be devoted to	**insist on**
be interested in	**look forward to**
be involved in	**object to**
be responsible for / have the responsibility of	**plan on**
choose between / among	**succeed in**
deal with	

   *The preposition *in* is implied. You need not use it; in fact, it is better usage to leave it out.

2 *Read the letter addressed to a management trainee in a large company. Underline the gerunds and the infinitives first. Then list the verbs or expressions that take the infinitive and those that take the gerund.*

Dear Ms. Rachel Smith,

   You have been working with our company for two years. During that time, you have provided excellent service to the firm. We are interested in <u>maximizing</u> the potential of our most promising new recruits. It is my pleasure to inform you that you have been chosen to receive one of our management trainee scholarships. We would like you to consider applying to an MBA program dedicated to preparing accounting and financial officers.

We are committed to offering you a full tuition grant for the MBA program of your choice. Because you already have experience working in the business world, we are sure that you will make the most of this opportunity to improve your understanding of the financial field. Please consider applying to schools that offer evening and weekend classes in our area. Prior to entering any program, you will need the approval of our Board of Directors, which reserves the right to advise you on these questions.

We hope you will accept our offer, and we look forward to hearing from you soon.

Sincerely,
Jonathan Weiss
Management Trainee Program

Expressions with Infinitives

1. _____
2. _____
3. _____

Expressions with Gerunds

1. _interested in maximizing_
2. _____
3. _____
4. _____
5. _____
6. _____
7. _____

3 *Using the expressions that are listed on pages 165 and 166, and that appear in the previous exercise, write seven sentences about why you would or would not like to have a career in business.*

1. _____
2. _____
3. _____

4. _____

5. _____

6. _____

7. _____

4 *Complete the essay with either the gerund or the infinitive of the verb in parentheses.*

Introductory Paragraph

The Advantages and Disadvantages of Private Business Schools

Students thinking of _____ business careers are required

_____ four to five years of work experience in the business world
2. (have)
(1. (pursue))

before they begin an M.B.A. program. When they are ready _____ to
3. (return)

school, it is important for them _____ thorough research on each
4. (do)

school that interests them. Because M.B.A. candidates in the United States can

choose between _____ at some excellent public and private
5. (study)

institutions, part of the decision-making process involves _____
6. (decide)

whether to enroll in a private or public institution. M.B.A. candidates who plan

_____ at large multinational corporations should make every effort
7. (work)

to attend a top private school. Despite the high tuition costs of private business

schools, they provide more competitive learning environments and more job

placement opportunities in the private sector.

Body

The disadvantages of private institutions are easy _____.
8. (identify)

Although private schools meet the needs of students who hope

_____ for large multinational corporations, what they offer comes at
9. (work)

a great cost. The price of a two-year program at a top private business school can

cost more than $100,000, while an M.B.A. program in a public school costs less

than half that amount. There is no doubt that the very high costs of private

business schools discourage many M.B.A. candidates from _____.
10. (apply)

Being faced with such a large new debt, when in most cases they have only started to pay back their college loans, is seen as a definite disadvantage despite the advantages of a competitive private school.

Competition attracts the best students, defined as those with the highest test scores and the most impressive portfolios. These students compete

_____ at the most expensive private business schools. Some of the
11. (enroll)

top private schools can review as many as 8,000 applications for admission in a given year, but no more than 15 percent of the applicants are usually admitted. Connected to this more competitive feature of the student profile is the diversity of the student population. Private institutions devote a lot of time and energy to

_____ a diverse representation of students from all geographic areas
12. (select)

of the United States and the world. This international "flavor" is also reflected in the

fact that private school students have the opportunity _____ in a
13. (participate)

great number of study abroad and internship programs with multinational corporations. Studying in a competitive atmosphere with the brightest students, both male and female, from many diverse backgrounds provides private business students with valuable insights and international experience.

These diverse insights and experiences are appreciated by the multinational

corporations who favor _____ at the top private schools. In a given
14. (recruit)

year, hundreds of recruiters come to private school campuses _____
15. (interview)

students. Not only do private school students have superb job placement opportunities, but they often receive higher paying job offers: The average starting salary for private school students can go as high as $150,000.

Conclusion

Studying for an M.B.A. degree at a top private school provides students with

definite advantages. Students who decide not _____ a private
16. (select)

institution because of the cost alone may be making a serious mistake because they may be able to earn back the initial investment quickly and have a higher-paying job at the same time. After a few years of _____ for a large

17. (work)

multinational corporation, their loans will be paid back and the advantages of their choice of a private business school will become clear.

C WRITING

In this unit, you read articles discussing two well-known businesses, Starbucks and Wal-Mart.

You will **write an essay in response to this question: What are the advantages and disadvantages of large chain stores and multinational corporations?***

PREPARE TO WRITE: Brainstorming

1 *Work in groups. In two separate columns, write down notes that point to the advantages and disadvantages of chain stores and large multinational companies. Use examples from the two readings as well as your own ideas.*

Advantages	Disadvantages
1. can offer many jobs (100,000 in Starbucks)	1. get trashed by anti-globalization activists
2. can help change the culture (support for national health care like Starbucks)	2. often pay employees too little; benefits too small
3.	3.
4.	4.
5.	5.
6.	6.
7.	7.
8.	8.

*For Alternative Writing Topics, see page 175. These topics can be used in place of the writing topic for this unit or as homework. The alternative topics relate to the theme of the unit, but may not target the same grammar or rhetorical structures taught in the unit.

2 *Examine your lists to identify common categories to which your thoughts belong. Group the various ideas under their respective categories. Try to find at least four categories.*

1. Making the economy more efficient
2. _____
3. _____
4. _____

◖WRITE: An Essay Showing Advantages and Disadvantages

1 *Reread the essay on pages 168–170 and discuss the questions with a partner.*

1. What is the writer's purpose in this essay?

2. Underline the thesis statement. According to the thesis statement, will the writer's focus in the essay be on the advantages or on the disadvantages?

3. Which body paragraph(s) deals with the advantages, and which body paragraph(s) deals with the disadvantages?

4. In the body paragraphs, what kind of support does the writer provide?

5. How does the writer show the logical connection between one topic and another?

6. Is the message in the concluding paragraph expected or unexpected? Why?

PURPOSE OF ESSAYS SHOWING ADVANTAGES AND DISADVANTAGES

Essays about advantages and disadvantages are similar to comparison and contrast essays, but there are some special points to remember.

- The aim of this kind of essay is to persuade, not simply to inform. You should *not* merely list the positive and negative aspects of the subject in a neutral way. You should take a stand.

- Your thesis statement should therefore take a clear position: Do the advantages outweigh the disadvantages, or are the disadvantages more important than the advantages?

- If the thesis statement states that the advantages are more important, then the body of the essay will devote relatively more space to the advantages. Conversely, if the thesis is focused on the disadvantages, that aspect will take up relatively more space in the essay than the advantages.

- The essay must provide enough support for the thesis so that the main points will be clearly justified and explained. As in all essays, the use of good transitions between the points under discussion ensures this clarity.

(continued on next page)

> **Thesis Statement**
>
> As you learned in Unit 2, the thesis statement communicates the main idea of the essay. It reflects the writer's focus and point of view, attitude, or opinion, and it also forecasts which aspects of the subject the writer will discuss to support the thesis in the body of the essay.

2 *Examine the thesis statement from the essay on pages 168–170. Answer the questions.*

Despite the high tuition costs of private business schools, they provide more competitive learning environments and more job placement opportunities in the private sector.

1. Is this an adequate thesis statement for an advantages and disadvantages essay? Why or why not?

   _____

   _____

2. The thesis tells the reader that the body paragraphs of the essay will deal with certain subjects. What are they?

   a. _____

   b. _____

   c. _____

3 *In your notebook, write an outline for an essay showing the advantages and disadvantages of large chain stores and large multinational corporations. Follow the steps:*

   • Use the guidelines for point-by-point outline organization on page 117 (Unit 5).

   • Write your thesis statement.

4 *Using what you have learned about writing advantages and disadvantages essays, write an essay that responds to this question:* **What are the advantages and disadvantages of large chain stores and large multinational corporations?** *Refer to the work you did in Prepare to Write and Write to write your first draft.*

◖ REVISE: Using Transitional Sentences

> **Transitional sentence**s show the logical connection between topics under discussion. Transitions may be needed within a paragraph ("internal transitions") or between paragraphs. When a transitional sentence connects the ideas of one body paragraph to the ideas of another body paragraph, it can be placed at the beginning of a paragraph (as a topic sentence) or at the end of a paragraph (as a concluding sentence). Transitions are especially important in essays showing advantages and disadvantages because the reader must be able to notice the shift between positive and negative factors.

1 *Go back to the essay on pages 168–170. First underline the transitional sentences connecting the body paragraphs in the text. Then underline the internal transitional sentence in body paragraph 2.*

2 *These two paragraphs come from the first draft of an essay on "The Advantages and Disadvantages of Being Self-Employed." Important transitional sentences are missing. Working with a partner, review the list of choices on the next page and mark them ✓ (acceptable) or ✗ (unacceptable). There can be more than one "acceptable" sentence in each set of choices. Discuss your answers with a partner.*

> Being self-employed permits a certain freedom that supports the development of a free spirit. Because there is no one in authority telling the self-employed person what to do, he or she enjoys a lot of independence. With independence, the individual is more willing to take risks. If a mistake is made, it is not the end of the world; something valuable will be learned from the experience. This passion for experimentation leads to creative undertakings. **(1)** _____
>
> _____. If he or she does not allow room or time for creativity as the business evolves, there will be no opportunity to place an original stamp on the product that is being marketed. Since the self-employed person has agreed to assume sole responsibility for his or her fate, creativity is an essential ingredient for future success.
>
> **(2)** _____
>
> _____. Because the self-employed person is at the same time both employer and employee, there is no safety net to "catch" him or her if he or she falls, and the financial and psychological stress that may be experienced can be a true test of nerves. That is why the individual must be assertive and yet humble enough to seek advice from financial consultants and mental health care professionals in order to be able to deal with these potential problems. **(3)** _____
>
> _____. Good character in an individual can be seen in his or her strong personality, ethics, positive self-image,

willingness to bend and appreciate the value of other people's ideas, along with the determination to work hard and achieve success. Only someone with many such qualities can effectively respond to the challenges that come with being self-employed.

1. Choices for Internal Transition of Paragraph 1

_____ a. Linked therefore to the self-employed person's independence is the individual's great potential for creativity.

_____ b. Can anyone doubt that creativity is the next step on the path to success in business dealings?

_____ c. Whether or not these creative urges come to fruition, they are an essential ingredient in success.

2. Choices for Topic Sentence of Paragraph 2

_____ a. Another undeniable problem facing an entrepreneur in the creation of a startup company is the financial burden.

_____ b. But creativity is not enough; a future businessperson must be strong in many other ways.

_____ c. In spite of the benefits that accompany independence and creativity, we must not forget that a self-employed person must cope with a great financial and psychological burden.

3. Choices for Internal Transition of Paragraph 2

_____ a. In this sense, going into business for yourself is a true test of character.

_____ b. Undoubtedly, the ability to respond to these stresses requires many positive character traits.

_____ c. Even though independence is a great benefit, being in business is very stressful.

3 Look at the draft of your essay. Does it have transitional sentences to guide the reader from one "topic" to another? If not, revise your essay accordingly.

◀ **EDIT: Writing the Final Draft**

Write your final draft. Carefully edit it for grammatical and mechanical errors. Make sure you used some of the vocabulary and grammar from the unit. Use the checklist to help you write the final draft. Then neatly write or type your essay.

✓ FINAL DRAFT CHECKLIST

- ○ Does your essay have an effective introduction, three or more body paragraphs, and a strong conclusion?
- ○ Is it obvious from the thesis statement whether the advantages outweigh the disadvantages or the disadvantages outweigh the advantages?
- ○ Does the thesis statement forecast the specific topics that are to be covered in the body paragraphs of the essay?
- ○ Do the paragraphs have transitional sentences that effectively show the reader the logical connection between topics?
- ○ Are gerunds and infinitives used correctly?
- ○ Have new vocabulary and expressions been used in the essay?

ALTERNATIVE WRITING TOPICS

Write an essay on one of the topics. Remember to provide a thesis statement and sufficient explanations, examples, and support to develop your main idea. Pay special attention to transitions. Use the vocabulary and grammar from the unit.

1. Write an essay showing the advantages and disadvantages of starting your own business rather than going to work for a company. Remember to take a stand on the issue.

2. Imagine the perfect career pattern for yourself. Would it involve working for several different companies, or for only one company during the course of your career? Would it involve building your own company? If so, what business would you create? Explain the steps you would take to create it.

3. Why is business important for the life of a country? What sacrifices, if any, must a country make so that businesses can thrive? You can use the history of a country you know to answer this question.

4. Do successful businesses have any civic responsibility? Do they have a responsibility to "give back" to the community in terms of jobs, contributions to social causes such as homelessness, medical research, the arts, the environment, and education? Why or why not?

5. Do research on some of the companies mentioned in this unit such as Starbucks, Wal-Mart, Patagonia, Timberland, Whole Foods, and Enron, or on companies in other countries. Compare their ideas on socially responsible business practices including how they treat employees, community needs, ecological concerns, etc.

6. How do you balance the demands of career and family? Does one need to be sacrificed for the other?

RESEARCH TOPICS, see page 265.

UNIT 8 When the Soldier Is a Woman . . .

1 FOCUS ON THE TOPIC

A PREDICT

What do you think women's lives are like in the military? Write a list of the problems you think women might face in the armed forces. Then make a list of the satisfactions you think they might find in military work. Compare your lists with a partner's.

How do you feel about women in the military? First answer the survey individually. Then work in groups of four or five people. Tally the answers from your group and discuss the reasons for each person's opinions.

WOMEN IN THE MILITARY:
WHAT SHOULD THEIR ROLE BE?

		Your Answer (Circle One)	Group Tally
1.	Women should be allowed to serve in the military.	Agree ____ Disagree ____	Agree ____ Disagree ____

Explain your answer: _____

_____

2.	Like men, women should be allowed to fight the enemy in direct combat.	Agree ____ Disagree ____	Agree ____ Disagree ____

Explain your answer: _____

_____

3.	Women with children should not be allowed to serve in the military.	Agree ____ Disagree ____	Agree ____ Disagree ____

Explain your answer: _____

_____

4.	Women officers should never command men.	Agree ____ Disagree ____	Agree ____ Disagree ____

Explain your answer: _____

_____

5.	Both women and men should have the right to refuse military service if it goes against their beliefs.	Agree ____ Disagree ____	Agree ____ Disagree ____

Explain your answer: _____

_____

C BACKGROUND AND VOCABULARY

Complete the paragraphs with words from the box. Choose synonyms for the words in parentheses.

ammunition	civilian	dreadful	missions
battalions	convoys	~~enlisted personnel~~	sparse
casualties	displayed	maintained	

Women have served in the American military for most of the last 100 years, mainly in secondary positions: as nurses, supply workers, and transport personnel. During World War II, some women flew Air Force planes as test pilots, trainers, and transport auxiliaries providing additional help. Some were officers, but most were

_____enlisted personnel_____. Their contributions were recognized and
    1. (not officers)

_____ to the nation in the Memorial to Women in Military
    2. (exhibited)

Service for America at Arlington National Cemetery in Washington, D.C.

During the Vietnam War in the 1960s and 1970s, only one in 70 American soldiers was a woman. In the 1990s, however, the figure was about one in nine. In the first Gulf War, women participated in the military, repairing tanks, flying

supplies, driving _____, doing intelligence work, flying
    3. (armed groups of vehicles)

helicopters, working with computers, and training to deal with

_____. Part of the reason for this greater participation of
    4. (the wounded or dead)

women is that technological advances replaced purely physical strength in many military operations, allowing women to fill new roles in jobs where their

participation had been very _____. In addition, in an effort to
    5. (small)

attract new candidates to the all-volunteer armed forces, the Army, Navy, and Air Force offer educational opportunities and significant financial incentives so that

troop strength can be _____ at the necessary levels.
    6. (kept)

When the Soldier Is a Woman . . . **179**

By the first decade of the 21st century, the number of women in the American military was almost one in seven. More than 160,500 American women soldiers served in Iraq, Afghanistan, and the Middle East from 2003 to 2007. Although they were not allowed to join the ground combat infantry or armor and field artillery units in wartime, women served on combat ships, flew combat

_____, and conducted door-to-door searches. They served in
    7. (assignments, tasks)

_____ alongside the men and faced the same dangers. Four
    8. (groups of soldiers)

hundred fifty women soldiers were wounded in Iraq and 71 died, many from enemy

_____ in a struggle with no clearly defined front. All the
    9. (bullets, bombs)

soldiers including the women, saw the _____ toll the fighting
                                       10. (terrible)

took on the _____ population.
           11. (nonmilitary)

② FOCUS ON READING

Ⓐ READING ONE: Women at War

List three topics that you would expect to read about in these letters written to Glamour magazine from American women soldiers who participated in the first Gulf War. Compare notes with a partner. After you finish the reading, check to see if your predictions were correct.

1. _____

2. _____

3. _____

Women at War

from *Glamour*

Women at war—what is it like? Via an ad in the military newspaper *Stars and Stripes*, *Glamour* magazine asked American women serving in the first Gulf War to write and describe their day-to-day life. What did they think about, dream about, worry about? Here are some of the letters received.

Letter 1

1 I am a First Lieutenant serving with coalition forces in the Middle East. Most of all I am afraid my husband will find out that I am within range of Iraq's Scud missiles. I don't want him to worry about me. Of course, I worry about chemical attacks. You move as fast as you can, but if you get the shakes during a red alert, you can't put on your GCE [ground crew ensemble]. You can't let the fear get to you.

2 I am a weather forecaster in charge of two men, both staff sergeants. Our job is to bring accurate weather information to air crews. Sounds easy, yes? No! **Sparse** satellite data really hurts, and the weather during the late winter/early spring is subject to rapid change.

3 I dream of not having to walk 100 yards to the shower. I dream of taking a long, warm bath. And wearing a dress would be marvelous. Also, eating at certain favorite restaurants in Oregon, my home state.

4 I write home all that I want to remember. The collection will be my "Desert Diary" to read to my husband and children on cold winter nights.

Thyra A. Bishop

Letter 2

5 I am an E-6 [Petty Officer First Class] in the Navy and the mother of two: a three-year-old boy and an eleven-month-old girl. It breaks my heart to be here, so far away from them. I put their pictures up on the wall in my room. I can barely look at them without crying, though. But I am fortunate because they are being very well cared for in the loving hands of their father. When all the death and destruction of this war starts to get me down, all I have to do is go to any of my fellow service members and see all the mail they have received from people they don't even know, the caring and concerned people of the U.S.A. When I think of all the yellow ribbons worn and all the American flags so proudly **displayed**, I get a great feeling in my heart.

Dawn Bell

Letter 3

6 I am a Second Lieutenant in the U.S. Army. I'm the executive officer [second in command] of a military intelligence headquarters company. I'm one of 17 females in a company of 127 personnel. My **battalion** flies aerial intelligence **missions**.

7 I keep myself busy by writing my fiancé, Jeff Devine, daily and planning our December seventh wedding.

8 My father is a Methodist minister in Appleton, Wisconsin. My parents are against the war and have marched for peace. They say that if the church doesn't stand up for peace, who will? That may seem strange to some people, as their only daughter is in Saudi Arabia. But the military paid for my college education, and I'm repaying that debt.

Jennifer Freese

Letter 4

9 Many people are curious to know how it is here for us females. Usually they ask the officers rather than the enlisted soldiers. **Enlisted personnel** are the backbone of the Army—we're the ones who get our hands dirty.

10 I am 24 years old, and I've been in the Army for almost two years. My biggest fear is being captured. We were told that if captured, we would be raped, tortured, and murdered. I could only say that they would have to murder me. I can't give up my ground to anyone.

(continued on next page)

11   I sometimes dream of shallow things like getting my hair and nails done or going shopping. When I see the natives and how poor they are, it hurts to see how I take some things for granted.

12   You do things here that you would never before dream of doing. If you're in a **convoy** that will not make many stops, you learn how to urinate in a Pringles or Planters can in a moving vehicle. It's really difficult, but you develop great balance.

Jillian Manderville

Letter 5

13   I am a 27-year-old soldier in the U.S. Army. Being in a Patriot [missile] unit, we have to move quite frequently. I saw torched bunkers, vehicles, shells from **ammunition**. It was truly unreal. The Iraqi soldiers were barely living from day to day on beans and rice. You could tell that they weren't expecting such an early ground war because they left their boots behind. You could also tell that an Allied tank not only shot at the bunker but ran right over the top of it. That is the price these soldiers had to pay. The thoughts that ran through me almost made me cry.

14   I honestly don't believe I'll continue my career in the Army, not because of the war but because the Army is tough and if you don't get tough with it and become strong, you are lost. I've learned to respect others, to survive in whatever conditions arise.

15   For those women who think that the service is for them, please think seriously about it. It's not a picnic. Getting up at 3 A.M. to move is scary, and deep down you know you have to go on and get it over with. I feel truly thankful to have made it through this war safely.

Carla Yvette Henry

Letter 6

16   I've been here for a month, and I really wish I were back home. I miss my daughters Kimberly and Candice. There are six of us on the midnight to 0800 shift. It's kind of lonely, but we always hope and pray that nothing happens because we're all working **Casualties**, which deals with personnel who are hurt, injured, or dead. We work eight hours a day, seven days a week. Before, it was twelve hours a day, but they worried about our getting burned out. The stress level in this place is very high.

17   They have just opened the sports complex so we can get a little recreation. The females can only go from 1300 to 1500 hours. We have to enter through the back door; the front door is for males. We're not allowed to drive **civilian** cars, only military vehicles, so to get anywhere they have public transportation for our use.

Barbara Ann Malone-Verduin

Letter 7

18   I am a sergeant in the Army. My job is equipment, records, and parts specialist. I make sure that equipment and parts are **maintained** properly and are at a fully mission-capable status.

19   My most **dreadful** moment was collecting two dead Iraqi soldiers and putting them in body bags. Normally, this wouldn't have been my mission. A crew who did this line of work was not available, so my unit asked for volunteers. I turned white as a ghost when I was asked to volunteer. But I felt someone should care for them properly instead of just letting them rot away as soldiers missing in action. At least their families would know their whereabouts. If I had died in this war, I would have wanted people to take care of my body. Despite the fact that they were the enemy, they were still human beings fighting this crazy war, who were just as frightened as all of us.

Lisa Richards

Letter 8

20   When Iraq invaded Kuwait on August 2, my unit—the 11th Air Defense Artillery Brigade at Fort Bliss, Texas—was put on alert. I was scared, not of the war, but because I didn't want to leave my family behind. Now it's two o'clock in the morning, 60 miles from the Iraqi border, and all I think about is whether I'm going to get out of here alive and be with my family again.

21   This is one of the hardest things I'll ever have to face. Sometimes when I'm lying on my cot I find myself gazing up at the ceiling, and I start crying because my son is now walking and running on his own and I'm not there to see it. He's growing up without me. But at least he's safe with his dad. (My husband got out of the Army in June of 1990, so he started playing the role of house-husband while I worked, paid the bills, and was still a mom.) The only things my son and I have together right now are the few opportunities I get to talk to him on the phone and the letters my husband writes.

22   I know every mother over here feels just as I do about being away from her children. My friend has five children; her husband is also at

home taking care of the kids, and she misses them dearly.

23 We try not to think about home too much, so we keep busy. Sometimes we don't even know what day it is. I just know it's been five months since I've been able to hold my baby and my husband—five months since someone told me he loved me—and still we don't know how much longer we will be here. A few months, maybe a year.

24 But we are strong, we are survivors. We are here to fight if we have to, to keep the rest of the world, especially U.S. citizens, from harm. When I do get out of here, I'll be able to pass down war stories to my son and be proud of them. The fact that I am an American woman in a male-dominated country and am being given the chance to fight for what I believe in shows our women have come a long way.

Veronica Martin

Letter 9

25 I think if you talk to women in the military, we see ourselves as soldiers. We don't really see it as man versus woman. What I'm doing is no greater or less than the man who is flying next to me or in back of me.

Army Major Marie T. Rossi
Aviator and soldier,
daughter and wife.
Killed in the Persian Gulf.

◖ READ FOR MAIN IDEAS

*Read the statements. Based on the reading, write **T** (true) or **F** (false) next to each statement.*

_____ 1. None of the women were worried about appearing unfeminine.

_____ 2. All the women decided to remain in the military after the war.

_____ 3. The women were afraid of the enemy and wanted revenge.

_____ 4. The military separated the men and women soldiers in their work teams.

_____ 5. All the women were patriotic.

◖ READ FOR DETAILS

Use the letter writers' exact words (with quotation marks) to explain their thoughts on the subjects. Also, identify the letter writer by name.

1. **Thinking about Fear**

   Choose direct quotes from letters 1, 4, 5, and 8 on this subject.

   a. *"Of course, I worry about chemical attacks." "You can't let the fear get to you." Thyra Bishop*

   b. _____

   c. _____

   d. _____

2. **Thinking about the Enemy**

   Choose direct quotes from letters 4, 5, and 7 on this subject.

   a. _____

   b. _____

   c. _____

3. **Discussing Their Jobs as Officers**

   Choose direct quotes from letters 1 and 3 on this subject.

   a. _____

   b. _____

4. **Writing about Discrimination against Women**

   Choose direct quotes from letters 6, 8, and 9 on this subject.

   a. _____

   b. _____

   c. _____

5. **Thinking of Their Children Back Home**

   Choose direct quotes from letters 2, 6, and 8 on this subject.

   a. _____

   b. _____

   c. _____

6. **Thinking about Their Husbands**

   Choose direct quotes from letters 1, 2, and 8 on this subject.

   a. _____

   b. _____

   c. _____

In a small group, review the letters in Reading One, and evaluate how dedicated each woman is to military service. Check (✓) the correct answer in the chart below. Underline clues in the letters that help to decide. Try to convince each other by referring back to the letters.

	VERY DEDICATED	SOMEWHAT DEDICATED	NOT VERY DEDICATED	NOT DEDICATED AT ALL
Letter 1				
Letter 2				
Letter 3				
Letter 4				
Letter 5				
Letter 6				
Letter 7				
Letter 8				
Letter 9				

◖ EXPRESS OPINIONS

Choose the one letter that affected you the most and explain your choice in a small group. Answer the questions.

- Did you identify with the writer of the letter? In what way?
- Do you share the writer's opinions or reactions?
- Did anything surprise you in the letter?
- Were you shocked by anything in the letter?
- What other reasons did you have for choosing this letter?

1 *Below is an article about the lives of women soldiers after they return home from a war in Eritrea, a country in East Africa. Before you read the article, discuss the question with a partner.*

How do you think women soldiers feel about their military experience after they return home?

Asmara Journal:
In Peace, Women Warriors Rank Low

By James C. McKinley (from the *New York Times*)

1 SOME DAYS NURIA MOHAMMED SALEH says she actually finds herself missing the war—not the fear and horror, not even the adrenaline kick and camaraderie of soldiering. She misses being treated like a man. Like thousands of other Eritrean women, Mrs. Saleh fought side by side with the men in the rebel army that freed this rocky land from Ethiopian rule in 1991. Like most women who are veterans here, she has found it hard to return to the deeply traditional and patriarchal society[1] she left behind as a teenager.

2 A few years ago, she recalled, she was hammering the enemy with mortar fire. Now she sweeps floors for a dollar a day in an office building near the capital she helped liberate. The only hints of her past are the shrapnel[2] scars around her lips. Mrs. Saleh is one of about 20,000 women who have been discharged from the Eritrean Army in the last two years as part of a larger demobilization of nearly 52,000 troops. Though about 3,000 remain in the army, the vast majority of women were sent home. Some had spent their entire adult lives in the Eritrean People's Liberation Front. Most have little education, having quit school to join the guerrillas.

3 The Front changed their lives, they said. The rebel commanders were Marxists by training and treated women as equals. The Front's soldiers were taught to ignore sexual, tribal, and religious differences. Women were trained to drive tanks, fight, and handle big guns. Though not many women had the education to become officers, a handful rose to command rebel battalions. Many married fighters from other religions and tribes.

4 Even outside the army in rebel-controlled regions, because the Liberation Front required most men to be in combat, women broke out of traditional molds, working as dentists, medical technicians, administrators, factory workers, mechanics, and teachers, a United Nations report said.

5 But if women who were guerrillas had hoped that fighting and dying in the war would change their status in Eritrean society, they have discovered instead that society's traditions die hard. Several said their families had rejected their mixed marriages and employers had been reluctant to hire them

---

[1] **patriarchal society**: a social system controlled only by men
[2] **shrapnel**: pieces of artillery, mortar shells, or hand grenades

for skilled jobs. Even more galling[3] for some women is that once they put on civilian clothes, men started expecting them to play subservient roles again.

6   Aster Haile was 12 when she joined the rebels. While she fought and worked for the front as a teacher, her sister spent the war in Saudi Arabia. After liberation, Ms. Haile said, she could not find work teaching, so she borrowed from her sister and opened a dress shop on Victory Avenue. Despite her military service, she said many men she meets still resist treating her like a businesswoman.

7   Other women who were veterans have banded together in cooperatives, pooling their savings and severance pay to start textile and honey-making businesses. Along with male veterans, they have been under-going retraining at government expense to work as truck drivers and carpenters.

8   Here in Asmara, the capital, one group of women who were fighters have opened a fish market, the Gejeret Fish Retail Shop, built with the help of grants from the United States and the United Nations. Nine women work there, having traded in their AK-47s for fillet knives. They share the profits with other female veterans who are partners. Each woman takes home about $72 a month. Ghenet Berhe, a 30-year-old mother, said she did not mind filleting fish, since the whole country is struggling to get back on its feet economically. But when she was asked if she missed her life in the rebel army, she smiled and said, "Of course. We had equality," she said. "We had common goals and common ends."

---

[3] **galling:** aggravating, frustrating

2 *Examine the incomplete statements. Decide with a partner which choices could complete the sentences according to the point of view expressed in the reading. Circle your choices. There is always more than one correct answer.*

1. Women veterans of the Eritrean Army miss their army days because _____.
   a. many became officers
   b. they didn't want to get married
   c. they were treated as equals to men
   d. they did not face religious or tribal discrimination

2. A subservient position is when you _____.
   a. take orders, not give them
   b. do unskilled labor
   c. don't own your own land
   d. are partners in a cooperative

3. During the war, women made progress because they could _____.
   a. take jobs only men had before
   b. train for skilled jobs
   c. choose their husbands more freely
   d. go to school more easily

4. Former women soldiers find life in peacetime frustrating because _____.
   a. they can't find good jobs
   b. their marriages have become unacceptable
   c. they are no longer traditional women
   d. they thought their country would be more grateful to them

C INTEGRATE READINGS ONE AND TWO

◀ **STEP 1: Organize**

Work with a partner. Go back to the reading selections and fill in the chart on the next page with notes giving relevant information showing the similarities and differences in the experiences and feelings of women in the army in the United States and Eritrea.

	TRUE FOR ONLY THE UNITED STATES	TRUE FOR ONLY ERITREA	TRUE FOR BOTH THE UNITED STATES AND ERITREA
Liked army life	Some wanted to leave the army; some liked it.	Most women loved their time in the army.	
Command positions			Some women were officers.
Gender in the army			
Education			
Married / Single			Some women were single and some were married.
After the army	Women were looking forward to their future lives outside the army.		
Patriotism			

Imagine you are Veronica Martin (Reading One, Letter 8). Write a letter to Nuria Mohammed Saleh (Reading Two) discussing your life in the military, being a woman, and your feelings about your country. Tell her about the similarities and differences between your life and hers. How do you see the future?

LIFE IN THE
ARMY

> Dear Nuria Mohammed Saleh,
>
> I am an American soldier in Kuwait. I came here because my unit of the National Guard was mobilized for war. _____
>
> _____
>
> _____

GENDER ISSUES

> I know that we share the experience of fighting alongside men. But our situation may be different. _____
>
> _____
>
> _____

PATRIOTISM

> Despite our differences, one thing is the same. We love our country. _____
>
> _____
>
> _____

THE FUTURE

> For me the future, _____
>
> _____
>
> _____

> I hope that someday soon you will be recognized for the contribution you have made to your country.
>
> Sincerely.
>
> Veronica Martin

③ FOCUS ON WRITING

Ⓐ VOCABULARY

◀ REVIEW

Today, women are an important part of the American armed forces, serving alongside men. About 15 percent of the members of the current United States military are women. About 203,000 women are on active duty. Of those, 35,000 are officers.

In a small group, try to relate the vocabulary in the first column to these concepts: **danger, teamwork, suffering,** *and* **peace.** *If a word relates to a concept, put a + sign in that column. If the word does not relate to the concept, put a − sign. If you are unsure, or if the word relates only partially to the concept, put a ? in the column. Explain your choices. Try to reach a group consensus.*

	DANGER	TEAMWORK	SUFFERING	PEACE
Ammunition	+	?	+	−
Camaraderie				
Casualties				
Civilian				
Coalition				
Convoy				
Enlisted personnel				
Front line				
Missing in action				
Red alert				
Shrapnel				
Survivors				

The suffixes *-al, -ial, -an, -ar,* and *-ary* mean "pertaining to," "related to," "connected with." When you add one of these suffixes to a noun, you create an adjective that means "pertaining to," "related to," or "connected with" the subject of the noun.

Example   education (noun)
              educational (adjective = "pertaining to education")

1 *Work with a partner. The noun forms related to the adjectives that appear in Readings One and Two are listed below. Add the correct suffixes to form adjectives. Make other necessary changes. Check your answers in the dictionary.*

1. medic _____   5. technique _____

2. militia _____   6. sex _____

3. tradition _____   7. tribe _____

4. patriarch _____   8. air _____

2 *Work with a partner. The following nouns appear in Readings One and Two. Change them to adjectives by adding the correct suffixes and making other necessary changes. Use a dictionary if you need to.*

1. volunteer _____   3. vehicle _____

2. recreation _____   4. minister _____

3 *There are many expressions in English that can use* **get**. *The following are only a few of the many examples. Find the correct meaning for each expression according to the way the expression is used in the readings, and circle your choice.*

1. "get the shakes" (Reading One, paragraph 1)
    a. become chilly
    b. become nervous
    c. become dizzy

2. "get to you" (Reading One, paragraph 1)
    a. approach you
    b. enter you
    c. bother you

3. "get me down" (Reading One, paragraph 5)
    a. depress me
    b. irritate me
    c. pull me under

4. "get our hands dirty" (Reading One, paragraph 9)
    a. become involved in illegal activity
    b. assume responsibility for all negotiations
    c. do all the heavy, physical work

5. "get it over with" (Reading One, paragraph 15)
   a. complete the task
   b. overcome all difficulties
   c. ignore all inconveniences

6. "getting burned out" (Reading One, paragraph 16)
   a. becoming exhausted or disinterested because of overwork
   b. becoming overly enthusiastic about work
   c. becoming inspired by too much work

7. "get back on its feet economically" (Reading Two, paragraph 8)
   a. assess its economic situation
   b. come to terms with its economic weaknesses
   c. recover its economic stability

4 Working in a small group, write a list of any other expressions with **get** that you know.

◀ CREATE

Complete the dialogue between a young woman and her father. The young woman has joined the military, but her father is not happy about her choice. Use at least eight of the vocabulary words listed below in the dialogue. Continue the dialogue on a separate piece of paper.

band together	~~enlist~~	get to you	missing in action	survivor
casualties	galling	grants	reject	traditional
civilian	get me down	handle	resist	~~volunteer~~

FATHER: _I can't believe that you are going to volunteer for the military. Why are you doing this? I don't understand._

DAUGHTER: _Dad, I never meant to hurt you in any way. I just want to support my country, and that's why I enlisted._

FATHER: _____

_____

DAUGHTER: _____

_____

FATHER: _____

_____

GRAMMAR: Direct and Indirect Speech

1 *Examine the two sentences and discuss the questions with a partner.*

- "The military paid for my college education, and I'm repaying that debt." (Jennifer Freese)

- Jennifer Freese said that the military had paid for her college education and she was repaying that debt.

    1. Do these two sentences have different meanings?

    2. Why are they written in a different way?

    3. Why does the second sentence have no quotation marks?

    4. How have the pronouns and verb tenses been changed?

DIRECT AND INDIRECT SPEECH

Direct speech is a quotation or recording of a person's exact words. Quotation marks are used to make this clear to the reader.

"The military paid for my college education, and I'm repaying that debt."

                               Jennifer Freese

Indirect speech paraphrases or reports what someone said without necessarily using the person's exact words. Quotation marks are not used. The verbs *agree, answer, believe, decide, explain, realize, say, tell,* and *think* are commonly used to introduce direct speech.

Jennifer Freese *said* that the military had paid for her college education and she was repaying that debt.

Changing Direct Speech to Indirect Speech

Verb forms and tenses and pronouns change when direct speech becomes indirect speech.

Direct Speech	Indirect Speech
1. Present tense changes to the past. "I **am** an E-6 in the Navy."	She said she **was** an E-6 in the Navy.
2. Simple past changes to the past perfect. "I **put** up pictures of my kids on the wall."	She said she **had put** up pictures of her kids on the wall.
3. Present perfect changes to the past perfect. "I **have been** here for a month."	She explained that she **had been** here for a month.
4. The future *will* changes to *would.* "I **will** read this diary to my children someday."	She thought that she **would** read this diary to her children someday.
5. The modal *can* changes to *could.* When *must* means *have to,* it changes to *had to. May, might,* and *should* remain the same. "I **can** barely look at them without crying."	She realized that she **could** barely look at them without crying.

2 *Rewrite the direct quotes in indirect speech. Compare your answers with a partner's.*

1. Lieutenant Veronica Martin is an Army Reserves Officer stationed at Fort Bliss, Texas. At her interview today, she said, "My unit, the 11th Air Defense Artillery Brigade, was put on alert last night."

   Indirect Speech: _____

   _____

2. She said, "I am scared but not of the war."

   Indirect Speech: _____

   _____

3. "I don't want to leave my family behind," she explained.

   Indirect Speech: _____

   _____

4. It is two o'clock in the morning, and Veronica Martin is 60 miles from the Iraqi border. "All I have been able to think about is my family," she said.

   Indirect Speech: _____

   _____

5. "Will I ever see them again?" she wondered.

   Indirect Speech: _____

   _____

6. "This is one of the hardest things I will ever have to face," she said.

   Indirect Speech: _____

   _____

7. "But the soldiers are strong," she told us. "We are here to fight if we have to, to keep the rest of the world, especially U.S. citizens, safe from harm," she added.

   Indirect Speech: _____

   _____

3 *Rewrite the indirect speech statements in direct speech. Compare your answers with a partner's.*

1. Lieutenant Martin's husband was interviewed about his wife's service in the Gulf War. Mr. Martin told us that he had been in the Army until last June.

   Direct Speech: _____

   _____

2. He explained he had started taking care of the children at that time.

Direct Speech: _____

_____

3. He said his son was learning to walk and run and that he missed his mother.

Direct Speech: _____

_____

4. He said they talked to her on the phone every two weeks.

Direct Speech: _____

_____

4 *Go back to Reading One, Letter 2, by Dawn Bell. Rewrite the letter as indirect speech. Compare your letter with a partner's.*

C WRITING

> In this unit, you read "Women at War" and "Asmara Journal."
>
> You will **write an opinion essay giving your views on women in the military using a summary of "Women at War" in the first paragraph.** You will answer this question: Should women be in the armed forces?*

PREPARE TO WRITE: Notetaking

Look back at your answers to the questions in Share Information, page 178. Have your opinions changed since you read and discussed the readings in this unit? Write notes in response to two questions: How did your opinion change? How did it stay the same?

WRITE: An Introduction Using a Summary

1 *This summary of "Asmara Journal" is an introductory paragraph for an essay on women in the military. Read the summary and answer the questions. Discuss your answers with a partner.*

SUMMARY

For many women in Eritrea, fighting for national independence in the army was a liberating experience, as James C. McKinley reports in his *New York Times* article, "Asmara Journal: In Peace Women Warriors Rank Low." Despite the threat of death and injury, in the words of Ghenet Berhe, "We had equality." Women had the opportunity to be trained and

---

*For Alternative Writing Topics, see page 201. These topics can be used in place of the writing topic for this unit or as homework. The alternative topics relate to the theme of the unit, but may not target the same grammar or rhetorical structures taught in the unit.

educated, and some even rose to positions of command. Traditional restraints on women's education and marriage choices were lifted. All this changed, however, with the end of military service. With the return to civilian status came a loss of respect for women and few opportunities for good jobs. Ms. Nuria Mohammed Saleh said she began to miss the war. But these women, who have proven themselves in combat, are banding together in cooperatives and resisting gender barriers in order to continue making a contribution to their communities.

THESIS STATEMENT **The story of Eritrean women shows that it is important for women to participate in military service because they need the confidence and professional experience; their efforts will help not only their country, but also the cause of gender equality.**

1. Underline the topic sentence of this paragraph.

2. Is there a reference to the original source material the summary is based on?

3. What main ideas were included in the summary? What details were left out?

4. Are there any direct quotes from the article? Are they in quotation marks and attributed to the person who said them? Was indirect speech used?

5. Where do we find the author's opinion?

PREPARING AND WRITING A SUMMARY

A **summary** contains the essential information from a text. Writing a summary can help you check if you have understood or remembered the main ideas of a reading passage. In addition, summarizing information from textbooks or course work is an essential tool in studying for examinations or preparing research papers. Summarizing facts and opinions is also important for business presentations, work meetings, and conferences.

As in the example paragraph, a summary of research often serves as an introduction to an essay developing your own point of view. That is, your summary leads to the writing of your opinion in the thesis statement. Therefore, when using the summary as the introductory paragraph for an essay, your own thesis statement must be added at the end of the summary.

This list outlines the steps for writing a summary.

1. Identify the main ideas.

2. Decide what you are going to leave out. Include only the essential points.

3. Reorganize the ideas in a way that makes your points clear. You do not have to follow the order of the original text.

4. Include a sentence at the beginning stating the subject of the summary. Also include in the summary the names of the original texts and/or the original author's name.

5. State only the author's opinions and not your own.

(continued on next page)

6. Use your own words. Do not copy from the text unless you use direct quotes and quotation marks or indirect speech.*

7. Make sure your tenses are appropriate and consistent when you use reported speech.

8. Make the summary no more than 25% of the original and, in many cases, much less.

9. Be sure to edit your work. Polish it to make the language flow smoothly.

---

*If you copy *without* using direct quotes, you will be guilty of plagiarism. Plagiarism means copying other people's ideas or words, either deliberately or inadvertently. In most American universities, plagiarism is severely punished. In academic work, to avoid plagiarism when using the Internet or any other source, put summaries of all material in your own words. If you use someone else's exact words, put quotation marks around the quote.

2 *Summarize each of the main ideas in three or four sentences. REMEMBER TO USE YOUR OWN WORDS unless you use direct quotes or indirect speech clearly attributing the words to the person who said them. Discuss your work with a partner.*

1. Summarize the women soldiers' experiences in the Eritrean Army. ("Asmara Journal")

   Fighting as a woman in the Eritrean Army meant risking one's life on the front lines, but it also meant learning new skills and gaining new opportunities. Women were able to break out of some of the restrictions they faced in traditional communities. Ghenet Berthe sums it up by saying, "We had equality. We had common goals and common ends." In this way, Eritrean women were able to gain the respect of men and assume responsible positions in service to their country.

2. Summarize the women soldiers' experiences when they became civilians. ("Asmara Journal")

3. Summarize all the women's comments about their children. ("Women at War")

4. Summarize all the women soldiers' thoughts about the enemy. ("Women at War")

3 *Using what you learned about writing summaries and having summaries serve as the introduction to an essay, summarize the main ideas from "Women at War" in the introduction of an essay and add your opinion (thesis statement) in response to this question: **Should women be in the armed forces?** Explain your position with one to three body paragraphs leading to a conclusion. Refer to the work you did in Organize, pages 188–189, Prepare to Write, page 196, and Write, pages 196–198, to write your first draft.*

1 *Read the sentences from the summary / introductory paragraph explaining one reason women join the military. With a partner, answer the questions.*

CONTEXT	Women were able to break out of some of the restrictions they faced in traditional communities.
QUOTE	Ghenet Berthe sums it up by saying, **"We had equality. We had common goals and common ends."**
PARAPHRASE	In this way, Eritrean women were able to gain the respect of men and assume responsible positions in service to their country.

    1. Where is the quote placed?

    2. Why is there a sentence before the quote?

    3. Why is there a sentence after it?

When you quote someone's words in your essay, you need to surround the quote with an explanation of its relevance and meaning:

- explain the **context** of the quote
- put the exact words in **quotation marks** and attribute them to someone
- **paraphrase** the quote: explain it in your own words and link it to your main idea

2 *Embed the quotes in two sentences of your own. Compare your answers with a partner's.*

    1. "You can't let the fear get to you." Thyra A. Bishop

    2. "I start crying because my son is now walking and running on his own and I'm not there to see it." Veronica Martin

    3. "For those women who think that the service is for them, please think seriously about it." Carla Yvette Henry

3 *Look at the first draft of your essay. Go back and check that you have embedded your quotes in every paragraph in which they appear in your essay.*

◀ EDIT: Writing the Final Draft

Write your final draft. Carefully edit for grammatical and mechanical errors. Make sure you used some of the vocabulary and grammar from the unit. Use the checklist to help you write the final draft. Then neatly write or type your essay.

✓ FINAL DRAFT CHECKLIST

○ Does your essay begin with a concise summary of the main points of the readings? Is there an appropriate reference to the source of the summary?

○ Does the thesis statement appear directly after the summary and give the reader a clear idea of the topics that will be discussed in the body paragraphs in support of the thesis?

○ Are the quotes adequately embedded in the essay?

○ Did you use your own words and did not copy the words in the article except when you used quotation marks?

○ Are the verb tenses consistent when using direct and indirect speech?

○ Have new vocabulary and expressions been used in this essay?

ALTERNATIVE WRITING TOPICS

Write an essay on one of the topics. Remember to provide a thesis statement and sufficient explanations, examples, and support to develop your main idea. Use the vocabulary and grammar from the unit.

1. Find a magazine or newspaper article about women in the military in a country other than the United States; or find an article about the history of the military. (You can use an excerpt from an encyclopedia or other reference materials.) Write a summary of the article. Use this summary in the introduction to an essay that expresses your point of view in the form of a thesis statement. Give a copy of the article to your teacher along with your finished essay.

2. Women of all ages are increasingly active in business, professional, and military life. Some people, both men and women, react to this trend by saying, "A woman's place is in the home." Do you agree or disagree? Explain your answer in a short essay.

3. Do you think letters from men who are soldiers would be similar to or different from the letters written by the women soldiers in this unit? Explain your answer in an essay, and refer to the readings.

4. Do you believe that military service should be required as a way to develop good citizens? If you believe that it should, would you require it for men only or for both men and women? Write an essay explaining your opinion, and refer to the experience of a country you know about.

5. Do you think a person has the right to refuse military service for religious or moral reasons? for political reasons? Write an essay to explain your view.

RESEARCH TOPICS, see page 266.

9 The Cellist of Sarajevo

①FOCUS ON THE TOPIC

A PREDICT

Look at the photo above and the title of the unit. What do you think this unit will be about? Write down your thoughts for a few minutes and discuss your ideas with a partner.

Work in a small group. Ask each other the following questions and explain your answers.

1. What kind of music do you enjoy? Jazz? Rock 'n' roll? Classical? Hip-hop?

2. What creative things do you like to do? Play a musical instrument? Paint? Write? Dance? Design or decorate? Sew? Something else?

3. Do you enjoy going to the movies, the theater, concerts, museums?

C **BACKGROUND AND VOCABULARY**

The boldfaced words are in Reading One. Before you read the passage below, read the words and study their meanings.

anticipation: expectation (of something good)

carnage: killing and wounding of many people, especially in a war

cherished: a cherished memory is one that is very important to you

defy: oppose; resist

exuberant: happy and cheerful, and full of energy and excitement

furor: sudden expression of anger among a large group of people

haunting: sad but also beautiful and staying in your thoughts for a long time

repertoire: all of the plays, pieces of music, etc. that a performer or group has earned and can perform

solitary: alone

soothe: make someone feel calmer and less anxious, upset, or angry

unassuming: showing no desire to be noticed or given special treatment

Work with a partner. As you read the background information for the subject of the unit, fill in the blanks with one of the new vocabulary words.

Whether we are professional artists or not, the creative arts play an important role in our lives. Through the attention that we pay to colors, materials, shapes and sounds when we select our clothes and decorate our homes, our creative instincts are continually at work. Our visual, auditory, and tactile choices help us to express our identity as we strive to make our mark in the world. They reflect our

_____cherished_____ values, our _____ feelings about being alive, and even our
     1.   **2.**
moments of sadness and grief.

It is also through creativity—through the language of music, for example—
that people reach out and connect with each other. Even the loneliest and most
_____ among us, those whose shy and _____ personalities never
     3.   **4.**
make them the center of attention, experience the power of music. Regardless of the
musical _____ people choose to play, music allows them to share
     5.
emotions and feelings that are common to us all. Music can _____ and
                     6.
comfort us in a harsh world.

One of the harshest realities that people must face is the cruelty and
destruction of war. Between March 1992 and November 1995, in the former
republic of Yugoslavia, the people of the city of Sarajevo suffered the agony caused
by the _____ of war. Once a prosperous, tolerant city where people of
     7.
many backgrounds lived together, Sarajevo was torn apart by ethnic conflict. People
had to call on all their strength to stay firm in their humanity and _____
                     8.
the appeals to hatred and violence. Somehow they found the strength to clean up
the bloody remains of the _____ in the streets and continue living. In
                 9.
_____ of a peace they hoped would come someday, the people of Sarajevo
    10.
sought the assistance of the international community, which eventually brought the
conflict to an end.

Although the war ended more than a decade ago, people are still deeply upset
by the dark _____ memories of those times. During the war, many artists
         11.
tried to ease the suffering of the people of Sarajevo by coming to their aid. The first
reading in this unit, which combines the beauty of music with the ugly sounds of
war, grew out of this struggle.

②FOCUS ON READING

A READING ONE: The Cellist of Sarajevo

Read the quotation from Georges Braque and answer the question. Then read Paul Sullivan's article, and keep Braque's statement in mind as you read.

The French painter Georges Braque (1882–1963) said, "Art is a wound that becomes light." What do you think this statement means? Write a few sentences in response, and discuss your ideas with a partner.

Paul Sullivan

The Cellist of Sarajevo
by Paul Sullivan (from *Reader's Digest*)

1   As a pianist, I was invited to perform with cellist Eugene Friesen at the International Cello Festival in Manchester, England. Every two years a group of the world's greatest cellists and others devoted to that **unassuming** instrument—bow makers,[1] collectors, historians—gather for a week of workshops, master classes,[2] seminars, recitals, and parties. Each evening, the 600 or so participants assemble for a concert.

2   The opening-night performance at the Royal Northern College of Music consisted of works for unaccompanied cello. There on the stage in the magnificent concert hall was a **solitary** chair. No piano, no music stand, no conductor's podium.[3] This was to be music in its purest, most intense form. The atmosphere was supercharged with **anticipation** and concentration. The world-famous cellist Yo-Yo Ma was one of the performers that April night in 1994, and there was a moving story behind the musical composition he would play.

---

[1] **bow makers:** people who make the flexible stick used to produce sound by players of the cello and other stringed instruments
[2] **master class:** form of teaching in which a celebrated musician instructs a group of pupils in front of other pupils or a paying audience
[3] **podium:** elevated platform

3   On May 27, 1992, in Sarajevo, one of the few bakeries that still had a supply of flour was making and distributing bread to the starving, war-shattered people. At 4 P.M. a long line stretched into the street. Suddenly, a mortar shell fell directly into the middle of the line, killing 22 people and splattering flesh, blood, bone, and rubble.

4   Not far away lived a 35-year-old musician named Vedran Smailovic. Before the war he had been a cellist with the Sarajevo Opera, a distinguished career to which he patiently longed to return. But when he saw the **carnage** from the massacre outside his window, he was pushed past his capacity to absorb and endure any more. Anguished, he resolved to do the thing he did best: make music. Public music, daring music, music on a battlefield.

5   For each of the next 22 days, at 4 P.M., Smailovic put on his full, formal concert attire,[4] took up his cello, and walked out of his apartment into the midst of the battle raging around him. Placing a plastic chair beside the crater that the shell had made, he played in memory of the dead Albinoni's *Adagio in G minor*, one of the most mournful and **haunting** pieces in the classical **repertoire**. He played to the abandoned streets, smashed trucks, and burning buildings, and to the terrified people who hid in the cellars while the bombs dropped and bullets flew. With masonry exploding around him, he made his unimaginably courageous stand for human dignity, for those lost to war, for civilization, for compassion, and for peace. Though the shellings went on, he was never hurt.

6   After newspapers picked up the story of this extraordinary man, an English composer, David Wilde, was so moved[5] that he, too, decided to make music. He wrote a composition for unaccompanied cello, "The Cellist of Sarajevo," into which he poured his feelings of outrage, love, and brotherhood with Vedran Smailovic. It was "The Cellist of Sarajevo" that Yo-Yo Ma was to play that evening.

7   Ma came out on stage, bowed to the audience, and sat down quietly on the chair. The music began, stealing out into the hushed hall and creating a shadowy, empty universe, ominous and haunting. Slowly it grew into an agonized, screaming, slashing **furor**, gripping us all before subsiding at last into a hollow death rattle and, finally, back to silence.

8   When he had finished, Ma remained bent over his cello, his bow resting on the strings. No one in the hall moved or made a sound for a long time. It was as though we had just witnessed that horrifying massacre ourselves. Finally, Ma looked out across the audience and stretched out his hand, beckoning someone to come to the stage. An indescribable electric shock swept over us as we realized who it was: Vedran Smailovic, the cellist of Sarajevo!

9   Smailovic rose from his seat and walked down the aisle as Ma left the stage to meet him. They flung their arms around each other in an **exuberant** embrace. Everyone in the hall erupted in a chaotic, emotional frenzy—clapping, shouting, and cheering. And in the center of it all stood these two men, hugging and crying unashamedly: Yo-Yo Ma, a suave, elegant prince of classical music, flawless in appearance and performance; and Vedran Smailovic, dressed in a stained and tattered leather motorcycle suit. His wild, long hair and huge mustache framed a face that looked old beyond his years, soaked with tears and creased with pain. We were all stripped down to our starkest, deepest humanity at encountering this man who shook his cello in the face of bombs, death, and ruin, **defying** them all. It was the sword of Joan of Arc—the mightiest weapon of all.

10   Back in Maine a week later, I sat one evening playing the piano for the residents of a local nursing home. I couldn't help

---

[4] **concert attire:** a tuxedo or formal dark suit worn by musicians at a concert
[5] **moved:** to feel a strong emotion, especially of sadness or sympathy

(continued on next page)

contrasting this concert with the splendors I had witnessed at the festival. Then I was struck by the profound similarities. With his music the cellist of Sarajevo had defied death and despair, and celebrated love and life. And here we were, a chorus of croaking voices accompanied by a shopworn[6] piano, doing the same thing. There were no bombs and bullets, but there was real pain— dimming sight, crushing loneliness, all the scars we accumulate in our lives—and only **cherished** memories for comfort. Yet still we sang and clapped.

11   It was then I realized that music is a gift we all share equally. Whether we create it or simply listen, it's a gift that can **soothe**, inspire, and unite us, often when we need it most—and expect it least.

---

[6] **shopworn:** not in the best condition after years of use

READ FOR MAIN IDEAS

Work with a partner. Read the statements and decide which three represent the main ideas of Reading One. Discuss the reasons for your choices.

1. Involving yourself in what you do best will always help you to emerge victorious from the most difficult situations.

2. Music can help solve political problems.

3. Music can give people the strength they need to soothe both physical and emotional pain.

4. Music can make people sympathize with the suffering of others.

5. Destroying things is not the only way to win a war.

6. Art creates a community of people.

READ FOR DETAILS

Work with a partner. Number the eight episodes in "The Cellist of Sarajevo" in the order in which they take place.

_____ Yo-Yo Ma plays a cello concert of David Wilde's work at the Royal Northern College of Music in Manchester, England.

__1__ Vedran Smailovic plays the cello with the Sarajevo Opera in the 1980s.

_____ The author plays the piano in a nursing home.

_____ David Wilde reads an article about Smailovic playing the cello in the midst of bombs; Wilde writes a cello composition in Smailovic's honor.

_____ Smailovic plays the cello in the streets of Sarajevo.

_____ The author is invited to perform at the International Cello Festival in Manchester, England.

_____ On May 27, 1992, a breadline in Sarajevo is shelled.

_____ Smailovic embraces Yo-Yo Ma in the concert hall.

◖ MAKE INFERENCES

Based on what you have read in "The Cellist of Sarajevo," answer the questions about the motivations and feelings of the people in the story. When you are finished, compare your answers with those of another student.

1. Why did Vedran Smailovic choose to make his "courageous stand for human dignity" in the streets of Sarajevo for exactly 22 days and always at 4 P.M. every day?

   _____

   _____

2. Why did David Wilde write a composition for unaccompanied cello rather than for a whole orchestra?

   _____

   _____

3. After Yo-Yo Ma's performance, how did the audience know for sure that Vedran Smailovic was the person he was asking to come to the stage?

   _____

   _____

4. Why did Yo-Yo Ma and Vedran Smailovic embrace each other and cry?

   _____

   _____

5. What was the author's purpose in describing exactly how Yo-Yo Ma and Vedran Smailovic were dressed?

   _____

   _____

6. How might we explain the author's idea that music is a way to defy death?

   _____

   _____

◖ EXPRESS OPINIONS

Discuss the questions in a small group. Share your group's conclusions with the rest of the class.

1. Some people might say that Vedran Smailovic acted foolishly rather than bravely. What do you think? Was he brave or foolish, or both?

2. Is music an international language? Do films use an international language? What do we mean by an international language of art?

3. Do very well-known performers, singers, actors, or artists have an obligation to society?

4. What current war do you know something about? Does this war concern you? Why? What can citizens and politicians do about it?

1 *Below is a passage from the novel* The Soloist *by Mark Salzman. Before you read, consider the questions and discuss them with a partner.*

1. Have you ever been able to do something very well (for example, a sports activity, playing an instrument, dancing) and then lost this ability because something happened to you or because you changed in some way, or do you know of anyone this has happened to?

2. How do you think people feel when they lose the ability to do something they really love doing? What can they do about it, if anything?

by Mark Salzman

1   An idea came to me, and I turned off the lights in the studio. In the darkness, I put the cello's spike into a loose spot on the carpet, tightened the bow, and drew it across the open strings. I took off my shirt and tried it again; it was the first time in my life I'd felt the instrument against my bare chest. I could feel the vibration of the strings travel through the body of the instrument to my own body. I'd never thought about that; music scholars always talk about the resonating[1] properties of various instruments, but surely the performer's own body must have some effect on the sound. As I dug into the notes I imagined that my own chest and lungs were extensions of the sound box; I seemed to be able to alter the sound by the way I sat, and by varying the muscular tension in my upper body.

2   After improvising for a while, I started playing the D minor Bach suite, still in the darkness. Strangely freed of the task of finding the right phrasing,[2] the right intonation, the right bowing, I heard the music through my skin. For the first time I didn't think about how it would sound to anyone else, and slowly, joyfully, gratefully, I started to hear again. The notes sang out, first like a trickle, then like a fountain of cool water bubbling up from a hole in the middle of a desert. After an hour or so I looked up, and in the darkness saw the outline of the cat sitting on the floor in front of me, cleaning her paws and purring loudly. I had an audience again, humble as it was.

---

[1] **resonating:** making a deep sound that vibrates the material of the instrument or the body
[2] **phrasing:** a way of linking the notes in order to bring out the melody of the music

3   So that's what I do now with my cello. At least once a day I find time to tune it, close my eyes, and listen. It's probably not going to lead to the kind of comeback[3] I'd fantasized about for so long—years of playing badly have left scars on my technique, and, practically speaking, classical musicians returning from obscurity[4] are almost impossible to promote[5]—but I might eventually try giving a recital if I feel up to it. Or better yet, I may play for Dr. Polk if our date at the concert goes well. Occasionally I feel a stab of longing, and I wish I could give just one more concert on a great stage before my lights blink off,[6] but that longing passes more quickly now. I take solace in the fact that unlike the way I felt before, I can enjoy playing for myself now. I feel relaxed and expansive when I play, as if I could stretch out my arms and reach from one end of the apartment to the other. A feeling of completeness and dignity surrounds me and lifts me up.

---

[3] **comeback:** starting a career again and returning to the heights of fame or celebrity
[4] **obscurity:** the state of not being known or remembered
[5] **promote:** get bookings or jobs for a client
[6] **before my lights blink off:** before I die

2 *Work with a partner. Write your answers to the questions.*

1. What did the narrator do for the first time in the darkness? (as he practiced playing the cello)

   _____

   _____

2. Why did the narrator believe that he was finally able to "hear" again?

   _____

   _____

3. What imagery does the narrator use to show that he has come out of his dry spell?

   _____

   _____

4. Why doesn't the narrator anticipate a grand musical comeback?

   _____

   _____

5. Why does the narrator's use of the expression "returning from *obscurity*" have a double meaning in this passage? (an especially clever and ironic use of language for the situation in question)

   _____

   _____

6. Why is the narrator happy now?

_____

_____

C INTEGRATE READINGS ONE AND TWO

◖ **STEP 1: Organize**

*Review Readings One and Two and complete this grid by putting notes in the appropriate places. If the information is not specified in the text for a particular category, put an **X** in the grid.*

	INSTRUMENT	LOCATION	CLOTHING	AUDIENCE	EFFECT OF MUSIC
Smailovic		Sarajevo / Manchester			
Yo-Yo Ma			formal concert attire	people in concert hall	
Sullivan	piano				soothes, inspires, unites
Salzman		apartment		cat	

◖ **STEP 2: Synthesize**

Work in pairs. Using the notes you took in Step 1, complete the short comparison and contrast essay by filling in the paragraphs with the information needed.

Music is a unifying and healing force for Vedran Smailovic, Yo-Yo Ma, Paul Sullivan, and Mark Salzman. Despite the different environments in which they play, music gives each of them the strength needed to face life's challenges.

Undoubtedly, all four artists would agree that they share an infinite love for their instruments. _____

_____

_____

_____

Where they play is often a question of circumstance. _____

_____

_____

But wherever they play, they are always artists communicating their deepest feelings about music.

Regarding the clothing they might wear when they play their music, here, too, the differences, although great, have nothing to do with the respect that they all share for the musical experience. For instance, _____

_____

_____

_____

Their audiences, whether large or small, are all moved by their performances.

_____

_____

_____

_____

It would therefore not be surprising to find that despite all the differences here, music has a similar effect on each of these individuals. _____

_____

_____

_____

_____

③ FOCUS ON WRITING

Ⓐ VOCABULARY

◀ REVIEW

Complete each of the sentences with one of the words from the box on the next page. Share your answers with a partner.

anticipation	exuberant	obscurity	resonating
comeback	furor	promote	solitary
defy	haunting	repertoire	soothe

1. The children's _____ was seen in their excited faces as they waited for the concert to begin.

2. The music had a _____ quality because its sad tones made the audience think of their unhappy past.

3. Handel's *Messiah,* Beethoven's *Fifth Symphony,* and Tchaikovsky's *1812 Overture* are all important parts of an orchestra's _____ of Western music.

4. Much of the classical music of the nineteenth century reflected the _____ and violence of revolutionary times.

5. Throughout history, creative artists have had to _____ the standards of society in order to produce new music and art.

6. When people are depressed, listening to music can _____ their pain.

7. The folk music made the people feel so happy and _____ that they became very hopeful about the future.

8. The artist is often a _____ figure, unknown or misunderstood by a society that offers no help.

9. These days, because of popular culture's interest in drama and gossip, it is difficult to _____ artists with unassuming or boring personalities, no matter how great their creative genius.

10. The _____ qualities of the violin vibrated so clearly through the musician's mind that he began to completely identify with his music.

11. People who have grown up in _____ do not easily adjust to becoming "superstars" after their talent has been discovered.

12. Making a _____ after a long time away from the theater can be a difficult task without a first-class manager.

◀ EXPAND

1 Work in a small group. Decide whether each adjective listed in the chart expresses the feeling of happiness, sadness, or anger. Some express more than one feeling. Put a check (✓) in the appropriate columns.

	HAPPINESS	SADNESS	ANGER
Agonized		✓	
Emotional	✓	✓	✓
Exuberant			
Haunting			
Mournful			
Moved			
Ominous			
Raging			
Screaming			
Slashing			
Solitary			

2 *Read the grammar box. Then do Exercises 1 and 2.*

PARTICIPLES USED AS ADJECTIVES

In the following sentences, both **moved** and **moving** are adjectives.

- The man was <u>moved</u> when he heard the cellist's story.
- <u>Moved</u> by the cellist's story, the man was close to tears.
- The <u>moving</u> story brought tears to the man's eyes.
- <u>Moving</u> the man to see the cellist's tragic situation, the story brought tears to the man's eyes.

The adjective *moved* modifies the noun *man*. The **-ed** suffix shows that the noun it modifies has been affected by something else. In this case, the man was moved by the story. The **-ed** adjective reminds us of the passive voice. It reflects a reaction ("to be moved by").

The adjective *moving* modifies the noun *story*. The **-ing** suffix shows that the noun it modifies has an effect on something else. In this case, the story moves the man. The **-ing** adjective reminds us of the active voice. The **-ing** adjective reflects an action ("the moving story" = "the story that moves us").

---

1. *Complete the paragraph by filling in the blanks with the correct adjective in parentheses.*

   The audience was settling into their seats, happy because the warm summer evening in Boston had had a _____ effect on them. But when the
   1. (relaxed / relaxing)

   refugees came on stage to tell their stories of war and pain and suffering, the

   audience was _____. The refugees told of _____
   2. (horrified / horrifying)   **3. (terrified / terrifying)**

   brutal soldiers and _____ panicked people running for their lives.
   4. (terrified / terrifying)

   The audience was _____ by tales of bravery and compassion, but this
   5. (inspired / inspiring)

   _____ story of senseless violence remained in their minds for a long
   6. (haunted / haunting)

   time.

2. *Complete the sentences based on the context of the previous paragraph. There is more than one correct answer for each item.*

   a. Horrified by the refugees' stories of pain and suffering, _____

   _____ .

   b. Terrifying the panicked people, _____

   _____ .

   c. Inspired by the refugees' tales of bravery and compassion, _____

   _____ .

d. Haunting the minds of the audience with visions of senseless violence, _____

_____ .

3 *Figurative language describes one kind of object in place of another to suggest a likeness. For example, in the sentence "The cello gave a sorrowful wail," the cello is making a human sound. The musical instrument symbolizes a human being.*

Explain the sentences from Reading Two. First identify the symbolism. Then write what you think the sentence as a whole means. Share your answers with a partner.

1. "I dug into the **notes**."
   (musical) **notes** = ___earth___

   a. sky   **b.** ocean   **c.** earth

   The cellist compares his musical instrument, the cello, to a shovel and

   the musical composition to the earth. At this time in his life, playing

   music is as intensely physical as breaking ground with a shovel.

2. "I heard the music through my **skin**."
   skin = _____

   a. feet   **b.** ears   **c.** eyes

   _____

   _____

   _____

3. "The **notes** sang out, first like a trickle, then a fountain."
   (musical) **notes** = _____

   a. stars   **b.** water   **c.** fire

   _____

   _____

   _____

4. "Occasionally I felt a stab of **longing**."
   longing = _____

   a. pain   **b.** joy   **c.** itch

   _____

   _____

   _____

5. "I wish I could give just one more concert on a great stage before my **lights** blink off."

lights = _____

a. eyes   **b.** appetite   **c.** life

_____

_____

_____

◖ CREATE

Write a short paragraph summarizing what Vedran Smailovic did for 22 days in Sarajevo. Use at least eight of the words from the box.

anticipation	furor	repertoire
carnage	haunting	resonating
defy	~~moved/moving~~	screaming
exuberant	ominous	solitary
feel a stab of longing for	raging	soothe

Vedran Smailovic made a stand for human dignity in a moving way.
_____

_____

_____

_____

_____

_____

_____

B   GRAMMAR: Reporting Ideas and Facts with Passives

1 *Examine the following sentences and discuss the questions with a partner.*

- <u>Many people say</u> that music is an international language.
- <u>Music is said to be</u> an international language.
- <u>It is said</u> that music is an international language.

1. Which sentences are in the active voice and which are in the passive voice?

2. In the second and third sentences, who says music is an international language?

3. Is there a difference in meaning among the three sentences?

USING THE PASSIVE VOICE

To Shift Focus

Using the passive voice shifts the reader's focus to *the thing being done* or *the process being described*, rather than to the specific agent. For this reason, in academic writing and scientific description, the passive voice is often used.*

- *Active:* A **craftsman dried** and **varnished** the wood for the cello.
- *Passive:* The **wood** for the cello **was dried** and **varnished.**

Using the passive voice relieves the writer of a certain amount of direct responsibility for what is said. For this reason, it is often used in reporting the news when the source of the news is not clear or cannot be told.

- *Active:* An **observer said** that the soldiers came from Sarajevo.
- *Passive:* **It was said** that the soldiers came from Sarajevo.

To Report Ideas and Facts

The passive voice creates a distance between the writer and the idea being communicated. That *impersonal* distance is the reason why the passive is preferred for reporting the ideas of others. The writer is reporting on something without adding his or her personal views, creating a sense of objectivity and impartiality.

- *Impersonal distance:* **Music is said to be** an international language.
- *Greater impersonal distance:* **It is said** that music is an international language.

GRAMMAR TIP: Because the writer is not interested in identifying the specific agent responsible for this statement, he or she uses the passive voice without *by* or an agent. In this example, "music is said to be an international language" has become a universal truth, and it is not necessary to identify the agent ("by many people," or "by great musicians," or "by experts," and so on).

Structures Commonly Used

Two structures can be used to form the passive:

Subject + passive form of the verb + *to be*

Music is said to be an international language.

The agreement of the subject (noun) and verb must be carefully considered. If the subject of the sentence is plural, the verb must be plural.

Musical *compositions* are said to be included in the box found in the composer's attic.

The second structure uses the impersonal pronoun *it* and *that* followed by an independent clause.

It* + passive form of the verb + *that

It is said that *music* is an international language.

Verbs Commonly Used

The verbs ***think, consider, regard, say, allege, believe, claim, know,*** and ***suggest*** are commonly used to report facts, ideas, and beliefs.

* If there is no specific reason to use the passive, the active voice is preferred in English.

2 *The sentences below are in the active voice. Rewrite each sentence in the passive voice. Examine both versions of the sentence and decide which is more effective. Give a reason for your decision.*

1. Many people say that the arts are essential parts of a child's education.

   It is said that the arts are essential parts of a child's education.

   This sentence is more effective in the impersonal passive voice because the agent ("many people") is very vague.

2. The government decided to give money to the school creative arts program.

   _____

   _____

   _____

3. The orchestra will have to dismiss many musicians beginning next week.

   _____

   _____

   _____

4. Sigmund Freud, the father of psychoanalysis, claimed that the imagination is the link to our innermost feelings.

   _____

   _____

   _____

5. Many teachers believe that an education in the arts develops sensitivity.

   _____

   _____

   _____

3 *With a partner, read the passage on how the arts are being used to help children. Decide whether the underlined sentences would be more effective if they were in the impersonal passive. (The passive voice is preferred only in specific cases. Most lively writing uses the active voice.) On a separate piece of paper, rewrite the sentences that should be changed.*

(1) People say that the creative arts have a healing effect on children. (2) We know that administrators at the Illinois Department of Children's Services are active supporters of this method. Last year they offered classes in art, theater, dance, and music to help children deal with their inner feelings. (3) The program was so successful that it quickly expanded.

(4) Several hundred children participated in the arts program this year. Children in the Illinois program show an awareness of how the arts are related to feelings.

According to their teachers, some children associate a specific color with a particular emotional state: red with anger, orange with happiness, and so on. (5) Teachers, administrators, and others in the program say that many children are learning how to relieve their tensions by drawing pictures about fighting instead of actually fighting. (6) They also claim that some of the children, noting that Leonardo Da Vinci and Michelangelo expressed both exuberant and mournful feelings in their art, are convinced there is a definite connection between these great artists and themselves. These insights are wonderful moments in building a child's emotional world.

C WRITING

In this unit, you read two narratives demonstrating the value that music can have in our lives.

You will **write a descriptive narrative essay about the effect that a work of art, such as a painting, a play, or a concert, has had on you.** You will place the experience in the context of your life as you explain why your experience with this work of art was so meaningful to you.*

◖ PREPARE TO WRITE: Asking Yourself Questions

Asking yourself questions is a prewriting technique that is very useful not only for focusing on your topic but also for narrative writing itself. By questioning yourself and writing brief answers in note form to your questions, you are able to explore your thoughts on the topic. The following questions should give you an idea as to how to follow this exercise. You may add other questions if you think of any. It is really up to you!

Questions	Answers in Note Form
WHAT kind of work of art will I focus on?	
is the name of the work of art?	
is the artist's message?	
do I want to say in my essay?	
is the purpose of my essay?	
WHO is the artist?	
went with me to see (hear) the work?	
WHEN did I see (hear) the work of art?	
was the work of art created?	
WHERE did I see (hear) it?	

---

*For Alternative Writing Topics, see page 229. These topics can be used in place of the writing topic for this unit or as homework. The alternative topics relate to the theme of the unit, but may not target the same grammar or rhetorical structures taught in the unit.

Questions	Answers in Note Form

WHY did I want to see (hear) it?
did I like it?
do I want to write about it?
did the artist create it?

HOW did I feel when I saw (heard) it?

Now freewrite about your topic based on the questions and answers you have here.

◖ **WRITE: A Narrative Essay**

1 *Work with a partner. Refer to the answers in Read for Details, page 208. Review "The Cellist of Sarajevo" and, on the lines provided below, place the numbers (which reflect the order in which the events actually took place) in the order in which they appear in the story's narrative. Then answer the questions.*

____ > ____ > _1_ > ____ > ____ > _6_ > ____ > ____

1. Why is the order of presentation of the events logical for the story that is being told?

2. What does the first paragraph explain? Why do you think the author feels the information he gives here is necessary for the reader to know at this time? How does it help the reader to understand the rest of the narrative?

3. How do the author's closing remarks in the conclusion connect with the information he gives at the beginning of the narrative? How do they permit him to communicate a lesson learned?

2 *Go back to Reading Two, page 210. Review the order of events in* The Soloist *and answer the questions:*

1. How does the author start the narrative?

2. How does the second paragraph connect with the first paragraph?

3. How does the final paragraph give a proper conclusion to the information given in the first two paragraphs? Why is the shift in verb tense significant?

4. Which of the two narratives, "The Cellist of Sarajevo" or *The Soloist*, is more simply constructed? Why?

STARTING NARRATIVES

The first paragraph of a narrative essay should do one of two things:
- Start the story
- Set the scene for the story

Both ways of starting a narrative are effective ways to begin. The story you want to tell should drive your choice of how you start your narrative. Sometimes the story itself will be enough to give the reader sufficient background to understand what is

---

happening. However, at other times you will need to set the scene for the reader so that you can influence the way the reader understands the characters and events of the story.

When the first paragraph starts the story, the next paragraph usually follows chronologically, in the order of time (see Unit 1). Note, however, that this does not mean that the plot has to be told from the first thing that happened to the last, although often that is the easiest way. When the first paragraph sets the scene for the story, the next paragraph is generally where the story starts chronologically.

For example, the author of *The Soloist* **starts the story** immediately. In the first paragraph, his narrator talks about "an idea" that "came to [him]" and tells about how he improvised before starting to play the D minor Bach suite, which is the subject of the second paragraph. More specifically, the first and second paragraphs have a cause-effect relationship. In the second paragraph, he shows how the preparation in the first paragraph was the cause of his great performance of the D minor Bach suite in the second paragraph. In the third paragraph, the narrator goes from these past-tense actions to a shift to the present as he explains how he approaches his music NOW because of the experience that he has just shared with us in the first two paragraphs.

The Soloist

INTRODUCTION: STARTING THE STORY
Idea of Playing in the Dark with Cello against Bare Chest ➤
Feeling of Body Becoming Part of the Cello ➤
Improvising ➤

BODY
Playing the D Minor Bach Suite ➤
Return of Musical Ear ➤
Great Performance ➤
Appreciative Audience (Cat Purring) ➤

CONCLUSION
Effect of Experience on Current Attitude towards Performance ➤
Declaration of Importance of Music in his Life

The author of "The Cellist of Sarajevo" **sets the scene** in the first paragraph. It is important for him to tell the reader in the first paragraph why he was at the International Cello Festival in Manchester, England. However, immediately thereafter, in the next five paragraphs, he also has to "set another scene." Before he can tell the moving story of Yo-Yo Ma's performance of "The Cellist of Sarajevo," he must take the reader further back in time with information about how Smailovic reacted to the massacre and how David Wilde was inspired to compose the piece. With the author's return home in the two final paragraphs, he closes the "frame" that the references to his trip provide in the essay, and he shares the lesson that he has learned. Although the narrative structure of "The Cellist of Sarajevo" seems a bit complicated because of its many "layers" in the past, it is so logically put together that it almost seems impossible that it could have been written any other way.

"The Cellist of Sarajevo"

INTRODUCTION: SETTING THE SCENE
The Author's Invitation to Cello Festival in Manchester, England ➤
Background Information about Vedran Smailovic and Sarajevo ➤
David Wilde and his composition of "The Cellist of Sarajevo" ➤

BODY
Yo-Yo Ma's Performance ➤
Yo-Yo Ma and Vedran Smailovic ➤

CONCLUSION
The Author's Return to Maine and Visit to Nursing Home ➤
Closing Remarks

---

3 *Imagine that the first paragraph of* The Soloist *is the first paragraph of the body. Write an introductory first paragraph that sets the scene for the story to follow. Share your paragraph in a small group. Discuss whether you think* The Soloist *is better with or without your introductory paragraphs. Give reasons.*

4 *Reread "The Cellist of Sarajevo" without the introductory first paragraph. In your groups, discuss the differences in the way the reader would understand the story. Explain which way you think is better. Give reasons.*

5 *Look back at your notes from Prepare to Write, pages 221–222. Write a brief paragraph explaining the purpose of your essay and how you believe you should organize it, either by starting the story immediately or by first setting the scene.*

6 *Prepare an outline. Show your strategy for the sequencing of events in the boxes.*

INTRODUCTION
Starting the story or *Setting the scene*?

BODY
Telling the main part of the story

CONCLUSION
Closing and communicating the message learned

7 *Using what you have learned about writing narratives, write a narrative essay on a work of art that had a great impact on you. Refer to the work you did in Prepare to Write, pages 221–222, and Write, pages 222–225, to write your first draft.*

◀ **REVISE: Using Descriptive Language**

Good writers use **descriptive language** when they want to give us the complete picture and to involve us fully in the story that they are telling. Writing without descriptive language just reports facts. This is good when the writer's primary goal is simply to communicate the facts of a situation. But if the goal is to go beyond the facts to move, inspire, and persuade the reader, the writer must use powerful descriptive language. Three ways the writer can create powerful descriptive language are to use well-chosen adjectives, to develop internal rhythms in the sentence by using parallel structure, and to vary sentence structure.

Adjectives

Adjectives can be used to describe feelings, to relate how any of the five senses—sight, smell, taste, hearing, and touch—were stimulated throughout an experience, and to report simple facts. They can also be used to reflect the writer's values and judgment.

Adjective phrases can also be used in descriptive writing. Adjective phrases begin with present participles ("-ing" forms of verbs) or with prepositions (*for, with, like,* and so on) and modify a noun just as adjectives do.

● "[Smailovic walked] into the midst of the battle *raging* <u>around him</u>."

Adjective clauses are also found in descriptive writing. They begin with *that, who,* and *which.*

● "He played . . . to the terrified people *who* <u>hid in the cellars</u> . . ."

Parallel Structure

Powerful descriptive passages have a certain music-like quality that is achieved when paragraphs have good internal sentence structure. Musical sentence rhythms are created by using **parallel structure**—by repeating patterns or sequences of action verbs, adjectives, nouns, adverbs, prepositional phrases, or adjective-noun pairs in one sentence. By threading sequences of images together—as a film editor does with the frames of a film—the writer is able to paint a complete picture and draw the reader into the world he or she is describing.

- "...<u>for</u> human dignity, <u>for</u> those lost to war, <u>for</u> civilization..."

Varied Sentence Structure

Varied sentence structure also contributes to good descriptive writing. The repetition of word patterns can be effective within the sentences themselves, but the repetition of the same grammatical sentence structure is not effective. Good writing should never have all the sentences in a paragraph starting in the same way. When this happens, the writing is very boring. Sentences should be both long and short, both simple and complex.

1 *Working with a partner, examine the paragraph from Paul Sullivan's "The Cellist of Sarajevo," and discuss the questions.*

> For each of the next 22 days, at 4 P.M., Smailovic put on his full, formal concert attire, took up his cello, and walked out of his apartment into the midst of the battle raging around him. Placing a plastic chair beside the crater that the shell had made, he played in memory of the dead Albinoni's *Adagio in G minor,* one of the most mournful and haunting pieces in the classical repertoire. He played to the abandoned streets, smashed trucks, and burning buildings, and to the terrified people who hid in the cellars while the bombs dropped and bullets flew. With masonry exploding around him, he made his unimaginably courageous stand for human dignity, for those lost to war, for civilization, for compassion, and for peace. Though the shellings went on, he was never hurt.

1. Why is this brief summary less interesting and effective than the whole paragraph above?

> Despite the bombs, a man named Smailovic played the cello in the streets of Sarajevo in memory of the dead.

2. Give examples of how the author makes a great effort to describe actions, places, and objects very carefully. Circle all the adjectives, adjective phrases, and clauses, and identify each one's purpose. Do they make facts more precise; communicate sights, sounds, or smells; tell about feelings; or communicate the author's value judgments?

3. Do you see examples of repeating patterns in his language? Underline all the parallel structures that give a certain music-like quality to the language.

4. Study the sentence structure in the paragraph. How many sentences start in the same way? Which sentence is the only one in the paragraph that begins with a subject-verb pattern? Why do you think this is the only sentence that starts in this way?

2 *Work in a small group. Using the techniques you have just learned, analyze the descriptive language in the paragraph from* **The Soloist.**

1. Underline the adjectives and adjective phrases.

2. Circle the repetitive patterns and parallel structures.

3. Discuss the variety of sentence structures in the passage.

> After improvising for a while, I started playing the D minor Bach suite, still in the darkness. Strangely freed of the task of finding the right phrasing, the right intonation, the right bowing, I heard the music through my skin. For the first time I didn't think about how it would sound to anyone else, and slowly, joyfully, gratefully, I started to hear again. The notes sang out, first like a trickle, then like a fountain of cool water bubbling up from a hole in the middle of a desert. After an hour or so I looked up, and in the darkness saw the outline of the cat sitting on the floor in front of me, cleaning her paws and purring loudly. I had an audience again, humble as it was.

3 *Look at the first draft of your essay. Have you used descriptive language to inspire the reader about the story you are telling? Did you include adjectives, adjective clauses, and parallel and varied sentence structures to make your writing more interesting?*

Write your final draft. Carefully edit it for grammatical and mechanical errors. Make sure you used some of the vocabulary and grammar from the unit. Use the checklist to help you write the final draft. Then neatly write or type your essay.

✓ FINAL DRAFT CHECKLIST

- ○ Does the introduction of your essay set the scene in an interesting and effective way?
- ○ Is there a logical connection between the introduction and the body?
- ○ Does the conclusion bring the essay effectively to an end and readily communicate your message?
- ○ Is the role of art in the essay clear?
- ○ Are the elements of descriptive language—parallel structure, varied sentence structure, adjective clauses—correctly integrated into the style?
- ○ Is the passive voice used to report ideas and facts?
- ○ Are *–ed* and *–ing* adjectives used correctly?
- ○ Is new vocabulary learned in the unit used? Are some words or expressions used figuratively?

ALTERNATIVE WRITING TOPICS

Write an essay on one of the topics. Use what you have learned about descriptive language to make your writing lively and effective. Use vocabulary from the readings and the passive voice.

1. What role does music play in your life? Has it been a source of comfort or help through a difficult period? In addition to comfort, what other emotions does music evoke?

2. Choose one of the quotes below, and write an essay explaining what it means to you. Use examples from your own life or your reading to explain your understanding. Say whether you agree or disagree with the quote.

   "Art is a wound that becomes light."   —Georges Braque

   "Art is a human activity having for its purpose the transmission to others of the highest and best feelings to which men have risen."   —Count Leo Tolstoy

3. Do you think that art and music should be an important part of the academic program in elementary and secondary schools? Should every child be required to learn to play an instrument and work on studio art? Why or why not? Discuss the advantages and disadvantages of making music and art a part of the academic curriculum for each child.

4. Choose one of the traditional arts of your native culture: quilt-making; pottery-making; beadwork or weaving; making mosaics; practicing traditional dances, songs, or theater. Describe this traditional handiwork, craft, or art, and tell what kinds of material it used and what it meant in the culture. What is the meaning of this art for people today?

RESEARCH TOPICS, see page 267.

UNIT 10 The End of Poverty

①FOCUS ON THE TOPIC

Ⓐ PREDICT

Look at the title of the unit and the photo collage. What do the photos show? What are some of the differences in the standard of living in developed countries and developing countries? Take five minutes to write down your thoughts about these questions. Share your answers with the class.

231

Below are statistics on the economic and social situations in different areas of the world. In the spaces provided, write a sentence giving your opinion on each of the questions on the next page. Discuss your observations and opinions in a small group.

GDP* per head in Dollars (Source: *The Economist: Pocket World in Figures 2007*)

United States	39,680	South Africa	1,190
Norway	38,450	Kenya	1,140
France	29,300	Mali	1,000
Japan	29,250	Ethiopia	760
Germany	28,300	Tanzania	670
South Korea	20,500	Malawi	650

Life Expectancy (Source: *The Economist: Pocket World in Figures 2007*)

Japan	82.8	Kenya	50.3
Norway	80.2	Mali	49.3
France	80.0	Ethiopia	48.5
Germany	79.3	Tanzania	46.6
South Korea	78.2	South Africa	44.1
United States	77.9	Malawi	41.1

Years of School Attendance (Source: *UNESCO Institute for Statistics*)

Norway	16.9	Japan	14.3
France	15.4	South Africa	14.1
Germany	15.3	Tanzania	5.0
United States	15.2	Ethiopia	4.3
South Korea	14.6	Mali	2.1

***GDP,** or **gross domestic product,** *is the total value of all the goods and services produced in a country, except for income received from abroad. This is different from the* **GNP,** *or* **gross national product,** *which is the total value of all the goods and services produced in a country, including income from abroad.*

1. How do the statistics for rich countries compare with those for poor countries?

   _____

   _____

2. How do you think these different economic indicators are related?

   _____

   _____

3. Does anything surprise you? Why or why not?

   _____

   _____

4. What do you think poor countries need in order to "catch up" with the developed nations?

   _____

   _____

C BACKGROUND AND VOCABULARY

Work in pairs. Read the sentences and circle the correct synonym for the boldfaced word from the choices given below. Use a dictionary if necessary.

1. Each year more than eight million people around the world face the **prospect** of dying because they are too poor to stay alive.

   a. possibility   **b.** hope   **c.** sight

2. Some economists fear that any plans to help the poor are just **fanciful** solutions that will never work out.

   a. expensive   **b.** practical   **c.** imaginary

3. Others are convinced that today's global prosperity makes it **feasible** to offer more help to the world's poorest people.

   a. probable   **b.** impossible   **c.** likely to work

4. They believe that it will take a **concerted** effort to solve some of the problems of impoverished countries; one nation cannot do it alone.

   a. careful   **b.** collective   **c.** clever

5. During the Cold War, more than $1 trillion was spent on aid to poor countries, but since the end of the Cold War, political interest has **waned.**

   a. decreased   **b.** increased   **c.** remained the same

6. The Bill Gates Foundation, set up by the founder of Microsoft, has given billions of dollars to **zero in on** health care in poor countries.

   a. look into   **b.** take away   **c.** concentrate on

7. Reducing the spread of tropical diseases would be a big step in the **eradication** of extreme poverty in the world.

   a. excusing   **b.** ending   **c.** establishing

8. **Monitoring** health programs in poor countries is an important step forward to ensure the well-being and safety of the entire world population.

   a. supervising   **b.** criticizing   **c.** organizing

9. Lack of basic education is a factor that can **inhibit** a country's economic development.

   a. hold out   **b.** hold on to   **c.** hold back

10. In the opinion of some economists, foreign aid is an essential **spur** to economic growth in today's developing world because developing countries lack capital for investment.

    a. stimulus   **b.** service   **c.** statistic

11. The uneven development typical of our economic system means that the difference between the most **affluent** and the poorest countries is growing bigger all the time.

    a. ancient   **b.** wealthy   **c.** humble

12. The United States is experiencing the largest gap between rich people and **impoverished** people in a hundred years.

    a. depressed   **b.** very poor   **c.** wealthy

2 FOCUS ON READING

A READING ONE: Can Extreme Poverty Be Eliminated?

Before you read, discuss the information and question with a partner.

Jeffrey Sachs, author of *The End of Poverty,* is Director of the Earth Institute at Columbia University and Special Advisor to the United Nations on the Millennium Development Goals. These goals, agreed on in 2000, set such targets as halving the proportion of people living on less than $1 a day by 2015.

Look at the title of the essay on the next page. Do you believe that extreme poverty can be eliminated? Why or why not?

Can Extreme Poverty Be Eliminated?

By Jeffrey Sachs from *Scientific American*

1   For the first time in history, global economic prosperity has placed the world within reach of eliminating extreme poverty altogether. This **prospect** will seem **fanciful** to some, but the dramatic economic progress made by China, India, and other low-income parts of Asia over the past 25 years demonstrates that it is realistic. Although economic growth has shown a remarkable capacity to lift vast numbers of people out of extreme poverty, progress is neither automatic nor inevitable. Market forces and free trade are not enough. Many of the poorest regions are caught in a poverty trap; they lack the financial means to make the necessary investments in infrastructure,[1] education, health care systems, and other vital needs. Yet the end of such poverty is **feasible** if a **concerted** global effort is undertaken, as the nations of the world promised when they attended the United Nations Millennium summit. The Millennium Project published a plan to halve the rate of extreme poverty by 2015 (compared to 1990). A large-scale public investment effort could in fact eliminate this problem by 2025. This hypothesis is controversial and I am pleased to have the opportunity to respond to various criticisms that have been raised about it.

2   Public opinion in affluent countries often blames extreme poverty on faults within the poor themselves—or at least with their governments. Culture was once thought to be the deciding factor:

United Nations Millennium Summit

religious divisions and taboos, caste systems, a lack of entrepreneurship, gender inequalities. Such theories have **waned** as societies of an ever-widening range of religions and cultures have achieved relative prosperity. Moreover, certain supposedly unchangeable aspects of culture (such as fertility choices and gender and caste[2] roles) do in fact change, often dramatically, as societies become urban and develop economically.

3   Most recently, commentators have **zeroed in on** "poor governance," or corruption. They argue that extreme poverty persists because governments

---

[1] **infrastructure:** a support system including roads, power, and ports, as well as health care and legal systems

[2] **caste:** division of society based on class differences of birth, rank, rights, profession, or job

(continued on next page)

fail to open up their markets, provide public services, and eliminate bribe taking. Developmental assistance efforts have become largely a series of good governance lectures. It is no good lecturing the dying that they should have done better with their lot in life. Although the debate continues, the weight of the evidence indicates that governance makes a difference but it is not the sole determinant of economic growth. According to surveys conducted by Transparency International, business leaders actually perceive some fast-growing countries to be more corrupt than some slow-moving African ones.

4   A second common misunderstanding concerns the extent to which corruption is likely to eat up the donated money. Some foreign aid in the past has indeed ended up this way. That happened when the funds were provided for political reasons during the Cold War. When assistance has been targeted at development rather than political goals, the outcomes have been favorable, ranging from the Green Revolution[3] to the eradication of smallpox and the recent near-eradication of polio. Aid packages would be directed towards those countries with a reasonable degree of good governance. The money would not be merely thrown at them. It would be provided according to a detailed and **monitored** plan, and new rounds of financing would be delivered only as the work actually got done. Much of the funds would be given directly to villages and towns to minimize the chances of their getting diverted by central governments.

5   Geography—including natural resources, climate, topography, and proximity to trade routes and major markets—is at least as important as good governance. As early as 1776, Adam Smith argued that high transportation costs **inhibited** development in the inland areas of Africa and Asia.

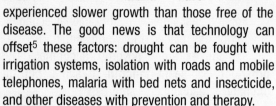

Other geographic features such as the heavy disease burden of the tropics, also interfere. Tropical countries saddled with[4] malaria have experienced slower growth than those free of the disease. The good news is that technology can offset[5] these factors: drought can be fought with irrigation systems, isolation with roads and mobile telephones, malaria with bed nets and insecticide, and other diseases with prevention and therapy.

6   Another major insight is that although the most powerful mechanism for reducing extreme poverty is to encourage overall economic growth, a rising tide does not necessarily lift all boats. Average income can rise, but if the income is distributed unevenly, the poor may benefit little, and pockets of extreme poverty may persist. Moreover, growth is not simply a free-market phenomenon. It requires basic government services: infrastructure, health, education, and scientific and technological innovation. Government spending, directed at investment in critical areas, is itself a vital **spur** to growth, especially if its effects are to reach the poorest of the poor.

7   Adding it up, the total requirement would be 0.7 percent of the combined gross national product (GNP) of the **affluent** donor nations, which is what all donor nations have long promised but few have given. If rich nations fail to make these investments, they will face famine, epidemics, regional conflicts, and the spread of terrorist havens. They will condemn not only the **impoverished** countries but themselves as well to chronic political instability, humanitarian emergencies, and security risks. As the UN Secretary-General wrote: "There will be no development without security, and no security without development."

---

[3] The *Green Revolution* of the 1960s and 1970s in Asia introduced high-yield grains, irrigation, and fertilizers, which ended the cycle of famine, disease, and despair.
[4] **saddled with:** burdened with a heavy responsibility or a difficult problem
[5] **offset:** to make up for, balance

*On the lines provided under "Objections to Sachs's Proposals" and "Sachs's Answers
to Critics," summarize in one sentence the information required, based on your
understanding of the reading. Compare your answers with a partner's. After you have
answered the questions in Express Opinions, you will be asked to come back to this
section and give "Your Opinion."*

Objections to Sachs's Proposals	Sachs's Answers to Critics	Your Opinion
1. The poor have only themselves to blame; their culture, habits, and attitudes are not appropriate.		
2. _____	Even if governments were excellent, they could not get their countries out of the poverty trap all alone. Aid money should be targeted directly to the villages rather than to the central governments and be carefully monitored.	
3. _____		
4. The free market is enough. You don't need government or international aid.		

Circle the best answer to complete each statement.

1. For impoverished countries, free trade _____.

   a. is not an important factor
   b. will bring prosperity for all
   c. is only part of the solution

2. People's cultural practices _____.

   a. never change because people respect their traditions
   b. may change with economic progress
   c. are not important for economic growth

3. Corruption is _____ a factor in economic decline.

   a. always
   b. sometimes
   c. never

4. _____ is NOT an example of targeted aid as Jeffrey Sachs proposes.

   a. The eradication of smallpox
   b. Giving political support
   c. Bringing better seeds, fertilizer, and irrigation to Asia

5. Aid will be given to countries _____.

   a. that can show they need it
   b. that have reasonably good government
   c. that are entirely free of corruption

6. _____ is a consequence of geography that CANNOT be helped by technology.

   a. The high cost of transportation
   b. Climate
   c. The lack of natural resources

7. Government spending _____.

   a. is necessary for investment in the infrastructure
   b. is not a good idea because it interferes with free trade
   c. should be avoided because of corruption

8. A good deal of the funds of the Millennium Project will be given _____.

   a. to governments
   b. to villages
   c. to aid agencies

◖ MAKE INFERENCES

*Mark the statements **T** (true) or **F** (false), based on the reading. Then write a sentence explaining your decision. Include points in the article that support your inference. Share your answers in a small group.*

_____ 1. Sachs's main intention in writing this article is to inform his readers of the facts about the world's poorest countries.

Support: _____

_____ 2. The author's target audience for this article is government leaders from developed countries.

Support: _____

_____ 3. Sachs's critics would probably argue that cultural factors make poverty permanent.

Support: _____

_____ 4. Sachs doesn't condemn the poor for their failings.

Support: _____

_____ 5. Jeffrey Sachs advocates giving people in Africa a "hand up" (a way to improve) rather than a "handout" (charity money).

Support: _____

_____ 6. Once incomes start rising, the government should get out of the economy.

Support: _____

_____ 7. Rich nations act in their own interests when they give aid to poor countries.

Support: _____

◖ EXPRESS OPINIONS

*What do you think of Sachs's proposal? Discuss with the members of your group what the political, economic, and moral reasons to help impoverished countries are. Then go back to Read for Main Ideas and, under "Your Opinion," rank Sachs's responses to the critics using a scale from **1** (least convincing) to **4** (most convincing). Discuss why you have ranked each idea in that way. Then share your group's opinions with the rest of the class.*

The following excerpt is taken from a review of a book by Barbara Ehrenreich entitled *Nickel and Dimed: On (Not) Getting By in America.* "To nickel and dime" is an idiom. Nickels and dimes are very small coins that are worth very little. "To nickel and dime" people is to pay them very little or have contempt for them. Another related meaning is to be petty or small-minded, particularly about money. Barbara Ehrenreich, a writer and social activist, went undercover for three months and lived in three different American cities to find out what it's like to be earning a minimum wage.

1 *Discuss the questions with a partner. Then read the excerpt.*

What do you think life is like for people in the United States who have to live on wages of $6 or $7 an hour? What is the meaning of "the working poor"?

Making Ends Meet

From a *New York Times* book review written by Dorothy Gallagher

1 In Key West, Florida, Ehrenreich found a job as a waitress at an inexpensive family restaurant. Her shift ran from 2:00 P.M. to 10:00 P.M. Salary: $2.43 an hour plus tips. To find an **affordable** rent, she had to move 30 miles out of town, a 45-minute commute on a crowded two-lane highway. How did her co-workers manage housing? One waitress shared a room in a $250 a week flophouse;[1] a cook shared a two-room apartment with three others; another worker lived in a van parked behind a shopping center.

2 "There are no secret economies that nourish the poor," Ehrenreich writes. "If you can't put up the two months' rent you need to get an apartment, you end up paying through the nose for a room by the week. If you have only one room, with a hotplate at best, you can't save by cooking up huge stews that can be frozen for the week ahead. You eat hot dogs and the styrofoam cups of soup that can be microwaved at a convenience store." Without health insurance from work, you risk a small cut becoming infected because you can afford neither a visit to the doctor nor antibiotics.

3 In the summer tourist slump, Ehrenreich found her salary with tips dropped from about $7 an hour to $5.15. At this rate, the only way to pay her rent was to get a second job. So, for a while she worked 8:00 A.M. to 2:00 P.M. and then rushed to her regular shift at the first restaurant – a 14-hour day of brutal physical labor, as anyone who has waitressed for a living knows. With such a schedule, she could not, of course, keep her decent housing so far from town. Ehrenreich's new home was an eight-foot-wide trailer parked among others "in a nest of crime," where "desolation rules night and day . . . There are not exactly people here but what amounts to canned labor, being preserved between shifts from the heat."

4 Moving to Maine, Ehrenreich took 2 jobs to make ends meet – a weekend job in a nursing home and a full-time job in a house-cleaning service. At Merry Maids, the cleaning service, the economics were as follows: the customer pays the service $25 an hour per cleaning person; the service pays $6.65 an hour to each cleaner. "How poor are my co-workers?" Ehrenreich asks. Half bags of corn chips for lunch; dizziness from malnutrition; a toothache requiring frantic calls to find a free dental clinic; worries about makeshift childcare arrangements because a licensed day-care center at $90 a week is beyond any cleaner's budget; no one

---

[1] **flophouse:** a very rundown, shabby place that rents you a bed or a small room by the night

sleeping in a car, but everyone crowded into housing with far too many others, strangers or family; "signs of real difficulty if not actual misery."

5   Soon, Ehrenreich starts having money troubles even with two jobs. Housing is the killer. She foresees a weekend without food unless she can find charitable help. More than an hour on the phone with various private charitable agencies (cost of phone calls: $2.50) nets her a severely restricted food voucher[2] – no fresh fruits, vegetables, chicken or cheese – worth $7.02.

6   Minneapolis is Ehrenreich's last stop. In this city, as in the other two, affordable housing was the major problem. Across the nation, the supply of housing for low-income families was decreasing: 36 units available for every 100 families in need. The old rule that one should pay no more than 30 percent of income for rent has become impossible. For most poor renters, the figure is more than 50 percent. In the Minneapolis-St. Paul region, where the minimum living wage for a parent and one child was calculated to be $11.77 an hour, Ehrenreich has a job at Walmart paying $7 an hour. Many of her fellow workers, even those with working spouses, work two jobs.

7   What does Ehrenreich conclude from her experiences? No surprises here. Even for a worker holding two jobs, wages are too low, housing costs too high, for minimally decent survival in the life of America's working poor.

---

[2] **food voucher:** a coupon given to you by the government that you can exchange for food at no cost to you

2 *Read the questions and select the best answers. In some cases there is more than one correct answer. Discuss your answers in a small group.*

1. Which of the following jobs did Barbara Ehrenreich have?
   a. waitress, cook, tourist guide, store employee
   b. cook, waitress, housecleaner, store employee
   c. waitress, housecleaner, nursing home attendant, store employee
   d. nursing home attendant, cook, tourist guide, housecleaner

2. Based on Ehrenreich's description of the trailer park in Key West, what are living conditions like for the working poor?
   a. dangerous
   b. congested
   c. depressing
   d. hot

3. What conclusions can we draw about Ehrenreich's job as a housecleaner?
   a. Homeowners pay the cleaning company $50 an hour for two cleaners.
   b. Only about 25 percent of the money goes to the cleaners; 75 percent goes to the cleaning company owners.
   c. Cleaning houses provides Ehrenreich with enough money to live on.
   d. The cleaning workers eat nourishing lunches.

4. What can we conclude about Ehrenreich's attempt to get help from private charities?

    a. She was successful in getting some food.
    b. It was easy to get help from charities.
    c. The charities provided the food she wanted to eat.
    d. The food voucher was really worth only $4.52 to her.

5. "There are not exactly people here [in the trailer park] but what amounts to canned labor, being preserved between shifts from the heat." What does this mean?

    a. The workers are treated well.
    b. Life in the trailer park is not fit for humans.
    c. Workers are housed only so that they can continue working.
    d. Employers use robots.

C INTEGRATE READINGS ONE AND TWO

STEP 1: Organize

Review Readings One and Two and complete this grid by putting notes in the appropriate places. Share your answers with a classmate.

	PROBLEMS WITH POVERTY	**SOLUTIONS TO POVERTY**
Developing countries	- disease - lack of capital to invest - -	- government investment in the infrastructure - directed aid packages - -
Developed countries	- low wages - lack of affordable health care - -	- - - -

STEP 2: Synthesize

Work in pairs. Complete the two paragraphs on the next page using the information in Step 1. Compare and contrast the problems of poverty in developed and developing countries and possible solutions to those problems.

The Experience of Poverty

The experience of not being able to live a decent life is something that poor people share no matter what country they live in. Nevertheless, there are significant differences between poverty in developed countries and developing countries. In developed countries

_____

_____

_____

In developing countries, the situation may be more desperate

_____

_____

_____

③ FOCUS ON WRITING

Ⓐ VOCABULARY

◀ REVIEW

Put the words in the word boxes where they belong in the text below and on pages 244–245. Check your answers with a partner's.

feasible	impoverished	prospect

The desire to help correct the worst injustices of the economic system in our own countries also leads us to reach out to help _____ people in
1.
other lands. What makes such an effort _____ today is the fact that
2.
so much of what people suffer from is preventable with science and technology.

However, not every economist supports the _____ of more foreign
3.
aid. Some criticize Jeffrey Sachs for exaggerating the role of donor aid.

monitoring	severely	spur

William Easterly at New York University _____ **4.** criticizes what he calls Sachs's "Big Plan" to cure all of Africa's ills. He claims that the bureaucracy of the United Nations is inefficient and wasteful. Even Sachs's assurance of careful _____ **5.** of all aid money does not convince some critics. They see Sachs as a technocrat who gives technical solutions to what are essentially unsolvable human and political problems. Paul Collier in *The Bottom Billion* agrees with many of Sachs's points, but emphasizes the role of trade as a _____ **6.** to economic development.

affordable	eradicate	inhibit

To show what can be done, Sachs's Millennium Project has set up 12 "research villages" in 10 African countries, with 66 more villages grouped around them. Each village will receive $250 per person in aid over five years. The money is carefully supervised by village councils and aid agencies to _____ **7.** any tendency to corruption. The Project is trying to show how a few _____ **8.** reforms like cleaner water and better fertilizer and seeds, which do not require a great deal of money, can improve people's lives. For the price of a cup of coffee in New York, a child can be free of disease for a year. Free bed nets may not _____ **9.** malaria completely, but in Sauri, Kenya, for example, they have reduced its incidence by 50 percent.

concerted	malnutrition	zeroing in on

A _____ **10.** effort from everyone in a village is the best solution. For example, after helping farmers to grow better crops, the Sauri village council

asked the farmers to give one free meal of maize and beans to every young child in school to fight _____. The result? With full stomachs, Sauri's
_____11._____
children went from 108th in district exam results to 2nd. By _____
_____12._____
the idea of villagers taking responsibility for the innovations, villagers say that now

everyone can find at least a little to eat.

affluent	available	fanciful

Is it _____ to think that these few villages will be enough to
_____13._____
make a difference on a whole continent? Will this make Africa too dependent on

money from _____ foreigners? For many economists, making help
_____14._____
_____ to poor countries so that they can climb onto the ladder of
_____15._____
economic growth is the challenge of this generation. How to do this is the subject of

a great debate.

◀ **EXPAND**

1 *Working in pairs, choose the sentences that best express the meaning of the underlined expressions. Refer to Reading Two to see how the expressions are used.*

1. Are you able to <u>put up</u> the rent, or do you need to borrow some money?
   a. Can you change the money?
   b. Are you able to afford the rent?
   c. Can you excuse this high rent?

2. If you don't have health insurance, you have to <u>pay through the nose</u> to see a doctor or a dentist.
   a. You have to pay cash.
   b. You have to pay less.
   c. You have to pay a lot.

3. We can't afford a regular babysitter, so we have <u>makeshift</u> childcare arrangements with neighbors and family.
   a. We use temporary solutions.
   b. We are able to use better childcare arrangements.
   c. We have to spend a lot of money.

4. Many people come here in the summer, but the winter tourist <u>slump</u> is badly affecting the economy of our city.

    a. Tourists are not coming at all.
    b. Fewer tourists are coming.
    c. Tourists are too fearful to come.

5. It is very difficult <u>to make ends meet</u> when you earn only $7 an hour.

    a. It is hard to meet others.
    b. It is hard to work in such conditions.
    c. It is hard to earn enough to cover your expenses.

Negative and Positive Connotations of Words

2 *The words in each pair below have approximately the same meaning, but one has a positive connotation, while the other has a negative connotation. Put a **P** next to the more positive word and an **N** next to the one with the more negative connotation.*

1. _____ **a.** stubborn   _____ **b.** determined

2. _____ **a.** economical*   _____ **b.** miserly

3. _____ **a.** scrawny   _____ **b.** slender

4. _____ **a.** foolhardy   _____ **b.** brave

5. _____ **a.** average   _____ **b.** mediocre

6. _____ **a.** self-satisfied   _____ **b.** self-confident

7. _____ **a.** statesmen   _____ **b.** politicians

---

* NOT a synonym for "economic" (relating to trade and industry)

3 *Circle the word that best completes each sentence. Pay special attention to connotation and context.*

1. Despite criticism, the United Nations is convinced of the need to make a (*stubborn / determined*) effort to reach the Millennium Goals.

2. Mothers in traditional societies are not so (*stubborn / determined*) that they will refuse new customs like vaccinations if it means saving the lives of their children.

3. A researcher who is (*self-satisfied / self-confident*) is full of conceit and arrogance.

4. We need to appear (*self-satisfied / self-confident*) when we speak in front of an audience at a professional conference.

5. A child who doesn't get enough food to eat is (*scrawny / slender*) and malnourished.

6. In magazine advertisements, affluent young people appear fashionably (*scrawny / slender*).

7. The (*average / mediocre*) American earns about $45,000 a year.

8. Because a lot of foreign aid during the Cold War was directed to the military, it brought at best only (*average / mediocre*) results in raising ordinary people's standard of living.

9. Jeffrey Sachs feels that giving aid to developing countries is the (*economical / miserly*) thing to do because the money spent now will save huge sums on security or immigration in the future.

10. It is difficult to get all countries to contribute their fair share to development goals because some are very (*economical / miserly*) with their money.

11. Millennium Project volunteers are (*brave / foolhardy*) people who travel far away to help the impoverished.

12. It would be (*brave / foolhardy*) to simply send money to needy areas without strict monitoring procedures.

13. (*Politicians / Statesmen*) do only what brings them popularity in the short term.

14. (*Politicians / Statesmen*), on the other hand, may defend unpopular or difficult causes because they know these causes are morally right.

◖ CREATE

Write a dialogue between Barbara Ehrenreich and Jeffrey Sachs about poor people and what they need. Use six vocabulary words, two idioms, and two more words with either negative or positive connotations.

BARBARA EHRENREICH: I am pleased to be able to meet you at last. I think that we are very concerned about the same kind of problem: the people who live in poverty. One big problem is that people don't seem to care about the poor. How can we get them to pay attention?

JEFFREY SACHS:

_____

_____

_____

_____

_____

GRAMMAR: Using Noun Clauses in Argumentative Essays

Examine the underlined clauses in the sentences and discuss the questions with a partner.

- <u>What Jeffrey Sachs hopes to see by 2025</u> is the end of extreme poverty in the world.

- <u>That our advanced science and technology can help us to make the achievement of this goal possible</u> is being considered seriously by <u>whoever wants to improve the human condition.</u>

- Critics of Jeffrey Sachs point to <u>what the results of past humanitarian aid efforts clearly show</u>: a failure to use the financial aid properly because of corruption.

- Nevertheless, despite past failures, <u>what Jeffrey Sachs says,</u> <u>that there are now new ways to eradicate extreme poverty in the world,</u> is probably true.

1. Does each clause have a subject and a verb? If so, what are they?

2. What words do these clauses start with?

3. What is the subject-verb word order in each of these clauses?

4. In the last sentence, there are two clauses underlined. How does the second clause "clarify" the first clause? What is the subject of this sentence?

NOUN CLAUSES

Noun clauses are like nouns in a sentence. Noun clauses can be subjects, objects of verbs or prepositions, or complements. The following words often introduce noun clauses: *what, that, who, whom, whether, why, where, how, whatever, whoever, whomever, wherever, however.*

Noun clause as SUBJECT	**What Jeffrey Sachs hopes to see by 2025** is the end of extreme poverty in the world.
Noun clause as OBJECT	We must consider seriously **what Jeffrey Sachs hopes to see by 2025.**
Noun clause as COMPLEMENT	This is **what Jeffrey Sachs hopes to see by 2025.**

Noun clauses can also be placed **in apposition** with each other (alongside each other):

What Jeffrey Sachs says, that there are now new ways to eradicate extreme poverty in the world, is probably true.

This sentence is a combination of these two sentences:

SUBJECT
What Jeffrey Sachs says is probably true.

SUBJECT
That there are now new ways to eradicate extreme poverty in the world is probably true.

Pattern for Noun Clauses in Apposition

What "X" insists,	that	+	opinion or idea being discussed,		is probably true.
(comma)			(that + *complete sentence*) (comma)		is indisputable.
asserts					does not make sense.
suggests					is worthy of consideration.
implies					etc.
etc.					

Combining the two noun clauses in one sentence permits writers or speakers to clarify exactly what they are referring to. This is a good technique to use when writing a persuasive or argumentative essay or participating in an oral debate.

GRAMMAR TIP: Like all clauses, noun clauses must have a subject and a verb. Although some noun clauses start with question words, the word order is not the inverted subject-verb word order that is used in questions. In all noun clauses, the subject comes before the verb. Note that sometimes the question word itself is the "subject" of the noun clause, as in "whoever wants to improve the human condition."

---

1 *Fill in the blanks with* **what, that, who, why, where, how,** *and* **whoever** *and the subject and the correct form of the verb in parentheses to complete this summary of CBS Worldwide correspondent Bob Simon's report entitled "Beatrice's Goat Fed a Dream."*

Beatrice's Goat Fed a Dream

Who would ever think that a goat could dramatically change the course of a person's life? This is _____what happened_____ to a Ugandan woman by the name
                                  1. (happen)
of Beatrice Biira. When she was nine years old, her parents could not afford to send

her to school. _____, in the small village of Kisinga, in the
                    2. (the family / live)
western part of Uganda, there were not enough jobs and not enough food to eat.

Beatrice and her family were hungry. _____ eating cassava and
                                           3. (the young girl / survive)
sweet potatoes every day was almost a miracle.

_____ Beatrice even at that young age understood that her
        4. (know)
hunger was for education as well as for food. Her luck changed when Beatrice's

family, one of the poorest in her village, was among 12 families chosen to receive a

goat from Heifer International, a charity in Little Rock, Arkansas. Beatrice's parents

were finally able to send her to the local school when she was ten years old.

Understanding _____ this opportunity for Beatrice is not
                5. (one goat / able to provide)
difficult. Because Heifer goats produce a great deal of milk, Beatrice's mother was

able to sell enough milk to send Beatrice to school.

Right from the start, with a combination of _____ her
                                              6. (reflect)
passion for an education and her intelligence, Beatrice impressed her teachers in the

local school. As a result, she won a scholarship to a high school in Kampala, the

country's capital. Soon after, she went to a private high school in New England, in

the United States. She is now a student at Connecticut College.

Undoubtedly, _____ now in her life in the United States is
              7. (Beatrice / enjoy)
very different from her life in Uganda. Nevertheless, it is in

_____ using the education she has received that makes this
  8. (she / envisage)
young woman special. Beatrice will not forget _____. Her
                                                9. (she / come from)
dream is to return to Uganda and give back to her community by creating a school

for disadvantaged children, or an orphanage, with a farm for cows and goats. This

should make _____ skeptical about donating aid to
              10. (be)
impoverished countries think again about the question. Just as the people in her

village celebrate "Passing on the Gift" by giving newborn goats to other families,

Beatrice will pass on the gift of her education to her countrymen in need.

Surely, _____, _____
         11. (Beatrice's story / prove)   12. (providing aid to people in poor countries / be)
sometimes very beneficial, cannot be overlooked.

2 *Do the following with the statements given below.*
- Make each statement part of a noun clause-in-apposition pattern as you show
  whether it is likely to be made by Jeffrey Sachs or one of his critics.
- Give your stand on the issue at the end of the noun clause-in-apposition pattern.
- Develop your argument further by adding a few sentences with examples and
  evidence that clarify your position.

1. There are now ways to eradicate extreme poverty in the world.

    What Sachs insists, that there are now ways to eradicate extreme

    poverty in the world, is probably true. We have the scientific training and the technical know-how to provide the impoverished around the world with enough food to eat. However, I question how we will make this happen. This can be a costly process.

_____

_____

_____

_____

_____

2. Foreign aid in the past has been eaten up by corruption.

_____

_____

_____

_____

3. The geography of a country can inhibit its development.

_____

_____

_____

_____

4. Free trade market forces will not resolve the problems of poverty in some countries.

_____

_____

_____

_____

5. Poverty on a large scale is a threat to world peace.

_____

_____

_____

_____

In this unit, you read Jeffrey Sachs's essay entitled "Can Extreme Poverty be Eliminated?" and Dorothy Gallagher's review of Barbara Ehrenreich's book, *Nickel and Dimed: On (Not) Getting By in America.*

You will *write an argumentative essay in response to the following question:* **Should affluent countries assume the financial burden of eliminating extreme poverty in the world, according to the proposal made by Jeffrey Sachs in his essay?***

◀ PREPARE TO WRITE: Listing

Working with a partner, write a list of arguments **FOR** *and* **AGAINST** *expecting affluent countries to assume the financial burden of eliminating extreme poverty in the world, according to the proposal made by Jeffrey Sachs in his essay.*

For	Against
1.	1.
2.	2.
3.	3.
4.	4.
5.	5.

Examining the list, determine which arguments you believe are more logical to your way of thinking. State here the position you are going to take in your essay: _____

_____

◀ WRITE: An Argumentative Essay

1 *Working with a partner, reread the introductory paragraph in Reading One. Then discuss the questions.*

> **(1)** For the first time in history, global economic prosperity has placed the world within reach of eliminating extreme poverty altogether. **(2)** This prospect will seem fanciful to some, but the dramatic economic progress made by China, India, and other low-income parts of Asia over the past 25 years demonstrates that it is realistic. **(3)** Although economic growth has shown a remarkable capacity to lift vast numbers of people out of extreme poverty,

---

*For Alternative Writing Topics, see page 260. These topics can be used in place of the writing topic for this unit or as homework. The alternative topics relate to the theme of the unit, but may not target the same grammar or rhetorical structures taught in the unit.

progress is neither automatic nor inevitable. **(4)** Market forces and free trade are not enough. **(5)** Many of the poorest regions are caught in a poverty trap; they lack the financial means to make the necessary investments in infrastructure, education, health care systems, and other vital needs. **(6)** Yet the end of such poverty is feasible if a concerted global effort is undertaken, as the nations of the world promised when they attended the United Nations Millennium summit. **(7)** The Millennium Project published a plan to halve the rate of extreme poverty by 2015 (compared to 1990). **(8)** A large-scale and targeted public investment effort could in fact eliminate this problem by 2025. **(9)** This hypothesis is controversial and I am pleased to have the opportunity to respond to various concerns that have been raised about it.

1. What kind of information do sentences 1 through 5 give the reader?

2. Why is sentence 6 important?

3. How do sentences 7 and 8 reinforce the statement made in sentence 6?

4. What purpose does sentence 9 serve?

ARGUMENTATIVE ESSAYS

Introduction and Thesis Statement

The aim of an **argumentative essay** is to convince the reader to agree with the author's point of view or opinion. An argumentative essay tries to be very persuasive by appealing to *reason* and *logic*.

An argumentative essay must introduce and explain the background to the issue or problem. The background information presents the issue and leads to the thesis statement. In the thesis statement, the author must take a stand and present his or her point of view *strongly* and *clearly*. Most commonly this is done through the use of modals such as *should (not), must (not), would be better if . . . , would like you to . . . .*

For instance, in the introduction to his essay, "Can Extreme Poverty Be Eliminated?" Jeffrey Sachs gives us the necessary background information in the first five sentences. Without this information, the reader would not be prepared to consider his thesis statement, which begins in sentence 6: "Yet the end of such poverty is feasible if a concerted global effort is undertaken, as the nations of the world promised when they attended the United Nations Millennium summit." He furnishes more background information to accompany his thesis in sentence 7. However, in sentence 8—"A large-scale and targeted public investment effort could in fact eliminate this problem by 2025"—he completes the thesis statement that he started in sentence 6. In sentence 9, Sachs gives us the procedure he will follow in supporting his thesis.

Sachs does not force the issue on his readers. He presents the arguments without the use of words *must (not), should (not),* etc. Instead, he wisely calls his idea a "hypothesis," which is something that needs to be proven, and the arguments against

(continued on next page)

his proposal the "concerns that have been raised about it." In so doing, he encourages the reader to join him in a necessary dialogue, with the hope that people will eventually accept the challenge of helping him to prove his theory. This reflects his optimism about what "could" happen if people all over the world took his hypothesis seriously.

Supporting Your Views

In most good argumentative essays, the writer's point of view is obvious in the first paragraph. However, an essay is not a mere opinion. The body of the essay should provide support or reasons for the author's point of view: factual details, explanations, examples, and even, in appropriate cases, anecdotes from personal experience.

Refuting Opposing Points of View

Writing an argumentative essay is like taking one side in a debate, either for or against. The writer must not only show that his or her ideas are correct; but must also show that opposing views are wrong. Refuting an opponent's views involves showing why the opponent's arguments, or "counterarguments," are incorrect. To be effective, an argumentative essay must contain a point-by-point **refutation** of the main arguments of the opposing view.

Concession

If an opponent has a valid point or expresses an idea that is true, the writer must, in honesty, concede it. It is very rare that the arguments on one side are *all* bad and on the other *all* good. After admitting that the opposition may have a good point, the writer can go on to show that overall, his or her reasons are superior to the opponents' views.

Every argumentative essay should have at least one concession to show some understanding of the ideas of the opposite side. The concession should not appear in the conclusion. Nor can it be allowed to change the main idea or divert attention from the thesis statement of the essay.

In paragraph 4, Jeffrey Sachs makes a concession. He agrees that corruption has been an obstacle to charitable aid efforts in the past. However, by offering his recommendation for a new method of giving by means of a "detailed and monitored plan" that would only be "directed towards those countries with a reasonable degree of good governance," he hopes to answer the objections of his critics.

Conclusion

The **conclusion** should follow logically from the arguments in the essay. It summarizes the main ideas and reaffirms the thesis. It may also offer further suggestions for consideration. For instance, in his conclusion, Jeffrey Sachs actually suggests that *we must eliminate extreme poverty in the world if we want to live relatively secure lives.*

As you develop your arguments and refute opposing points of view, you can organize your essay in one of three ways:

1. Make your own arguments, followed by the counterarguments and refutations.

2. Alternate between your own arguments and the relevant counterarguments and refutations.

3. Discuss the counterarguments and refutations, then follow with your own arguments.

For instance, in paragraph 3 of his essay, Sachs goes from a reference to the *counterargument* ("poverty persists because governments fail to . . .") to his own *argument* ("the weight of the evidence indicates that governance makes a difference but it is not the sole determinant of economic growth") to a *refutation* ("According to surveys conducted by Transparency International, business leaders actually perceive some fast-growing countries to be more corrupt than some slow-moving African ones").

Working with a partner, go back to Reading One and underline the counterarguments Sachs deals with. Then evaluate his rebuttals. Discuss whether or not Sachs has done a good job in refuting the criticisms of his position.

2 *Write an outline for your essay. Circle your thesis here:*

"Affluent countries **should assume the financial burden of** eliminating extreme poverty in the world."

"Affluent countries **should not assume the financial burden of** eliminating extreme poverty in the world."

Now write in complete sentences your arguments, counterarguments, and refutations here:

Arguments

_____

_____

Counterarguments

_____

_____

Refutations

_____

_____

Write at least one concession here:

Concession

_____

_____

_____

You should try to have at least three arguments, with their respective counterarguments and refutations.

3 *When you have finished, share your plan with a partner. Discuss which of the three organizational patterns described above will be best for you to follow.*

4 *Using what you have learned about writing argumentative essays, write an essay in response to the question asked at the beginning of Focus on Writing. Refer to the work you did in Prepare to Write, page 252, and Write, pages 252–256, as you organize your notes into logical patterns.*

◖ REVISE: Using the Language of Concession

There should be at least one concession in your essay where you acknowledge a good point in your opponent's argument.

The following phrases can introduce concessions:

Concession	Writer's Argument
It is true that / I concede that / I agree that corruption has been a major challenge to individuals or institutions that have tried to give aid to countries suffering from extreme poverty.	**Nevertheless,** this should not stop us from looking for ways to help people whose lives depend on our support.
Undoubtedly, / Admittedly, poor countries also suffer from civil wars, bad leadership,and ethnic conflicts.	**However,** donors should not use problems as an excuse to do nothing.

In the above sentences, the writer concedes and continues to pursue his main argument with transitional discourse connectors. Concessions can also be made with the contrastive conjunctions, **although** and **even though,** which contrast two opposite ideas in the same sentence. The argument appears in the main clause, NOT the subordinate clause. The concession comes in the subordinate clause (the clause with **although** and **even though**). The argument can come before or after the concession: "Although the most powerful mechanism for reducing extreme poverty is to encourage overall economic growth, a rising tide does not necessarily lift all boats." (Jeffrey Sachs, "Can Extreme Poverty Be Eliminated?")

Concession	Writer's Argument
Although the most powerful mechanism for reducing extreme poverty is to encourage overall economic growth,	a rising tide does not necessarily lift all boats. (overall growth doesn't help every country or every person)
Writer's Argument	**Concession**
A rising tide does not necessarily lift all boats	**even though** the most powerful mechanism for reducing extreme poverty is to encourage overall economic growth.

1 Work with a partner. Refer to the Read for Main Ideas section, pages 237–238, where you have outlined "Objections to Sachs's Proposals" (AGAINST Jeffrey Sachs's proposals) and "Sachs's Answers to Critics" (FOR Jeffrey Sachs's proposals). Using the language of concession shown above, choose three arguments for each point of view, and write sentences that include a main argument and a concession.

For Jeffrey Sachs's Proposals

1. Although the corruption of centralized governments prevented financial aid from going to where it was needed most in the past, future financing will be closely monitored and sent in installments directly to the villages where people will be working on important development projects.

2. _____

_____

_____

3. _____

_____

_____

Against Jeffrey Sachs's Proposals

1. It is impossible to believe there will be no corruption in the villages where people live with so many basic needs even though the close monitoring of future financial aid has been promised.

2. _____

_____

_____

3. _____

_____

_____

2 *Examine the model paragraph of a Concession and Reply. Working with a partner, answer the questions that follow as you consider how the kinds of sentences you have practiced in the previous Exercise and in Exercise 2 of the Grammar section, pages 250–251, can contribute to a well-developed concession / reply paragraph.*

It is true that the desire for survival is a force that can quickly change into dangerous rage. **What Jeffrey Sachs suggests**—that terrorism will increase on a global scale if attempts are not made to eradicate extreme poverty—**may be correct.**

Concession ➤ People who are trapped in one way or another eventually rebel if they are kept from improving their condition. **However, even though the security of the world may be at risk if nothing is done to help people of poor**

Main Argument (Reply) **countries,** affluent countries should not be expected to send large amounts of financial aid to impoverished nations. Solving poor countries' problems this way will not be easy because finding countries in Africa that demonstrate good governance seems difficult. For instance, people who live in Ethiopia, Somalia, Eritrea, the Sudan, and Darfur are not only the victims of hunger but also of the horrors of civil war. Because of this situation, even sending skilled administrators, teachers, engineers, health and agricultural workers to these countries, which would be a better idea than sending them money, is not possible at this time. Undoubtedly, Jeffrey Sachs knows that his argument is a bit weak when he uses the words "*a reasonable degree* of good governance" (italics added). How "reasonable" would it be for donor countries to expect a good return on their investment? In the current climate, it is hard to believe it would be very reasonable at all.

---

1. A concession / reply paragraph has three main parts: a part that **states** the ideas of an opponent, a part that **refutes** most of the ideas of the opponent, and a part that **agrees** with some aspects of an opponent's ideas. Where do these parts appear in the paragraph?

First: _____

Second: _____

Third: _____

2. Underline the sentence that has a noun clause-in-apposition format. Which of Jeffrey Sachs's opinions does the writer refer to there? How does the writer react to that viewpoint?

3. In what sentence does the writer start to disagree with Sachs? Why does the writer's tone in that sentence seem to be diplomatic and tactful?

4. What is the writer's main opinion in the paragraph? Does the writer support this opinion well? Why or why not?

◀ **EDIT: Writing the Final Draft**

Write your final draft. Carefully edit it for grammatical and mechanical errors. Make sure you used some of the vocabulary and grammar from the unit. Use the checklist to help you write the final draft. Then neatly write or type your essay.

☑ FINAL DRAFT CHECKLIST

○ Does your introduction give the necessary background information and thesis statement?

○ Does the thesis statement clearly reflect the writer's stand on the issue?

○ Are the arguments, counterarguments and refutations presented in a logical manner?

○ Does the essay have at least one concession/reply paragraph?

○ Does the conclusion restate the thesis and offer the reader other ways to consider the problem?

○ Are noun clauses and noun clauses in apposition used effectively in the essay?

○ Have new vocabulary, expressions, and positive and negative connotations been used in the essay?

ALTERNATIVE WRITING TOPICS

Write an essay on one of the topics. Use the vocabulary, grammar, and argumentative essay structures from the unit.

1. *"If a free society cannot help the many who are poor, it cannot save the few who are rich."*

   John F. Kennedy, President of the U.S.

   What do you think President Kennedy meant by this quote? Does it apply only to people in one country? Does it apply to the world in general? Do you agree or disagree with this idea? Give examples to illustrate your point of view. Remember to include refutation and at least one concession.

2. "Neither a borrower or a lender be," says a character in Shakespeare's *Hamlet*. What are some reasons why we shouldn't borrow or lend money? What things can happen if you borrow or lend money? Do you think this also applies on the world economic level? Explain.

3. Some people give money to those who beg on the streets. Do you agree or disagree with this behavior? Is there a difference between giving money to the homeless on the streets and sending money to people in impoverished countries? Explain.

4. Some people feel that "charity begins at home." What is the meaning of this quote? Do you agree or disagree? How would that apply to Jeffrey Sachs's proposals?

5. As an investigative journalist, Barbara Ehrenreich wrote *Nickel and Dimed* by living the lives of the people she was writing about—in this case, America's working poor. What kind of investigative journalism would you like to do, and how would you do it?

RESEARCH TOPICS, see page 268.

RESEARCH TOPICS

UNIT 1: Mickey's Team

◀ RESEARCH: An Addiction

Preparation

Reading Two gives the characteristics of all addictions. Choose one addiction and explain why you are interested in learning about this addiction:

_____

_____

_____

_____

_____

Research Activity

1. Do an Internet search or go to the library, and find out how many people are reported to have this addiction. Get statistics for the population of the United States or another country. Also, find out in which country this particular addiction is the biggest problem, and why.

2. Then find out how people are able to recover from this addiction. Where do they go for help? How long does it take? How much does it cost? How successful are these interventions?

Sharing Your Findings

Write a report summarizing your findings and present a five-minute oral report.

UNIT 2: Lies and Truth

◀ RESEARCH: The History of Lie Detectors

Preparation

Because security has become such an important issue all over the world, inventors have been struggling to develop technology that can uncover the "lies" that may leave us in great danger.

To understand how we should apply such technology in the future, it is important to learn about the history of lie detectors, to know who their inventors are and how they have succeeded or failed.

Research Activity

Do research on the Internet about the history of lie detectors. Who are the most famous inventors? What were their motives? How did they succeed and how did they fail in inventing such protective devices? What are the developments in lie detection today?

To proceed, take these steps:

1. Go to a search engine (for example, www.google.com, www.yahoo.com).
2. Key in "lie detector inventors."
3. Read the leads that are of interest to you.
4. Take notes as you find the answers to the above questions.

Sharing Your Findings

Summarize your research findings in a report that you will give to the class.

UNIT 3: The Road to Success

◀ RESEARCH: Interview with a Successful Person

Preparation

Speaking to successful people can help us all to find ways to achieve success.

1. Write the name of a successful person it would be possible for you to interview:

   _____

2. Write at least three reasons why you believe understanding this person's personal success will help you as you strive to realize your dream:

   a. _____
   b. _____
   c. _____

3. Create questions that you want to ask this person. Brainstorm with a partner as you formulate at least five questions in preparation for your interview.

   a. What strategy did you follow to reach your career goals?
   b. What mistakes did you make, and what did you learn from them?
   c. _____
   d. _____
   e. _____

Research Activity

1. Explain to the person you are interviewing why you chose to interview him or her.

2. Take notes as you listen to the person's responses to your questions.

Sharing Your Findings

1. Examine your notes taken during the interview.

2. Write a summary of the interview. What have you learned? What can be applied to your own career?

3. Prepare a formal presentation to give to the class.

UNIT 4: Silent Spring

◀ RESEARCH: A Product or Idea that Has Started a Trend

Preparation

Choose a product or original idea that started a trend in society and created a need so great that it changed the way we live or think about things. It can be anything from fast food to blockbuster movies to technology to a famous book. You can choose one of the trends mentioned in this chapter or discover your own. You can write about today's trends or trends in history.

- Identify the product or idea and the trend it created.
- Identify the company, individual, or government that helped create this product or idea, and give its history.

Research Activity

1. Find the history of the product or idea.

2. Explain the popularity and success of the product or idea.

3. What was special about the person who thought of the product or idea? Why did this person succeed in getting it to become popular?

4. Indicate your opinion about this trend: Do you think it is positive or negative for society?

Sharing Your Findings

When you have found the information you need, create a poster explaining the origin and evolution of the trend you chose, and present the poster to the class.

In designing the poster, make sure you have included a title and all the important information. Show cause and effect. Pay attention to the layout. Work with computer graphics or color markers, crayons, and ink. Use visual imagery that will attract the viewers' attention.

◀ RESEARCH: Your Family History

Preparation

In what way has your family been touched by history? Prepare to write an essay in response to this question. Interview family members—in person, by mail, or by e-mail—to gather information for your essay. Before starting your research, brainstorm with a partner other questions you believe would be worth investigating. Here are some questions to consider.

- Has your family always lived in the same place? What influenced the decision to stay or go?
- Has your country undergone any great changes in the last 50 years? wars? revolutions? divisions? reunifications? changes in the political system? What effect have these events had on your family?
- Have the economic circumstances of your family changed in recent generations? What are the reasons for these changes?
- How has your family adjusted to change?
- Do you think it is important for children to know the history of their family?
- Has your family ever had any secrets that were not immediately told to the younger generation? Why were certain facts not discussed in your family?
- Is there any documentation that you would like to show to illustrate your family's history? This can include photos, newspaper articles, or magazines from the period. It can include personal items if you and your family agree about using them.

Research Activity

When you interview family members, be sure to take good notes. You may want to request permission to use a tape recorder if you are interviewing in person. Ask them if they have any photos, newspaper articles, official announcements, letters, or personal records that you can include with your essay.

Sharing Your Findings

Write an essay in which you summarize your findings and explain how this information has affected you. Include relevant documentation. Discuss the main points of your essay with the class.

◖ RESEARCH: The Nature of a Particular Religion

Preparation

In Reading Two you read a general definition of religion. There are many religions in the modern world. Choose one religion with which you are not familiar, and find out as much as you can about it. Begin with the following questions, and add to them as you do your research.

- Does this religion have a belief in a creator? Is there one god or many?
- What kind of behavior is expected of believers? What is the definition of "a good life" according to this religion?
- Where is this religion practiced in the world?

Research Activity

If possible, interview a member of the religious community you are interested in, or conduct your research in the library or on the Internet. Be sure to consult several sources so you can reduce the likelihood of prejudice or distortion in your treatment of the religion.

Sharing Your Findings

1. After you have taken notes about the religion you chose, write up your findings as a definition essay. The title can be, for example, "What Is the Hindu Religion?" or "What Is Zen Buddhism as Practiced in Japan?" or "What Is the Baptist (Protestant) Religion?"

2. Form a small group, and share your essay with the other members of the group. Comment on each other's essays, and discuss what you have learned.

UNIT 7: In Business, Size Matters

◖ RESEARCH: Attitudes toward Business

Preparation

Create a questionnaire to use in interviewing several people at your school about what they think of business. For instance, you might want the students you interview to consider the following questions:

- Do people in business have to be aggressive and ambitious?
- Is corruption a common problem in business?
- Should businesses be socially responsible to the community?

Work in groups. First discuss what you think of business. Then write at least five *Yes / No* opinion questions that you would like to have in your questionnaire.

Research Activity

When you conduct your survey, count the *Yes* and *No* responses to each question and take notes on the comments the interviewees (the students you interview) make. You can use the following grid to write your questions, tally responses, and record comments.

QUESTIONS	YES	NO	COMMENTS
Example: Would your family be happy if you went into business?	ℍℍ ///	ℍℍ	• Business brings financial security. • People in business have no time for family life.
1.			
2.			
3.			
4.			
5.			

Sharing Your Findings

Write a group report on the results of your survey.

1. In the introduction, explain the purpose of the survey and share the questions you asked.

2. In the body, give a summary of the number of *yes* and *no* replies you received for each question and the comments the interviewees made.

3. In the conclusion, give your interpretation of the information you collected.

4. Share the results of your research with the class in an oral presentation.

UNIT 8: When the Soldier Is a Woman ...

◖ RESEARCH: Policies Toward Women in the Army

Preparation

Choose a country not represented by any of the students in the class, and research the policies in that country toward women in the army. Before starting your research, brainstorm with a partner for questions that you believe would be worth investigating.

Here are some questions you may want to consider:

1. Are women allowed to serve in the military in this country? In what capacity? Can women do combat duty? What is the percentage of women soldiers?

2. Does this country have compulsory (required) military service, or do citizens volunteer for the military? Are women drafted?

3. Are there provisions for conscientious objectors—people who, because of religious or moral beliefs, refuse to engage in physical combat? Is some sort of alternative service to the country possible? Can women participate?

4. Does this country have military schools to prepare people for the military? Can women enroll?

5. Can women become officers? Can they command men as well as women?

6. Can women soldiers be married? Can they be mothers?

7. Does one's military service have an effect on one's future career in this country? Is there respect for the military in this country?

Research Activity

After you have prepared a list of questions, go to the library or do an Internet search. When you do your research, be sure to take detailed notes about the information you find and the sources you use.

Sharing Your Findings

Write a summary of your findings to share with the class. Follow the guidelines for writing summaries in the *Focus on Writing* section of this unit.

UNIT 9: The Cellist of Sarajevo

◀ RESEARCH: Interview with a Musician

Preparation

The character in *The Soloist* was haunted by the loss of his musical ear and the exuberant feeling of accomplishment that he used to have when he gave concerts to audiences that cherished his flawless performances. We leave him on a positive note as he seems to have rediscovered his musical gift. He now anticipates the possibility of playing for new audiences, either on the concert stage or in the privacy of his own home.

Work with a partner. Interview a professional musician, if possible, to find out how he or she feels about the instrument he or she plays. If you cannot interview a professional musician, you can interview someone for whom music is a serious hobby, or a rock guitarist who plays in a student band—someone who plays an instrument all the time even though he or she is not a professional.

Before conducting the interview, brainstorm with your partner to come up with questions you may want to use in the interview. In addition to your own questions, you may want to ask:

1. What was your first experience with the instrument?

2. At what age did you first take lessons?

3. How do you feel about the instrument?

4. What feelings do you have when you play for an audience and when you play for yourself?

5. Which do you enjoy more—playing with other musicians or playing alone?

Research Activity

To find a musician, you may want to consider the following possibilities:

1. Ask friends to introduce you to a professional musician or someone who plays an instrument.

2. Consult the orchestras or the music schools in your area.

3. Contact the host of a local radio program who interviews musicians on the air.

Talk with your partner, and consider what other resources may be available to you.

Sharing Your Findings

After you have conducted the interview, work together and write a summary of your findings. Use descriptive language as you explain how the person you interviewed feels when he or she plays an instrument, either in public or at home.

UNIT 10: The End of Poverty

◖ RESEARCH: Data about the Poor in Industrialized Nations

Preparation

In preparing to write her book, Barbara Ehrenreich went under cover to investigate the living conditions of America's working poor. Ironically, in the United States, the richest nation in the world, there are still many people who live in poverty. The same is true for people who live in other developed nations.

Identify at least five developed countries here:

1. _____

2. _____

3. _____

4. _____

5. _____

Research Activity

Follow these steps in conducting your research:

- Find data on the poor in these five countries: what percentage of the population they represent; how many of them work and how many of them do not work; what the poverty line is in each country; what services the poor are given from the government in order to survive; where they live, and so forth.

- Then choose one of the countries and find an issue that is now being argued in this country about the treatment of the poor. Read about the arguments that are dividing people on ways in which to address this issue.

Sharing Your Findings

When you have found the information you need, write a summary of the results of your research. Evaluate your findings by referring to data that you thought was surprising and data that you thought was "expected." Give your opinion about the issue that is now being argued in the country that you did specific research on. Include whatever recommendations you may have to improve the conditions in this country and the others covered in your report.

GRAMMAR BOOK REFERENCES

NorthStar: Reading and Writing Level 5, Third Edition	*Focus on Grammar Level 5,* Third Edition	*Azar's Understanding and Using English Grammar,* Third Edition
Unit 1 Past Unreal Conditionals	**Unit 23** Conditionals; Other Ways To Express Unreality	**Chapter 20** Conditional Sentences and Wishes: 20-4
Unit 2 Double Comparatives	_____	**Chapter 9*** Comparisons: 9-10 * From *Fundamentals of English Grammar,* Third Edition
Unit 3 Identifying and Nonidentifying Adjective Clauses	**Unit 11** Adjective Clauses: Review and Expansion **Unit 12** Adjective Clauses with Prepositions; Adjective Phrases	**Chapter 13** Adjective Clauses
Unit 4 Adverb Clauses and Discourse Connectors	**Unit 17** Adverbs: Functions, Types, Placement, and Meaning **Unit 20** Connectors	**Chapter 17** Adverb Clauses: 17-2 **Chapter 19** Connectives that Express Cause and Effect, Contrast, and Condition: 19-1, 19-2, 19-3, 19-4
Unit 5 Adverb Clauses of Comparison And Contrast	**Unit 18** Adverb Clauses	**Chapter 17** Adverb Clauses: 17-3, 17-4 **Chapter 19** Connectives that Express Cause and Effect, Contrast, and Condition: 19-6

NorthStar: Reading and Writing Level 5, Third Edition	Focus on Grammar Level 5, Third Edition	Azar's Understanding and Using English Grammar, Third Edition
Unit 6 Definite and Indefinite Articles with Count and Non-Count Nouns	**Unit 7** Count and Non-Count Nouns	**Chapter 7** Nouns: 7-7,7-8
Unit 7 Specific Uses of Gerunds and Infinitives	**Unit 15** Gerunds **Unit 16** Infinitives	**Chapter 14** Gerunds and Infinitives, Part 1 **Chapter 15** Gerunds and Infinitives, Part 2
Unit 8 Direct and Indirect Speech	**Unit 22** Direct and Indirect Speech	**Chapter 12** Noun Clauses: 12-6, 12-7
Unit 9 Reporting Ideas and Facts with Passives	**Unit 14** The Passive to Describe Situations and to Report Opinions	**Chapter 11** The Passive: 11-1, 11-2, 11-3
Unit 10 Noun Clauses	**Unit 21** Noun Clauses: Subjects, Objects, and Complements	**Chapter 12** Noun Clauses: 12-1, 12-2, 12-3, 12-4, 12-5

CREDITS

Notes